The Rise of Anti-Americanism

Is anti-Americanism one of the last respectable prejudices, or are accusations of anti-Americanism a way to silence reasonable criticism of the United States? This new volume brings together an international team of well-known scholars from the United States, UK and Australia to examine the rise of anti-Americanism.

Is the recent rise in anti-Americanism principally a reaction to President George W. Bush and his administration, or does it reflect a general turn against America and Americans? Have we moved from the American century to the anti-American century, with the United States as the 'whipping boy' for a growing range of anxieties? Can the United States recapture the international good will generally extended towards it in the days following 11 September 2001? These key questions are tackled by this new book, which offers the first comprehensive overview of anti-Americanism in the twenty-first century.

Examining anti-Americanism and its principal sources, this study details how the Bush administration has provoked a recent upsurge in anti-Americanism with its stances on a range of issues from the Kyoto Protocol to the war in Iraq. This study also highlights how the spread of anti-Americanism reflects deeper cultural and political anxieties about Americanization and American global power that will persist beyond the Bush administration.

Providing a detailed and comprehensive overview of anti-Americanism and its associated dilemmas, this book will be invaluable to students and scholars of American politics and International Relations.

Brendon O'Connor is a Senior Lecturer in the Department of Politics and Public Policy, Griffith University, Queensland, Australia.

Martin Griffiths is Associate Professor of International Relations in the Department of International Business and Asian Studies, at Griffith University, Australia. He is the Editor of the *Encyclopaedia of International Relations and Global Politics* published by Routledge, 2005.

The Rise of Anti-Americanism

Edited by Brendon O'Connor
and Martin Griffiths

Routledge
Taylor & Francis Group

LONDON AND NEW YORK

First published 2006 by Routledge
2 Park Square, Milton Park, Abingdon, Oxfordshire, OX14 4RN

Simultaneously published in the USA and Canada
by Routledge
711 Third Avenue, New York, NY 10017

Routledge is an imprint of the Taylor & Francis Group

© 2006 Brendon O'Connor and Martin Griffiths for selection and
editorial matter; individual contributors, their contributions.

Typeset in Baskerville by Taylor & Francis Books

British Library Cataloguing in Publication Data
A catalogue record for this book is available from the British Library

Library of Congress Cataloging in Publication Data
A catalog record for this book has been requested

ISBN 0–415–36907-X (hbk)
ISBN 0–415–36906–1 (pbk)

ISBN13 9-78-0-415-36907-X (hbk)
ISBN13 9-78-0-415-36906-1 (pbk)

Taylor & Francis Group is the Academic Division of T&F Informa plc.

Contents

Contributors

John Chiddick is Lecturer in International Relations in the Department of Politics at La Trobe University, Australia.

Richard Crockatt is Professor of American Studies at the University of East Anglia.

Martin Griffiths is Associate Professor of International Relations in the Department of International Business and Asian Studies, at Griffith University, Australia.

John Higley is Professor of Government and Chair of the Department of Government at the University of Texas at Austin. He is also the Jack S. Blanton Chair in Australian Studies, and Director of the Center for Australian and New Zealand Studies.

Iyanatul Islam is Professor of International Business in the Department of International Business and Asian Studies at Griffith University, Australia.

Tony Judt is the Erich Maria Remarque Professor of European Studies at New York University.

John Kane is Associate Professor in the Department of Politics and Public Policy at Griffith University, Australia.

Brendon O'Connor is Senior Lecturer in the Department of Politics and Public Policy at Griffith University, Australia.

Andrew O'Neil is Senior Lecturer in International Relations in the School of Political and International Studies at Flinders University, Australia.

Inderjeet Parmar is Senior Lecturer and Director of the Centre for International Politics in the Department of Government, International Politics and Philosophy at the University of Manchester.

Robert Singh is Professor of Politics at Birkbeck College, University of London.

Alan Wolfe is Professor of Political Science and Director of the Boisi Center for Religion and American Public Life at Boston College.

Acknowledgements

A number of the chapters in this book were first presented as discussion papers at a Fulbright symposium in Brisbane, Australia in 2002. We would particularly like to thank the Australia-American Fulbright Commission and the Executive Director Mark Darby for supporting the symposium, which provided an excellent basis for the development of this book.

Chapter two is a revised version of a paper that was first published as 'A brief history of anti-Americanism' in the *Australasian Journal of American Studies*, 2004, vol. 23, no. 1, pp. 77–92. It is reproduced with the permission of the editors. An earlier version of chapter seven was first presented to the First International Sources of Security Conference in Melbourne in November 2004. Chapter thirteen was first published as 'Anti-Americans abroad' in *The New York Review of Books*, 1 May 2003, pp. 24–7.

Brendon O'Connor would like to thank Professor Patrick Weller and the Department of Politics and Public Policy at Griffith University for support throughout the preparation of this book. Finally, we could not have completed this book without the support of our families. To Katherine, Kylie, Finnegan and Jade, and all those who came to our aid when deadlines loomed, our deepest thanks go to you.

Brendon O'Connor and Martin Griffiths

Brisbane
October 2005

Introduction

Making sense of anti-Americanism

Brendon O'Connor and Martin Griffiths

Anti-Americanism remains an elusive phenomenon, despite the widespread use of the term, and the common perception that it signifies what George Orwell would have called an increasing 'tendency' in public discourse. Nonetheless, like so many words and phrases that litter the contemporary landscape of political commentary (think of 'globalization' or 'Islamic fundamentalism'), the term is a clumsy attempt to describe a rising sensibility whose contours and causes are the subject matter of this book. The term itself is composed of two words, the first meaning 'against' and the second, well, therein lies a problem. If one could identify a movement, ideology or even a vague set of beliefs to bring some order to the term 'Americanism', then it would be relatively easy to identify its opposite. In their absence, defining anti-Americanism is a difficult exercise. Nonetheless, the term is part of our vocabulary and we need to have some way of grasping its meaning and significance in the highly charged debates that surround the role of the United States in the world.

Rather than define the term by its substance, anti-Americanism is more usefully understood as an attitude towards the United States that both refuses to be deterred in its judgement by doubt or the acknowledgement of complexity, and which subscribes to what Brian Fawcett (in his reflections on Noam Chomsky) calls 'a Standard Total View (STV) of the United States as a demonic purveyor of more or less total evil'.[1] Thus mere opposition to American policies is not sufficient to constitute anti-Americanism, which contains an emotional element of anger or resentment. Moreover, anti-Americanism can be motivated by completely opposed points of view: for example, dislike of America because it is 'overly religious', or because it is 'overly secular'. In short, anti-Americanism is a disposition or sensibility rather than a substantive set of beliefs or arguments. It should also be noted that one person's reasonable criticism of the United States is another person's anti-Americanism. Anti-Americanism is both a descriptive and a pejorative term. It is rightly used to describe hatred of America and often misused by its critics to dismiss genuine criticisms of the United States. Thus a key issue is how to distinguish criticism based on anti-Americanism from criticism based on other grounds. Genuine anti-Americanism implies an across-the-board abhorrence of American politics, culture and people. Such a breadth of antipathy is a tall order given the diversity of American society.

Recognizing this, Zeldin has described anti-Americanism as pathological, arguing that '[t]o hate a whole nation, to love a whole nation, is a clear symptom of hysteria'.[2] Similarly Toinet suggests that the use of the term anti-Americanism 'is only fully justified if it implies systematic opposition – a sort of allergic reaction to America as a whole'.[3]

Furthermore, anti-Americanism must be understood as the product of a relationship between a target ('America') and its critics ('anti-Americans'). It is not difficult to identify characteristics of the target that are often used to justify anti-Americanism. Many Americans are parochial. They belong to the most powerful state in the world, yet they know little about the world they dominate. In poll after poll, young Americans find it difficult to locate other countries on a map, few speak a foreign language, and the educational system is weak in the teaching of world history. The foreign policy of the United States is accompanied by a rhetoric of freedom, human rights, and democracy that it often contradicts in practice, both at home and abroad. Global inequality is growing, both within and between countries, feeding the resentment of the 'have-nots' against the power and wealth increasingly concentrated in the United States. In addition to its parochialism, the United States is increasingly arrogant and unilateral in its foreign policy, disregarding international organizations such as the United Nations, international law in its attack on Iraq, and its obligations to help clean up the global environment. Since 11 September 2001, the United States has used its armed forces to project its 'hard power' overseas against Afghanistan, Iraq, and has threatened to do so against other 'rogue' states. Since its military power is the one dimension of its superiority that dwarfs all others, there is a temptation to resort to precipitate military action at the expense of more complex but perhaps more effective instruments of foreign policy, including diplomacy and international law. In its 'war on terror', the United States has selectively unleashed its military machine (on which it spends more money than virtually the rest of the world combined) against states that it unilaterally decides are members of the 'axis of evil'.

One could add further items to the list, but these characteristics of the target are its main flaws in the eyes of its critics. The problem is that if anti-Americanism involves a *relationship* between a target and its critics, merely dwelling on the former tells us nothing about why some of the latter are anti-American and others merely critics. After all, it is perfectly possible to endorse some of the criticisms and yet be 'pro-American'. As Michael Walzer has shown, the most effective form of social criticism engages with its target's own proclaimed values, drawing our attention to the gap between ideals and practice, and examining ways to close that gap.[4] According to those whom we might label 'anti-anti-Americans', something else is at work in the mind of the anti-American.

Anti-anti-Americans argue that anti-Americanism is the product of many factors, but two in particular are worth noting. The first is that anti-Americanism is a kind of religion for those who hate religion. It appeals to those on the far left of the political spectrum who no longer have to defend the indefensible (the Soviet Union), and can turn their energies against the United States without ever articulating a coherent ideological project for the left. Secondly, and this may explain a good deal of anti-Americanism in countries other than the United States, it provides a convenient scapegoat for internal problems.

Even thought of as an 'ism' rather than a prejudice, the broad range of views that are called anti-Americanism make the concept more incoherent and amorphous than the standard usually expected of ideologies or belief systems. The clearest version of an anti-American ideology has arguably been put forward by Osama bin Laden and al-Qaeda, with the events of 11 September 2001 being quintessential anti-American acts. Al-Qaeda's anti-American belief system principally blames the United States and its client rulers for the world's various injustices. In political debates in the West this viewpoint is associated most readily with writers such as Noam Chomsky, John Pilger and Tariq Ali. However, the criticisms of these authors generally focus on American politics, not American culture or the American people. As a result they would all reject the label of anti-Americanism, as would most non-fanatics. But if 9/11 can be construed as the exemplar of anti-Americanism at work, does it make much sense to imply that all anti-Americans are complicit with terrorism?

This book seeks to shed light on this and other questions raised by the phenomenon of anti-Americanism in the early twenty-first century. The book is divided into two parts. Part One examines the nature of the beast. Brendon O'Connor begins by noting that anti-Americanism is not a novel tendency. It has a history that starts with the creation of the United States in the late eighteenth century. O'Connor usefully distinguishes between four phases of anti-Americanism. Whilst he acknowledges the utility of Naím's identification of five distinct types of anti-Americanism (politico-economic, historical, religious, cultural, and psychological), O'Connor demonstrates that the strength of each type varies in different historical periods.[5] Disturbingly, he notes that over time the focus of anti-Americanism has become more diffuse as it has increased in intensity. What began as a cultural critique from Europe has evolved into a mindset that can motivate terrorism. Robert Singh's chapter delves deeply into the diversity of criticism that is concealed by the term 'anti-Americanism'. He argues that beneath the apparent ubiquity of hostility towards the United States (only some of which can be understood as a response to American power and the conduct of the Bush administration since 9/11) one can discern at least three dominant types of reaction. These include a sustained leftist critique of US capitalism and its promotion of an American project of globalization, the resentment of what he calls 'rival nationalisms' whose distinctive identities are struggling to emerge within an international order dominated by the United States, and (particularly in Europe) a reaction against what is understood to represent American cultural imperialism. In addition to deconstructing anti-Americanism into these three types of reaction, Singh makes the important argument that the target of criticism is partly to blame for the simplistic images of America projected both at home and abroad through the media of film and television. Fortunately, most people are able to make a distinction between

America as a country and the character of its government, and therefore experience no cognitive dissonance arising from their consumption of hamburgers as they march the streets in protest at the foreign policy of the Bush administration. Nonetheless, Singh observes that anti-Americanism is unlikely to disappear simply on the basis of a change in government in Washington. It is fuelled not only by the parochialism of many Americans but also the widespread ignorance of the United States by those who hold it responsible for many of the world's problems.

John Kane's chapter revisits the history of anti-Americanism traced by O'Connor, but this time with a more specific focus. Notwithstanding the shifting contours of anti-Americanism and the need to understand its discrete elements, Kane argues that the tendency has been consistently marked by ambivalence. The United States is hated in part because it is also loved. Ambivalence, argues Kane, is a function of the American myth of 'exceptionalism'. Seymour Martin Lipset has suggested that America is more than a country – it is an ideology.[6] Lipset suggests that liberty, egalitarianism, individualism, populism and laissez-faire beliefs are at the core of American exceptionalism, which Kane argues is not just a unifying myth designed to conceal domestic social and political conflict in the United States. In his historical overview, Kane suggests that the myth is shared by those for whom the United States represents the idea of enlightenment and progress. Kane's argument is important because it sheds light on one of the peculiar characteristics of America; its civic nationalism whose universal ideals ensure that it is held to a standard of conduct that we could not even begin to apply to most other countries.

Part One of the book concludes with two complementary chapters by Iyanatul Islam and John Chiddick, both of whom are concerned with the nature of anti-Americanism in the Muslim world, and the Middle East in particular. Iyanatul Islam devotes a good deal of attention to what we earlier, and somewhat clumsily, called the 'anti-anti-Americans', for whom anti-Americanism is best understood as an irrational mindset that has little to do with the actual role of the United States in the world. Iyanatul Islam is specifically concerned with the work of two American scholars (Samuel Huntington and Bernard Lewis) who have promoted the idea that Islam and America are on a collision course for reasons that have little to do with the history of American foreign policy. Both Iyanatul Islam and Chiddick are concerned with the ways in which the charge of 'anti-Americanism' can be used to silence or to marginalize legitimate criticisms of the United States. Just as the United States is far more diverse than anti-Americans are prepared to concede, Iyanatul Islam argues that the same is true for the Muslim world. In exploring the contours of anti-Americanism in the Middle East, Iyanatul Islam points to the dangers of what he calls American 'orientalism'. He argues that it is a discourse that both conceals the diversity of Muslim societies and their shifting relationship with the United States and also blinds us to the long history of US foreign policy in the Middle East. Iyanatul Islam argues that the 'roots of Muslim rage' (to invoke Bernard Lewis) are not merely a function of Arab backwardness and the failure of Islam to accommodate modernization, but are inextricably linked to American foreign policy, particularly its close relationship with Israel. In making his case, Iyanatul Islam also draws our attention to some of the ways in which American orientalism is sustained in the United States. He suggests that Islamic anti-Americanism cannot be disentangled from American foreign policy, nor can it be muted by a rhetorical commitment to replace military force with 'soft power'. Chiddick concurs with this view. His chapter is specifically concerned with the degree of intractability of anti-Americanism in Arab countries. To what extent is it linked to America's support for Israel throughout the cold war and beyond? Again, in contrast to the view of Bernard Lewis and other American orientalists, Chiddick argues that shifts in anti-American sentiment in the Middle East closely track US policy towards Israel vis-à-vis Arab states as well as the Palestinians.

The chapters by Iyanatul Islam and John Chiddick link the two parts of the book. Whereas Part One is an examination of the nature of anti-Americanism, the contributors in Part Two are concerned with the sources of contemporary anti-Americanism, especially the role of American foreign policy. Martin Griffiths begins with an examination of what might be called the paradox of American power. He suggests that we live in a novel era in which the traditional logic of world politics and the balance of power appears to be suspended. Griffiths argues that the United States is a unique hegemon in world affairs, which has been able to build an international order that inhibits the emergence of any viable competitor. In this context, despite the long history of anti-Americanism explored by other contributors to this volume, Griffiths suggests that the virulence of contemporary anti-Americanism is in part the resentment of the impotent. However, it is not a phenomenon that the United States can ignore in light of the goals that the Bush administration is claiming to promote as part of its 'war on terror'. Griffiths suggests that the achievement of those goals is hampered by a fundamental tension between the attempt to create a world of viable states and a foreign economic policy that perpetuates the political and economic division between core and periphery states. He argues that the quagmire of Iraq is symptomatic of this contradiction at the heart of American foreign policy.

If Griffiths calls into question the ability of the United States to maintain its image as a fundamentally benign hegemon in the world post-9/11, the following chapters suggest that we are unlikely to see a decline in anti-Americanism as the United States rethinks its foreign policy in light of Iraq. Richard Crockatt returns to the theme of civilizational conflict explored by Robert Singh and Iyanatul Islam. He distinguishes between two contrasting ways in which the term 'civilization' has been used since 11 September 2001. On the one hand it has been used by the Bush administration and some American commentators to refer to a distinctively 'American civilization' that is allegedly at war with Islamic fundamentalism. On the other hand the term has been used more broadly to refer to 'the civilized world' that includes America but also includes other states and societies that share its abhorrence of terrorism. Crockatt argues that the challenge for the United States is to provide leadership to the 'the civilized world' in a way that accommodates the latter's diversity rather than promoting America's own particular interests. He argues that the Bush administration has so far failed to provide the necessary leadership. Andrew O'Neil suggests that the main reason for this failure lies with the 'grand strategy' of the United States adopted by the Bush administration since 9/11. Beneath all the 'world order' rhetoric of US foreign policy makers, O'Neil traces an overriding concern by the Bush administration to sustain American power for the foreseeable future. Whilst the doctrinal innovations of pre-emption and unilateralism suggest a radical shift in American strategic thinking in light of the attacks of 11 September 2001, O'Neil identifies a fundamental continuity of American purpose. 9/11 provided the United States with an opportunity to sweep aside the vacillations of American foreign policy during the Clinton era, and replace them with a new set of doctrines to deal decisively with a novel set of challenges. According to O'Neil, the rise of anti-Americanism is seen by some in the Bush administration as a small price to pay, particularly if other states can do little to counter the global hyper-power.

Whilst O'Neil argues that any change in American foreign policy will have to arise from the failure of its grand strategy to accommodate the challenges represented by 'rogue states' such as North Korea and Iran (as well as its inability to reconstruct Iraq), John Higley suggests that it would be naïve to expect much change from an elite that he argues is becoming increasingly entrenched in the United States government. In what is perhaps the most depressing chapter of the book, at least for those who believe that anti-Americanism is to a significant degree the consequence of the Bush administration and its policies, Higley argues that the present administration should not be regarded as a mere aberration. Whilst the voting patterns in the 2004 presidential election appear to reflect an increasingly divided America, Higley argues that what he calls the 'Bush elite' is a remarkably united political class 'without precedent in American history'. He traces its emergence over the past thirty years, and demonstrates how 9/11 provided the elite with a unique opportunity, not only to pursue a grand strategy abroad, but also to cement its power at home. This opportunity was facilitated by the narrowing of the differences between the Democrats and the Republicans on the key issues of immigration and multicultural affairs, defence spending, foreign alliances and interventions, surveillance and civil liberties. Moreover, the defence and taxation policies pursued by the Bush administration are likely to lock the United States into a more centralized and militaristic path. If Higley's analysis is correct, it will take much more than a setback in Iraq to shift the fundamental worldview of the administration.

In his contribution to the book, Inderjeet Parmar explores the role of the 'Big Three' American foundations (Ford, Rockefeller, and Carnegie) in combating anti-Americanism. Complementing Higley's argument, Parmar suggests that the foundations constitute a crucial component of the United States' hegemonic role in the world. He traces how the foundations have adapted from the cold war to the 'war on terror', and analyses how they wield their financial power to promote a particular vision of US-led globalization, thereby attempting to moderate (some would say conceal) the contradictions in American foreign policy identified by Griffiths.

In his examination of the bonds between individual members of the Bush elite, Higley mentions in passing its members' 'strong religious coloration'. This brings us to the penultimate chapter of the book, by Alan Wolfe, who tackles head-on the degree to which anti-Americanism can justifiably be motivated by the view that 'militant believers of Islam in the Middle East are similar to Christian fundamentalists in the United States'. For many observers, the United States is not only undermining liberal democracy in its 'war on terror' but it is also becoming a more fundamentalist country, thereby replacing the secular dichotomy between capitalism and communism (the cold war) with a new religious conflict of competing religions – Islam and Christianity. However, in contrast to Higley's pessimism regarding the future of the American polity, Wolfe provides a more optimistic chapter to this book. He suggests that the tension between American religion and American culture, or between tradition and modernity in the United States, is often overdrawn by critics. Based on his examination of how Americans 'live' with their religious beliefs, Wolfe suggests that it is highly unlikely that America's secular culture will be overtaken by a resurgent Christian fundamentalism. Instead, he argues that Americans are unique in their ability to adapt religious tradition to the demands of culture rather than the other way round. Finally, Tony Judt draws the book to a close. Casting a critical eye over recent texts published in France, Judt notes the 'recurring themes, fears, and hopes' that animate anti-Americanism among French intellectuals. However, he suggests that the conduct of the Bush administration since 9/11 has added something new to the mix of irrationality and considered criticism that constitutes anti-Americanism in our time. Judt suggests that US foreign policy, particularly its invasion of Iraq in 2003, has shifted what he calls the 'tectonic plates' of world politics. Whether it has done so sufficiently to generate the concerted European reaction that Judt warns may now take place, remains to be seen.

On 12 September 2001 the headline of *Le Monde* proclaimed that 'we are all Americans now'. Four years later one could be forgiven for thinking that many people who shared that sentiment in 2001 would today redescribe themselves as anti-American. In this book we have brought together a group of individuals who would describe themselves as neither pro- nor anti-American, but whose examination of the rise of anti-Americanism constitutes a modest attempt to transcend this simplistic dichotomy.

Notes

1 B. Fawcett, *Unusual Circumstances, Interesting Times*, Vancouver, BC: New Star Books, 1991, p. 175.
2 D. Lacorne, J. Rupnik, M. Toinet, and T. Zeldin, *The Rise and Fall of Anti-Americanism*, Basingstoke: Macmillan, 1990, p. 35.
3 Ibid., p. 219.
4 M. Walzer, *The Company of Critics*, New York: Basic Books, 2002.
5 See M. Naím, 'Anti-Americanism', *Foreign Policy*, January/February 2002, vol. 132.
6 S. Martin Lipset, *American Exceptionalism*, New York: Norton, 1996.

Part I

Understanding anti-Americanism

1 The anti-American tradition

A history in four phases

Brendon O'Connor[1]

This chapter provides an historical examination of anti-Americanism from its beginnings to the current day. I argue that anti-Americanism is not a comprehensive or coherent belief system or ideology, but rather a series of criticisms and prejudices regarding the United States that have haphazardly been labelled anti-Americanism. Chronologically the term is first associated with European cultural laments about Americans' lack of manners and their general vulgarity and then, as America becomes a global power, more politically and economically based criticism comes to the fore. Finally, in recent times what has been labelled 'anti-American terrorism'[2] has reared its head.

This chapter does not pretend to be a comprehensive overview of all forms of anti-Americanism across the globe as each nation has its own story to tell (see Robert Singh's chapter in this volume). What I have drawn on are the dominant or most noted types of criticism of America throughout history. This history is based on what other commentators and scholars have labelled 'anti-Americanism', a position that has distinct advantages given that there is no widely agreed upon definition of the term. Scholarship on the topic has been largely patchy and impressionistic, particularly until very recently. The most detailed study of the subject – Paul Hollander's *Anti-Americanism* (1995) – is a one-sided attack on anti-Americanism as an irrational position largely adopted by the misguided left. Similarly lacking in balance is Stephen Haseler's *The Varieties of Anti-Americanism* (1985), which counsels Americans to largely ignore the criticisms of foreigners (whom Haseler principally sees as being envious of America's global power).[3] Arguably the best book written on anti-Americanism during the twentieth century was *The Rise and Fall of Anti-Americanism* (1990), an edited collection of French scholarship on the topic. In this volume Marie-France Toinet suggests that the use of the term anti-Americanism 'is only fully justified if it implies systematic opposition – a sort of allergic reaction – to America as a whole'.[4] Alvin Rubinstein and Donald Smith offer a broader definition. They see anti-Americanism 'as any hostile action or expression that becomes part and parcel of an undifferentiated attack on the foreign policy, society, culture and values of the United States'.[5] Bringing us much closer to the common use of the term is Robert Singh's suggestion (in chapter two of this book) that anti-Americanism is rather like Justice Potter Stewart's famous definition of pornography – we instinctively know it when we see it.

Because there is no agreed upon definition, what differentiates anti-Americanism from reasonable criticism of the United States is often confused or sometimes deliberately distorted. Since 11 September 2001, defenders of the United States have been particularly prone to label criticisms of the United States 'anti-American' in order to silence legitimate debate. At the same time, increasing numbers of people are expressing their frustrations and anger with the United States in a manner that is fairly labelled anti-American.[6] Another conceptual problem is that an aversion to America often coexists, within a nation or an individual, with an embracing of America. This ambivalence – the coexistence of attraction and disdain – has been long felt. For example, Alexis de Tocqueville, generally considered an admirer of American democracy, wrote, 'I know of no other country, where, by and large, there exists less independence of mind or true freedom of discussion than in America'.[7] For many Europeans, America represented a bright new beginning, a return to the innocence and perfection of the Garden of Eden; something reflected in early American place names such as New Haven, New Jerusalem, New Hope, Providence and Eden. However, this new world naturally had its doubters and disparagers from its beginnings, and more so as it became a rival and later a cultural and political threat. Cornelius de Pauw, in the late eighteenth century, 'complained that the discovery and conquest of the New World was "the greatest tragedy" ever to befall humanity'.[8]

To give order to the strong and critical opinions that have long existed regarding America, I develop an overview of anti-Americanism that distinguishes between four identifiable phases. The first phase extends from the inception of America as a European settlement to the end of World War Two. In this period anti-Americanism was largely culturally oriented criticism premised on European superiority and American cultural inferiority. The second phase is that of the cold war (1945–1989). What was called anti-Americanism in this period was more politically and ideologically oriented criticism. This tended to be leftist, ranging across a broad spectrum from Soviet propaganda to anti-Vietnam War protest movements. In this period the false and disingenuous labelling of objections to American policies as 'anti-American' became more prominent. The third phase of anti-Americanism started in 1989 with the end of the cold war. This period saw a greater emphasis on the ill effects of American capitalism and Americanization and continues today as anti-Americanism is inextricably linked to the anti-globalization movement. The most recent phase of anti-Americanism can be dated to 11 September 2001 with the arrival of terrorist anti-Americanism as a significant and widely acknowledged force. What is important to stress is that these phases are not hermetically sealed off from each other; early forms of criticism continue across time, reinforcing new forms of anti-Americanism. As a result we often see a combination of these forms of anti-Americanism such as when George W. Bush is mocked as a 'toxic Texan'. Both his policies on environmental matters and his Texan self-image are combined in this caricature.

America: 'uncultured but cocksure'

Criticism of the United States started to form into a set of proto anti-American ideas and stereotypes in the late eighteenth and early nineteenth centuries as the United States became something more than a colonial or religious outpost. The earliest forms of anti-American comment tended to be cultural criticism of the lack of taste, grace and civility in American habits and everyday life. European writers such as Charles Dickens and Frances Trollope built up a picture of Americans as rude and indifferent to manners or polite conversation.[9] The French diplomat and bishop Talleyrand (1754–1838) anticipated two centuries of European commentary when he declared that the United States comprised 'thirty-two religions and just one dish'.[10] Summing up the criticisms of nineteenth century European intellectuals about America's lack of civility and taste, Norwegian writer Knut Hamsun commented that 'America is a very backward country culturally'.[11] However, what infuriated Europeans the most was that this American backwardness and uncouthness was combined with what they regarded as a cocksure arrogance. Reflecting on this unpleasant combination, Simon Schama observes that '[b]y the end of the nineteenth century, the stereotype of the ugly American – voracious, preachy, mercenary, and bombastically chauvinist – was firmly in place in Europe'.[12] In short, Americans were seen as overconfident and self-important and, according to Schama, it was this American 'egocentricity' that most aggravated Europeans.

The assertion of European superiority has long been a theme of transAtlantic relations, with the United States being depicted as the antithesis of Europe. The German-Israeli historian Dan Diner describes America as:

> ... the counter-world to Europe, a complementary continent of occidental civilization and a screen upon which to project all the images and metaphors arising from its contrast to Europe; a screen upon which to project isolated portions of self-hatred owing mainly to modernity, but blamed only on the New World.[13]

The early forms of anti-Americanism pitted an idealized version of European culture against a stereotype of an uncultured but brazen America.[14] This battle between so called 'high' and 'low' culture, and the later more nationalistic battle over the Americanization of other cultures have remained central themes of anti-American discourse. Beyond plain rivalry, nineteenth century criticism of America also attacked American materialism and industrialism as perils to European sensibilities and the European lifestyle. In these critiques, Europe is depicted as the aesthetic bulwark against rampant American materialism and industrialism.[15] Although no longer the preserve of a conservative elite, this nineteenth century critique of a cultured Europe and a philistine America is still visible today in the anti-globalization movement. The protests of the French farmer and anti-globalization celebrity, Jose Bove, are a modern example of this long tradition of European anti-Americanism.[16]

Some would say little has changed regarding how Europeans view their trans-Atlantic cousins, except that the stereotypes are now provided by Hollywood and American television sitcom producers, rather than by European novelists and commentators. However, during the twentieth century, criticism of America became much more politically oriented as the United States emerged as a global power after World War One. The French in particular found it galling that, on top of their late entry into the war, the Americans had come out such clear global winners. In his intellectual history of early and mid twentieth century France, Tony Judt suggests that anti-Americanism developed from a general critique into a recognized 'ism' in the 1930s in France. He argues that, like earlier nineteenth century criticism, this 1930s anti-Americanism was largely conservative in its origins with strong romantic overtones. American society was criticized for becoming something akin to Chaplin's *Modern Times* writ large, with its materialism and industrialism seen as a real threat to the beauty and variety of Western culture.[17] For most of these critics, Europe was and always would be the soul of Western civilization; however, for some anti-Americans the Orient was romanticized as the antidote to the American way.[18] Important criticisms of American materialism, corporatization, and conformity that emerged in this period were pushed to the sidelines after 1945 with the discrediting of the European right and the rise of the communist threat.[19] Furthermore, in the 1930s a particular strand of anti-Americanism had become an extension of anti-Semitism. In the minds of certain critics, Jews were associated with rootless modernity and capitalism, with the worst outcome of these forces being America. Summing up this tendency, Judt translates French right-wing columnist Robert Brasillach's answer to the question of what separated France from America. 'The answer is threefold: its hypocrisy (a frequent charge), its dollars, and international Jewry'. Judt goes on to note that '[a]s the last bastion of Jewish power in the world, the United States was the enemy of revolutionaries and reactionaries, anti-modernists and socialists alike'.[20] This list of enemies points to the plasticity of America as a target for criticism, blame and grievance.

America: the new imperialist

After World War Two, as America became fully engaged in international politics and involved in a global cold war with the Soviet Union, political anti-Americanism became more significant. Much of this criticism of America tended to be leftist, with communism being in many ways the opposite and natural enemy of the American creed. Reflecting on this ideological conflict, Seymour Martin Lipset has written that America is more than a country – it is a creed or in fact an 'ism'.[21] During the cold war, America, like the Soviet Union, symbolized an ideological approach to economic life and, to a lesser extent, political life. These two superpowers and their belief systems were often pitted against each other in a 'you are either for or against us' fashion reminiscent of the rhetoric of the current Bush administration. Thus at its simplest level to be pro-Soviet was to be anti-American (or in American domestic parlance un-

American). Although this is a very reductionist approach, it is one largely adopted by Paul Hollander in his book *Anti-Americanism*. Recruitment to the pro-Soviet cause, however, was undoubtedly hindered by the behaviour of the Soviet regime. Nonetheless communist parties in Europe, particularly in France, had some success arguing that America was intent on global military and economic domination and needed to be opposed. Possibly the most noted early cold war 'anti-American' rallies were large protests organized by the French Communists against the Korean War. These included a sizable anti-war gathering when the American military commander General Ridgeway visited Paris in 1952. The French Communists lambasted Ridgeway, dubbing him the 'Bacterial General' based on their claims that America was engaged in germ warfare in Korea.[22] By the time of the Vietnam War a much broader range of leftist parties, in Europe and elsewhere including Australia, were heavily involved in organizing anti-war activities, which were frequently criticized as being anti-American.

Not all post-1945 criticism of America was leftist. An interesting case in point is French political opposition to American foreign policy in the early cold war. French commentary and politics from the 1930s through the early cold war era have created the broadly held view that anti-Americanism is significantly a French tradition, buoyed in France in particular by a resentment of American power.[23] However, the right-wing Gaullist Party and its leader General de Gaulle (the French President from 1958–1969) challenged American policy in a number of areas including the US push to rearm Germany under a European Defence Community (EDC) proposal in the early 1950s. De Gaulle also opposed proposed changes to the NATO troop command, and ultimately organized France's partial withdrawal from NATO. De Gaulle's decision to recognize Communist China in 1964, his opposition to American policy in Vietnam, and his criticism of Israeli conduct in the 1967 war also put him clearly at odds with the United States. These conflicts represented both a difference of outlook and interests; furthermore they were part of an attempt to reassert French independence and honour,[24] all of which seen through American eyes made France a difficult ally.

Gaullism in post-war Western Europe was unique; it certainly had no other right-wing parallels, beyond rather marginalized groups or individuals such as the British Conservative MP Enoch Powell. Generally in Western nations it was left-wing parties and movements that propagated anti-Americanism, as was most evident in the Korean and then the Vietnam anti-war movements. These movements helped create a new and virulent critique of America opposed to what was seen as the unjustified and imperialistic use of American force. In the case of the Vietnam War protesters tried (and were drawn to) a variety of means and tactics, certainly not all of which were anti-American; nonetheless some undoubtedly were, as the *Washington Post* columnist E. J. Dionne regretfully remarks in this quote about the American anti-Vietnam War movement:

> Critics of American foreign policy have nearly always been labelled 'anti-American' by their foes; being cast into the political darkness is one of the

risks of dissent. But rarely have dissenters cooperated so willingly to validate the claims of their enemies. By embracing anti-Americanism as a noble cause, the farther fringes of the New Left divided and set back the anti-war movement.[25]

As John Kane has persuasively written, the Vietnam War was a time when the image of a virtuous America lost much credibility both internally and amongst friends and allies.[26] The Vietnam conflict has undoubtedly also had a long political legacy. What was interpreted in Australia as the anti-Americanism of the anti-Iraq War movement of 2003 has, from its slogans to its general worldview, a good deal in common with the anti-Vietnam War movement. This is not surprising given the impact the anti-Vietnam War movement had on the generation of Australian baby boomers. The conflict was also a watershed for Australia as a country with an independent voice on major foreign policy issues. Jean Bethke Elshtain similarly notes the parallels between the anti-Vietnam and anti-2003 Iraq War protests in the United States.[27] However, one important difference was that many of the anti-Vietnam War protesters were sympathetic towards Ho Chi Minh and his government whereas in 2003 Saddam Hussein's regime had very few supporters. Despite the obvious significance of the Vietnam War, the most detailed work on anti-Americanism – Hollander's *Anti-Americanism* – barely discusses the anti-Vietnam War movement. This seems a clear weakness and reflects the rather haphazard scholarship on anti-Americanism. Instead of Vietnam, Hollander pays considerable attention to objections to American policy in Nicaragua in the 1980s,[28] and also looks in detail at criticisms of America in the United Nations forums in the 1970s.[29] Both of these cases illustrate the lack of good will and trust between America and foreign governments and foreign opinion makers. Hollander particularly focuses on American and European pro-Sandinista supporters whom he largely depicts as being driven by a combination of knee-jerk anti-Americanism and socialist fantasies about Nicaragua. In Hollander's account this outlook has little to do with the reality of American foreign policy or the behaviour of the Sandinista leadership but instead reflects the psychological needs of many of the Sandinistas' Western supporters. This critique is reminiscent of the neo-conservative criticism of New Class liberals in America as promoters of the causes of the poor for their own self-aggrandisement.[30] For all Hollander's criticism of the allegedly one-eyed anti-Americanism of the pro-Sandinista movement, his account is far from being a neutral or comprehensive assessment of the rights and wrongs of US policy in Nicaragua. Instead it is a polemic against a certain type of leftist sympathizer whom Hollander is seeking to discredit with accusations of anti-Americanism.

Arguably world opinion softened towards America in the late 1970s, particularly in France where anti-American sentiment seemed on the wane.[31] Even while the French Minister of Culture took the significant step of imposing quotas on American television programmes and films, some noted former socialists amongst the French intelligentsia were moving towards a more pro-American stance. These included Bernard-Henri Levy and Andre Glucksmann, who denounced French radicals for naïvely sympathizing with Maoist China and other brutal regimes. According to a number of accounts, the French left in general was shaken by the 1974 publication of Alexander Solzhenitsyn's *Gulag Archipelago*, which 'severely undermined residual sympathies for the Soviet Union, just as the later revelations about communist behaviour in Cambodia shook liberal sympathies for Third World socialism'.[32] It was in this milieu that Levy emerged as an intellectual celebrity in France, where he continues to be well known and one of the leading anti-anti-Americans.[33] At the national political level the French Socialists, led by President François Mitterrand, supported the US-NATO policy of installing Cruise and Pershing missiles in Western Europe. This sympathetic outlook towards American strategic policy in Europe stood in stark contrast to the policies of the West German SPD and the British Labour Party, both of which strongly opposed these weapons being placed in their respective countries.

In Britain and West Germany in the 1980s, the presence of American bases and nuclear weapons became issues of considerable public antipathy and long-standing protest such as at Greenham Common.[34] However, at the same time the conservative Kohl and Thatcher governments staunchly defended their alliance with the United States throughout the 1980s. A 'backlash' against American bases spread to a number of places including the Philippines[35] and more recently to Japan and South Korea. Chalmers Johnson has written ominously about the potential the latter two countries hold for anti-Americanism in his book *Blowback* – a title, and term, that has become synonymous with recent claims of anti-Americanism. The term 'blowback' was first used in a political sense by the CIA in reference to America's involvement in the 1953 overthrow of the Iranian Prime Minister. 'The word', writes James Risen, 'has since come into use as shorthand for the unintended consequences of covert operations'.[36] Johnson and others have suggested, for example, that the CIA's support of the Afghan *mujahedeen* and Osama bin Laden resulted in perhaps the most stunning incident of anti-American blowback – the terrorist attacks of 11 September 2001.[37] As this last example suggests, criticisms of America's use of its military and political power have continued beyond the end of the cold war and remain a major source of what is often labelled anti-Americanism. The key difference in these current foreign policy debates and conflicts is that the Soviet Union no longer exists as an alternative pole or source of support.

Beyond the cold war: are we all Americans now?

The end of the cold war was widely predicted to usher in a new era of harmony on political and ideological matters. Hollander predicted that there would be a reduction of anti-capitalist sentiment, which for him is one of the key strands of anti-Americanism.[38] However, rather like predictions of the 'end of ideology' a generation earlier, these pronouncements turned out to be premature. Rather, new issues have led to unparalleled disagreements between former NATO allies with the 2003 Iraq conflict being the most obvious example. At a general level the end of the cold war was followed by what has been widely dubbed the era of globalization. The anti-Americanism of this period is frequently associated with the anti-globalization movement and its fears of a world dominated by American capitalist interests and American culture.[39] These anti-globalization concerns often extend beyond anxiety over US dominance, but nonetheless the rhetoric and protests of these movements more often than not single out US multinational corporations, US influence on the International Monetary Fund and the World Bank, and the United States' failure to sign the Kyoto protocol when seeking a place to lay the blame for the world's ills. Similarly, it is America that is most at fault for world poverty, environmental degradation, and global conflict. Some of these criticisms are fair and justified; others are indiscriminate and are rightly called anti-American. Amongst many in the anti-globalization movement, 'America' has become a code word for all the various ills of the world, reminiscent of its use in the mid nineteenth century in certain French circles.[40]

Against a backdrop of widespread scepticism about America in the post-cold war period, the attacks of 11 September 2001 elicited an ambivalent response from the rest of the world, which took many Americans by surprise. Reflecting the noted insularity of their society, many Americans seemed largely unaware of how America and Americans were viewed around the globe. In the wake of 9/11 the president and society were to ask 'why do they hate us?' in reference to terrorists and their supporters. The answer to this question may, however, be much simpler to understand than anti-Americanism in the general populace.

Anti-American terrorism

The violent anti-Americanism symbolized by the 9/11 attacks has undoubtedly made the subject of anti-Americanism much more serious than the parlour room denouncements of American manners and culture of an earlier era. However while 11 September 2001 marked a new phase of anti-Americanism, the concerns of the previous phase have continued largely unabated. The beginnings of violent anti-Americanism can be traced to earlier events such as politically motivated attacks on, and murders of, Americans in Beirut from the 1970s onwards, the Iranian hostage crisis of 1979–1980, the 1993 detonation of a van bomb in the underground car park in the World Trade Center, the 1998 car bomb attacks on the US embassies in Nairobi and Dar es Salaam, and the 2000 suicide bombing of the USS *Cole* in Aden Habour, Yemen. All of these attacks had anti-American motivations as Barry and Judith Colp Rubin argue in their recent book on anti-American terrorism,[41] but they were considered more as random events before 11 September 2001. The term 'anti-American terrorism' was barely mentioned in pre-9/11 literature and the Rubins and others have animated this earlier history in light of the events of 9/11.

Following 9/11 many theories abounded about why the attacks had occurred.[42] Elshtain has noted a tendency to not take Osama bin Laden and al-Qaeda at their word and instead look for deeper and possibly more complicated reasons for the attacks.[43] For Elshtain this tendency is largely due to the inability of most commentators to take religious messages (such as al-Qaeda's declared *jihad* against America) seriously; as a result they see such statements as 'window dressing'. Instead they seem to believe that the 'the heart of the matter lies else-where, in leftover colonial ire or antiglobalist chagrin'.[44] Elshtain's argument that more attention needs to be paid to the statements and actions of al-Qaeda and other radical Islamic organizations is an important addition to the post-9/11 discourse which has often been characterized by commentators and politicians bringing too much of their own political baggage to bear on why the attacks occurred. Although Elshtain is right to highlight the importance of religious motivations, as I will illustrate below, it is the intersection of religious and territo-rial concerns that most animates the statements and actions of anti-American terrorists.

In analysing 9/11 one of the crucial issues involves cause and effect. In other words, what actions and political positions taken by the United States principally precipitated the terrorist attacks? It seems that both official assessments in America, Australia and Britain *and* radical interpretations from some leftist academics cast the net far too wide. George W. Bush, John Howard and Tony Blair have all said that those responsible for the 9/11 attacks hate America (and like-minded nations) because of their freedoms and liberties – in short because of their way of life. Certain left-wing scholars have cited colonialism, poverty, glob-alization, and twentieth century American foreign policy as the causes of the attacks. However, a series of speeches, interviews and videoed comments by Osama bin Laden and other al-Qaeda leaders reveal seemingly more delimited and specific reasons for targeting America than much of the standard commen-tary acknowledges. These speeches state their grievances directly and with considerable repetition; they condemn America for its 'occupying of the country of the two Holy places', for its alliance with the Jews in oppressing and killing Palestinians and occupying the sacred al-Aqsa mosque and Dome of the Rock in Jerusalem, and for its policies in Iraq which have led to the death of 600,000 children (later claimed by bin Laden to be one million children). It is these poli-cies that al-Qaeda clearly states justify the killing of Americans, with once again the clear aim being America's retreat from the Muslim world. Bin Laden bluntly states that 'what happened on September 11 is nothing but a reaction to the continuing injustice being done to our children in Palestine, Iraq, Somalia, southern Sudan, and elsewhere, as well as Kashmir and Asia'.[45] While this state-ment refers to a wide variety of conflicts, the underlying message is consistent – let Muslims govern their societies without outside interference.

Bin Laden and others in the al-Qaeda leadership seem to believe that America can be forced to retreat and that it has far less stomach for war than the Soviets whom al-Qaeda helped to defeat in Afghanistan. In his 1996 statement entitled 'Declaration of War' bin Laden paints the Americans as cowards.

> When the explosion in Beirut took place [in] 1983 ... you were turned into scattered bits and pieces at that time; 241 mainly Marines [and] soldiers were killed. And where was this courage of yours when two explosions made

you to leave Aden [after the attack on the USS *Cole*] in less than twenty-four hours! But your most disgraceful case was in Somalia, where – after vigorous propaganda about the power of the United States and its post-cold war leadership of the new world order – you moved tens of thousands of international force[s], including 28,000 American soldiers, into Somalia. However, when tens of your soldiers were killed in minor battles and one pilot was dragged in the streets of Mogadishu you left the area carrying disappointment, humiliation, defeat, and your dead with you.[46]

This claim that Americans can be forced to retreat is repeated by bin Laden elsewhere and is clearly similar to the belief systems of other terrorist organizations (such as Hamas) that their enemies will retreat if violence is used against them. In a recent comprehensive study of suicide terrorism from 1980 to 2001, Robert Pape concludes that the aim in nearly all of the 188 cases during this period was territorial. In most cases territory (or greater self-rule) was ceded in a response to the suicide terrorism, further fuelling the terrorists' belief that terrorism pays.[47] A number of conclusions can be drawn from these findings. Pape argues for a tougher line with terrorists, making it clear their demands will not be met and focusing on improving 'homeland security' to detect terrorist activity. Alternatively, a more interventionist approach to violent territorial disputes could be adopted where a United Nations arbitration process is established. A further alternative is NATO and American armed intervention as occurred in the former Yugoslavia.

Bin Laden's criticisms of America, like some earlier forms of anti-Americanism, also propound conspiracy theories regarding the Jewish influence over America. In a variety of speeches he talks of the Jewish-crusader or Zionist-American alliance, and in a video dated 2000 he goes much further, describing America as a puppet of Israel.

> The American government is independent in name only. We believe that it represents and is controlled by Israel. If we take a look at the most important ministries in the current government [the Clinton administration], such as the defence department and the state department, and the sensitive intelligence services and others, we find that the Jews have the final say in the American government. The Jews manipulate America and use it to execute their designs in the world, particularly in the Muslim world.[48]

Other al-Qaeda members reiterate similar views to bin Laden[49] as do other radical Islamic organizations such as the World Islamic Front[50] and Islamic Jihad.[51] Along with the Jewish conspiracy theories, these organizations share with bin Laden a central aim of forcing Western powers out of the Middle East. Ali A. Muhammad, an Islamic Jihad member, describes the organization's objective as being 'just to attack any Western target in the Middle East, to force the governments of the Western countries just to pull out' based on the Beirut experience of America pulling out after the killing of US Marines.[52]

Interestingly these direct speeches and testimony from al-Qaeda and other radical Islamic organizations comment little on American society and its freedoms and liberties. Instead their central tenet is the removal of America from the Middle East. Yet President Bush and his supporters maintain that the terrorist attacks are an attack on the American way of life rather than an extreme means of forcing changes in American foreign policy. My analysis here in no way means to excuse the brutality of al-Qaeda's terrorist actions. Rather my aim is to highlight the weaknesses of much of the writing on the causes of the 9/11 attacks. At the same time I acknowledge that there are limits to understanding the 'logic' of the actions of such terrorist organizations.

In many regards the terrorist attacks of 11 September 2001 were quintessential anti-American acts, which satisfy all of the competing definitions of anti-Americanism. In targeting the Pentagon and the World Trade Center, the terrorists deliberately attacked two famous symbols of American power as well as indiscriminately killing civilians who were predominantly Americans. When asked by interviewers to justify the 9/11 attacks, bin Laden claims that the evils committed by America justified a suspension of Islamic laws regarding murder. Furthermore, he states that American civilians are a legitimate target because they vote for their leaders and their taxes fund American forces (and help fund Israel's military forces, which are used to 'massacre Palestinians').[53] Theodore Zeldin has described anti-Americanism as pathological, arguing that '[t]o hate a whole nation, or to love a whole nation, is a clear symptom of hysteria'.[54] Although al-Qaeda's terrorist anti-Americanism fits this pathology, its outlook even in all its irrationality is arguably more strategically oriented towards a set of territorial aims than Western leaders have generally acknowledged.

Conclusion

From laments about bad manners to denouncements for the supposed occupation of sacred Muslim sites in the Middle East, criticism of America has a varied and broad history. The cultural criticisms with which I began this examination have remained constant in anti-American discourse, particularly as the spectre of Americanization is increasingly resisted. Once America emerged out of a period of infancy and isolation to being recognized as a 'great power' by the rest of the world, political and economic concerns also became a central plank of the anti-American thinking; and finally most recently we have seen the emergence of anti-American terrorism. My historical classification of different periods of anti-Americanism has similarities with Moises Naím's identification of five 'pure' types of anti-Americanism: politico-economic, historical, religious, cultural, and psychological.[55] However, beyond such historical or thematic classifications of anti-Americanism, much work is still required to differentiate real anti-Americanism from what would be better described as criticism. A narrow definition of anti-Americanism that defines it as an indiscriminate attack on America is probably the most useful conceptual starting point. Most discussion on anti-Americanism lacks a precise definition and as a result the history of zanti-Americanism has been recorded and retold in a largely impressionistic fashion. This has contributed to the incoherent nature of much so-called 'anti-American' comment, with the term being used too broadly and thus too regularly. As these broad categories of anti-Americanism suggest, hating certain aspects of the United States is perhaps understandable, but to hate the nation and its people as a whole is irrational. Such blanket hatred generally relies on a series of stereotypes or caricatures that often tells one more about the individual or group passing judgement than it does about America. None of this is to suggest that America is always right, honourable or just, but rather I would suggest the slide from criticism into anti-Americanism distinguishes no one. Prejudiced rhetoric weakens otherwise justifiable critiques of America's many faults. At the same time it hinders the ability to appreciate the promise that America still holds for itself and the world.

Notes

1 Thanks to John Chiddick and Katherine Delaney for their most useful comments on this chapter.
2 See B. Rubin and J. C. Rubin (eds.), *Anti-American Terrorism and the Middle East*, Oxford: Oxford University Press, 2002.
3 P. Hollander, *Anti-Americanism: Irrational and Rational*, New York: Transaction, 1995; S. Haseler, *The Varieties of Anti-Americanism*, Washington, DC: Ethics and Public Policy Center, 1985.
4 Marie-France Toinet, 'Does anti-Americanism exist?', in D. Lacorne *et al* (eds.), *The Rise and Fall of Anti-Americanism*, Basingstoke: Macmillan, 1990, p. 219.
5 A. Rubinstein and D. Smith, 'Anti-Americanism in the Third World', *Annals (AAPSS)*, 1988, vol. 497, p. 35.
6 For anyone who doubts whether people from a wide variety of nations really dislike the United States, these recent surveys are worth consulting: BBC (2003) *What the World Thinks of America*. Available <http://news.bbc.co.uk/2/hi/americas/2994924.stm> (accessed 12 December 2004); Pew Research Centre (2003) *America's Image Further Erodes, Europeans Want Weaker Ties*. Available <http://people-press.org/reports/display.php3?ReportID=175> (accessed 12 December 2004).
7 Toinet, 'Does anti-Americanism exist?' pp. 223–4.
8 D. Diner, *America in the Eyes of the Germans*, Princeton, NJ: Markus Wiener Publishers, 1996, pp. 3–4.
9 S. Schama, 'The unloved American', *The New Yorker*, 3 March 2003. Available <http://www.newyorker.com/printable/?fact/030310fa_fact> (accessed 18 November 2004). For a more complicated view of Dickens' position on America see George Orwell's 'Charles Dickens', in G. Orwell, *The Collected Essays*, vol. 1, Harmondsworth: Penguin, 1970, pp. 474–5.
10 T. Judt, 'Anti-Americans abroad', *The New York Review of Books*, 1 May 2003, p. 24.
11 K. Hamsun, *The Cultural Life of Modern America*, Cambridge, MA: Harvard University Press, 1969 [1889], p. 15. Similarly in Germany Nikolaus Lenau in the 1830s and Friedrich Kurnberger in his novel *Der Amerika-Mude* (1855) presented a picture of an America lacking in cultural worth that was fairly widely accepted (see Diner, *America in the Eyes of the Germans*, p. 33).
12 Schama, 'The unloved American'.
13 Diner, *America in the Eyes of the Germans*, p. 5.
14 T. Judt, *Past Imperfect*, Berkeley, CA: University of California Press, 1992, pp. 188–9.
15 Ibid; See also Diner, *America in the Eyes of the Germans*.

16 S. Meunier, 'The French exception', *Foreign Affairs*, vol. 79, no. 4, July/August 2000.

17 Judt, *Past Imperfect*, pp. 190–1.

18 This tradition was continued throughout the twentieth century by those who promoted the Third World and indigenous lifestyles as an alternative to Western materialism. In America the contrast was often with Eastern mysticism and Buddhism, an outlook popularized by the American counterculture from the Beats onwards (see J. Kerouac, *Dharma Bums*, London: Deutsch 1959).

19 Concerns about American capitalism and modernity continued to be expressed by intellectuals despite the discrediting of French and German Romanticism. Arguably the Frankfurt School theorists such as Marcuse, Adorno, Horkheimer and Habermas offered the most significant critiques in the post-1945 period. Such concerns remained rather marginal; nonetheless they were to become an important component of the intellectual heritage of both the environmental movement and later the anti-globalization movement.

20 Judt, *Past Imperfect*, p. 194.

21 S. Martin Lipset, *American Exceptionalism*, New York: Norton, 1996.

22 A. Werth, *France 1940–1955*, New York: Henry Holt, 1956, pp. 577–9.

23 There was also lingering resentment about the behaviour of American troops. For instance in France it was commonly thought that the American army was more generous in handing out rations to German prisoners of war than it was to French citizens (see Lacorne, *The Rise and Fall of Anti-Americanism*).

24 R. Crockatt, *America Embattled*, London: Routledge, 2003, p. 58.

25 E. J. Dionne, *Why Americans Hate Politics*, New York: Simon and Schuster, 1992, p. 52.

26 J. Kane, 'American values or human rights?', *Presidential Studies Quarterly*, vol. 33, no. 4, 2003, pp. 772–800.

27 J. Bethke Elshtain, *Just War Against Terror*, New York: Basic Books, 2003, p. 72.

28 Hollander, *Anti-Americanism*, pp. 259–306.

29 Ibid., pp. 343–55.

30 See B. O'Connor, *A Political History of the American Welfare System*, Lanham, MD: Rowman and Littlefield, 2004, pp. 103–8.

31 Lacorne, *The Rise and Fall of Anti-Americanism*; Crockatt, *America Embattled*, pp. 58–9.

32 P. Sheenan, 'Paris: Moses and polytheism', *The New York Review of Books*, 24 January 1980. Available <http://www.nybooks.com/articles/7558> (accessed 10 December 2004).

33 A. Gopnik, 'The anti-anti-Americans', *The New Yorker*, 1 September 2003.

34 Opposition to nuclear weapons and American bases in Britain has been a long-standing concern of the Campaign for Nuclear Disarmament (CND) established in the UK in 1958. The protests of the 1980s were often referred to as CND's 'second wave'.

35 Whereas the end of the cold war took some of the bite out of European objections to American bases, it had the opposite effect in the Philippines, which took the opportunity under a new leader not to renew the American naval base in Subic Bay. The issue of American bases continues to be a source of tension in many parts of the world. In a recent *Australian* newspaper editorial (which is very positive about Australia's defence relationship with America and a proposal to have more American military equipment and personnel in Australia for training purposes), the idea of an American base in Australia is dismissed. 'Nobody needs to get themselves excited about the prospect of thousands of Marines overpaid, oversexed and over here.' (*The Australian* 'Joint facility can strengthen the US alliance', 19 January 2004). This repeats a common objection to the presence of American troops that lingers in popular consciousness from memories of World War Two across the globe.

36 Quoted in C. Johnson, *Blowback*, London: Time Warner, 2002, p. xii.

37 Ibid., pp. xii–xvii. This finding is disputed by Elshtain, *Just War Against Terror*, p. 80; and by P. Bergen, *Holy War*, New York: Free Press, 2001.

38 Hollander, *Anti-Americanism*, p. 445.
39 B. Barber, *Jihad vs. McWorld*, New York: Ballantine Books, 1996; G. Ritzer, *The McDonaldization Thesis*, London: Sage, 1998.
40 Judt, *Past Imperfect*, p. 188.
41 Rubin and Rubin, *Anti-American Terrorism and the Middle East*.
42 K. Booth and T. Dunne (eds.), *Worlds in Collision*, Basingstoke: Palgrave Macmillan, 2002.
43 See the Special Issue of the *Australian Journal of Politics and History*, vol. 49, no. 3, 2003. This series of articles makes little mention of Osama bin Laden's and al-Qaeda's justifications for the 9/11 attacks and instead too often imprints the authors' own politics on why these attacks occurred. The worst offender is an article by Geoff Dow and Winton Higgins that provides a very tangential set of explanations for the causes of the 9/11 attacks ('What have we done wrong?', *Australian Journal of Politics and History*, vol. 49, no. 3, 2003, pp. 380–97).
44 Elshtain, *Just War Against Terror*, p. 86.
45 'Interview with Osama bin Laden', (27 December 2001), in ibid., p. 265. Elsewhere bin Laden condemns the UN promoted division and separation of East Timor from Indonesia (see 'Broadcast by Osama bin Laden', (3 November 2001), in ibid., p. 259).
46 Osama bin Laden 'Declaration of war', (August 1996), in ibid., p. 140.
47 R. Pape, 'The strategic logic of suicide terrorism', *American Political Science Review*, vol. 97, no. 3, 2003, pp. 343–62.
48 Osama bin Laden, 'Al-Qa'ida recruitment video', (2000), in Rubin and Rubin, *Anti-American Terrorism and the Middle East*, p. 178.
49 Suleiman Abu Ghaith, 'Al-Qa'ida statement', (13 October 2001), in ibid., pp. 254–5.
50 World Islamic Front, 'Statement: Jihad against Jews and Crusaders', (23 February 2001), in ibid., p. 149.
51 'Testimony of Ali A. Muhammad', (21 October 2000), in ibid., pp. 209–10.
52 Ibid., p. 210.
53 'Dawn Interview with Osama bin Laden', (10 November 2001), in ibid., p. 261.
54 T. Zeldin, 'The Pathology of anti-Americanism', in Lacorne, *The Rise and Fall of Anti-Americanism*, p. 35.
55 M. Naím, 'Anti-Americanisms', *Foreign Policy*, vol. 132, January/February 2002.

2 Are we all Americans now?

Explaining anti-Americanisms

Robert Singh

In 1980, the British comedian Rowan Atkinson, in a sketch entitled 'The Devil' performed during his one-man show in Belfast, played Lucifer welcoming sinners to their new home in Hell. After running through a list of reliably dubious categories – bank managers, thieves, adulterers, lawyers – his biggest laugh came when he asked, after a suitably prolonged pause, 'Now, Americans: are you here?' (When performing the same show in Boston a few years later, an equally heartfelt burst of applause from his American audience greeted his substitution of 'Americans' with 'the French'.)

If expressions of antipathy towards America and Americans display a remarkably long historical pedigree, the international response to the terrorist attacks of 11 September 2001 and the subsequent American-led wars in Afghanistan and Iraq have generated a new level of academic and popular commentary on 'anti-Americanism'.[1] The term itself is now so ubiquitous as to be part of the language of contemporary international politics although, like that other much-used term, 'legitimacy', it remains difficult to define. Although some scholars argue that the phenomenon 'finds its most sophisticated intellectual expression in the West in France',[2] if recent empirical surveys are to be believed anti-Americanism is evidently a global phenomenon. References to anti-Americanism, however, though frequent across the political spectrum, rarely seek to examine its fundamental character beyond assertions that – if it exists – it has ultimately either been 'born in the USA' because of US arrogance or thrives outside the United States because of non-American mendacity, resentment and unthinking enmity.

At a moment when a common refrain is 'I'm not anti-American, but ...' it might therefore appear redundant to inquire as to whether, as *Le Monde* suggested on 13 September 2001, 'we are all Americans now'. The response that such an assertion invariably elicits across the non-American world is as emphatically negative as the explanation is clear, simple and forceful: US foreign policy. On some accounts, this is a matter of the administration of President George W. Bush having abandoned its predecessors' multilateral approaches for a 'Bush Doctrine' of 'regime change', preventive war and unapologetic unilateralism in the service of American primacy. For others, antipathy towards America is simply the price to be paid for power, the Bush experience merely representing a more intense form of that encountered by successive American administrations since at least 1945 (and by dominant world powers throughout history). As Walter Laqueur argues, '[t]o be hated is a consequence of being great and powerful. It can be remedied not by becoming gentler, only by becoming weaker'.[3]

This conventional wisdom, however, may be more conventional than wise. Although the existence of broadly based and deeply rooted antipathy towards aspects of the American nation, people and public policies is undeniable, this is neither new nor consistently coherent as a worldview. Nor is anti-Americanism uniform in its focus, intensity or origins. Rather, there exist distinct forms, causes and expressions of antipathy that derive from an abiding ambivalence about America: anti-Americanisms rather than anti-Americanism. These, in turn, reflect distinct encounters with American nationalism. They are responses to specific effects of particular US foreign policies, and in some cases are projections of internal problems onto an American 'other' as the locus of responsibility for maladies whose origins are in large part as much intra- as inter-national. What limited intellectual unity anti-Americanisms possess is a function of a shared ambivalence about America. But the particularistic expressions of anti-Americanism differ wherever one cares to look.

The analysis that follows first examines the problem of defining anti-Americanism and rejects the notion that anti-Americanism represents a coherent worldview. I then examine the reasons for the phenomenon's apparent ubiquity. I argue that anti-Americanism assumes distinct forms according to the intensity, breadth and nature of the grievances levelled against America. If ambivalence about America provides the unifying thread of anti-Americanisms, anti-Americanisms are also – necessarily – dualistic phenomena in Europe, Latin America and Africa as much as in the Arab and Islamic worlds. In this sense, post-9/11 American foreign policy provoked a new wave of anti-Americanism, facilitating the widespread public expression of antipathy towards the United States that had been muted in the decade following the end of the cold war.

Anti-Americanism(s): 'designer prejudice' or ideology?

Antipathy towards 'America' is an identifiable and influential global phenomenon. In 2002 and 2003 mass protests against American foreign policy towards Iraq were staged from Sydney and London to Buenos Aires. Public and private discussions on whether and how to resist America's military, economic and cultural dominance occurred across otherwise disparate continents. Critical essays and polemics about America achieved bestseller status, ranging from broad explorations of anti-American hostility to examinations of why Americans are disproportionately fat.[4] Bush's State Department convened a symposium on anti-Americanism in 2002 and the administration hired public relations consultants to improve America's international image. Public figures around the world ventured their opinions on America while America's role and power featured prominently in several national election campaigns from 2002–2005. Anti-Americanism had reached the highest counsels of government and become worthy of renewed academic scrutiny.

Despite (or because of) its status as America's closest ally the British case is especially instructive in examining changes in perceptions of America. In the immediate aftermath of 9/11, President Bush declared to a joint session of Congress that his nation had 'no truer friend than Great Britain' while Prime Minister Tony Blair asserted that the UK would stand 'shoulder to shoulder' with America. By May 2002, however, Blair was sufficiently moved to publicly attack the growing anti-Americanism across Europe. He declared that '[t]here's no way Britain is ever going to be anything less than a full friend and partner of America, in Europe, out of Europe, whatever'.[5] Similarly, in May 2003 Britain's Foreign Secretary Jack Straw expressed his concern about how 'trite anti-Americanism' had 'become fashionable' in the UK, while NATO Secretary General Lord Robertson defined anti-Americanism '… not as a criticism of individual policies or even an individual president. It's a sort of racialist view that the USA is wrong in principle and wrong in practice'.[6] If, even in the UK, anti-Americanism has moved beyond private discussions to become part of national political discourse, such comments may perhaps be taken as clear symptoms of a spreading strain. But whether they indicate the rise of an identifiable and coherent phenomenon, and, if so, which sources best explain its increasing incidence, is less obvious than critics and proponents of anti-American sentiments typically concede.

One illustration of the difficulty of analysing anti-Americanism can be gleaned by considering Richard Posner's comment (made in 2001) on Aldous Huxley's novel, *Brave New World*: 'The society of happy, thoughtless philistines depicted by Huxley seems merely an exaggeration of today's America'.[7] Uttered by an Arab or a European, this statement might justifiably be regarded as an expression of anti-Americanism. However, Posner is an American conservative federal court judge and prolific scholar. Is he 'anti-American', 'un-American', 'elitist' or merely 'critical'? If the latter, when does the expression of negative views about America by non-Americans legitimately merit the designation 'anti-American'? Discussions of anti-Americanism frequently presume that the phenomenon is readily understood – many commentators use the term without any attempt at definition.[8] Like Justice Potter Stewart's notorious 'definition' of pornography, we instinctively 'know it when we see it'. But while anti-Americanism is a term at once excessively precise and overly vague, as Christopher Hitchens has noted, 'we do seem to need a word' for what it represents. As he observes, '[t]here are those in the Islamic world for whom the slogan "Death to America" is a real and meaningful invocation. There are those in Europe and elsewhere for whom the word "American" occasions a wrinkle in the nostril. And there are those, in America itself, for whom their country can do no right'.[9]

Three main problems nonetheless impede analysis of anti-Americanism. First, regarding content, anti-Americanism can encompass opposition to: the public policies – foreign and/or domestic – of the current administration; the administration's strategies and tactics; America's singular global influence (military, diplomatic, economic, and/or cultural); market democracy, a form of political economy that America is widely held to be exemplar of and primary ideological cheerleader for; 'American' values (individualism, democracy, equality of opportunity, private property, the rule of law, and populism); and/or antipathy to Americans as people (anti-Americanism as brute prejudice, stereotyping or bigotry).

Second, to attach the '-*ism*' suffix to a markedly heterogeneous range of attitudes, beliefs and values that are antipathetic to America or Americans implies a systematic coherence in both America/'Americanism' as well as non-American worldviews that is *prima facie* implausible when ascribed to hundreds of millions of people within and outside the United States. For example, many Europeans who adamantly opposed the war on Iraq rejected the charge of anti-Americanism and continued to consume American food, TV, movies, music and clothes – as did many anti-war Americans. Conversely, many nations whose ruling elites and masses mostly appear to loathe American cultural – as opposed to technological – products nonetheless remain in substantive terms close, albeit *sotto voce*, allies of America (Saudi Arabia, Egypt, Kuwait). Moreover, individual affirmations or denials of anti-Americanism may be poor guides to 'objective' evaluations. That is, an avowed 'anti-American' may nonetheless wear American clothes, articulate American slang, listen to American popular music and consume American food. Conversely, a more 'selective' anti-American may be 'in denial' about his or her cognitive dissonance: an antipathy to American cultural products may well complement or fuel more expressly political attitudes that cause all things American to be greeted by a combination of resignation, ridicule and anger.

Third, mass publics' 'idea' of America is neither uniform nor always well informed. If nations are 'imagined communities' then America is, arguably, especially imaginary to many outside – as well as within – the United States. The vivid images conveyed by American cultural products – especially television, film and music – not only represent the American 'reality' for millions but also present a more vaudevillian spectacle than the more complex and mundane realities experienced daily by most Americans. Basic facts about American life – from the extent of government regulation of the market to the relative responsibility of gun owners – rarely intrude on many non-American perceptions of the nation as rapaciously individualistic, violent, selfish, ignorant and philistine. America's marked diversity abets – inadvertently – such selective evaluation. For every William Fulbright there is a Dick Armey ('I've been to Europe once. I don't need to go again').

It is therefore especially important that informed, dispassionate and reasoned criticisms of government policies are distinguished from a deeper, broader and more settled hostility to America and Americans as such. The difficult question – where reasonable persons may disagree – is where that dividing line is most appropriately located.

Anti-Americanism is conventionally represented as a more or less systematic and coherent entity, a worldview with core beliefs, values and lenses by which America is judged as wanting, on a continuum ranging from mildly deficient to utterly depraved. It generally entails strong (rather than mild) disapproval, enmity or animosity for the United States, its government, policies, people, values and/or 'way of life'. As such it comprises a multi-dimensional set of attitudes that are at once political (anti-'imperial'), economic (anti-capitalist, anti-'Anglo-Saxon' free markets and/or anti-globalization), religious (anti-religiosity and/or anti-secularism), cultural (anti-Hollywood, popular TV, film and music and/or 'mass' culture), and ethical (anti-'decadence' and depravity but also anti-Puritanism). The capaciousness of these sources of critical commentary provides anti-Americanism with remarkable elasticity – as Lyndon Johnson once said of the Gulf of Tonkin resolution, like grandma's nightdress, it 'covers everything'.

Which criticisms provide the most reliable source(s) of anti-Americanism, and how broad and intense these are, however, relies heavily on factors internal to the hosts exhibiting the '*ism*'. The extent to which America is admired, feared or loathed hinges substantially on the host nation/region's particular encounters with America, and its socioeconomic and political fortunes. Secular Europeans, for example, invariably combine a mixture of bafflement, derision and offence regarding American religiosity and the extent to which policies such as capital punishment separate America from its 'advanced' industrial democratic peers. America's cultural products – from cop shows and baseball caps to rap – rarely register as a major cause of ire (outside elites). By contrast, within Arab and Muslim communities, it is not only US foreign policy but also the perceived lack of religious underpinning of American public life, its decadence and unrestrained individualism that compound the antagonisms. Equally, whereas Europeans tend to look poorly on America's refusal to ratify the Kyoto accords or support the International Criminal Court, insufficient environmentalism forms less of a priority in Arab, Muslim or Chinese concerns about US foreign policy.

Much as the sources of anti-Americanism are therefore multiple and diverse, so recent worldwide expressions of anti-Americanism assume distinct forms along a continuum, from passive dislike and private disapproval through mild gestures of resistance (boycotting Nike) to mass activism (protest marches such as those of anti-globalization demonstrations in Seattle in 1999) and violence (wrecking McDonalds and KFC stores and, ultimately, targeting Americans for terrorist strikes – 9/11 was, after all, the most extreme and 'pure' expression of anti-Americanism possible as, on a far smaller but equally lethal scale, is the deliberate targeting of individual Americans for hostage-taking and extra-judicial executions in Iraq). Once again, which activities predominate is location-specific. Burning the American flag is a protest ritual against a cultural and political 'Other' that is more common in Tehran than Tbilisi or Turin.

As the sources and expressions of anti-Americanism have received increasing attention, two principal sources of division are identifiable within the scholarly and popular literatures concerning its anatomy and origins.[10] The first concerns whether anti-Americanism represents a 'rational' worldview or whether the phenomenon is simply too inchoate and ambivalent (even contradictory) to meet even a minimal test of intellectual coherence. Among those who view the phenomenon as coherent, Philippe Roger and Jean-François Revel argue that anti-Americanism represents a more-or-less systematic view of America.[11] Salman Rushdie regards anti-Americanism as 'an ideological enemy that may turn out to be harder to defeat than militant Islam'.[12] The British critic John Lloyd denies that anti-Americanism is merely criticism of US policies but rather represents a 'narrative' of leftist critics who see America as 'an imperial predator whose actions – all actions – are conditioned by this aspect of its being'.[13]

Contesting these depictions of coherence are scholars for whom anti-Americanism is a convenient but misleading 'catch-all' term that obscures more than it reveals – its capacious elasticity providing the explanation of its global ubiquity. In its strongest guises, these critics view anti-Americanism as more an emotive than a reasoned response. Clive Christie, for instance, describes anti-Americanism as a 'designer prejudice for our times' that is 'perfectly self-contained. It provides an all-encompassing explanation for global events and can easily accommodate contradictions and even absurdities'.[14] Richard Crockatt, similarly, regards anti-Americanism as 'nothing more or less than the expression of an awareness of cultural difference', albeit a version that is 'expanded and intensified by the disparity in size, power and cultural influence between the United States and other nations'.[15]

Such divergent views on anti-Americanism's structural coherence also reflect differences over its motivating forces. For example, one of the strongest critics of US foreign policy, Arundhati Roy, claims that anti-Americanism is 'in the process of being consecrated into an ideology' for strategic reasons, by conservative Americans themselves, to condemn all critics of US foreign policy for being blinded by hatred of America.[16] From the opposite end of the political spectrum, but partially vindicating Roy's characterization, Paul Hollander has defined anti-Americanism in holistic terms as 'an unfocused and largely irrational, often visceral aversion toward the United States, its government, domestic institutions, foreign policies, prevailing values, culture, and people'.[17] Michael Medved even describes anti-Americanism as 'the world's most dangerous, powerful and pathological hatred' that 'needs to be punished and rooted out, not respectfully analysed' – but regards it, nonetheless, as 'irrational'.[18]

Such marked disagreements over coherence and motivation are powerfully suggestive of the multiple meanings that underpin anti-Americanism as a construct. The notion of anti-Americanism as – rightly or wrongly – something more sweeping and socially embedded than opposition to specific government policies demands the types of comprehensive definitions offered above. But these typically risk failing to adequately explain the particularistic nature of many forms of antipathy towards America. Equally, while individuals can combine vitriolic criticism of US policies with avowed warmth towards America and Americans, a loathing of Americans as a people or culture can be logically combined with a *realpolitik* embrace of US foreign policy (Egypt and Saudi Arabia are obvious examples).

Beyond its incoherence, the second prominent feature in the literature on anti-Americanism – distinct but related to the first – more directly concerns the sources of anti-American sentiment and, in particular, whether these are a product of America's failures or successes: self-inflicted wounds or envious counter-attacks by resentful non-Americans. Critics typically draw on a range of historical, sociological and psychological interpretations to explain the phenomenon.

In the former camp one finds a range of commentators from the relatively selective, policy-specific critics within the Academy (such as Joseph Nye and G. John Ikenberry) to those – mostly leftist, Islamic or non-academic – writers for whom little if any good has, or could, ever emerge from America (such as Noam Chomsky, John Pilger, Gore Vidal, Tariq Ali, and Harold Pinter). In the latter group, however, anti-Americanism represents less a self-inflicted American wound than some type of collective international psychological flaw: envy, resentment and jealousy – a contempt bred in some cases by familiarity and in others by fear. Tony Blair, for example, attributed European anti-Americanism to 'jealousy about America's position'.[19] Walter Russell Mead echoes this theme in arguing that whilst America's 'shortcomings and failures' inflame and disseminate anti-Americanism, its source is 'American success, American power, and America's consequent ability to thwart the ambitions of other states and impose its agenda on the rest of the world'.[20] An Indian philosophy professor has extended this 'love/hate' dichotomy still further:

> It may be that many hate America, not because it is evil, but because it has become part of them. They have invited it in, it moves their will, as it does of many, and they cannot escape it. The desires and aspirations America produces have become our desires and aspirations. Our resistance becomes more virulent because it has become less effective.[21]

The sources of anti-Americanism are complicated still further by its status as an inherently dualistic phenomenon. On the one hand there are the 'brute facts' of American history, as the republic has evolved from what Condoleezza Rice described as its 'birth defect' of slavery through civil war and segregation to the present day in which policies from abortion regulation to environmental protection regularly excite non-American criticism. On the other, there exist developments that are predominantly internal to nations, regions and hemispheres that encounter American political, economic and cultural influences. In the case of European states such as the UK and France, the end of colonial empires, mass immigration from former colonies, and the development of the European Union; for many Middle Eastern states, the end of colonialism, the rise of authoritarian regimes, the waxing and waning of Arab (pan-)nationalisms and Political Islam, and wars both within and between secular, Arab, nationalist, and Islamic regimes. If, therefore, the specific forms and diverse roots of anti-Americanism around the globe can in principle coalesce, it is rare that they do so with any meaningful unifying coherence beyond ambivalence. Following Tolstoy's observation that unhappy families each exhibit their own particular form of unhappiness, it therefore seems preferable to frame the remainder of the analysis in terms of a plurality of anti-Americanisms – a set of unhappy families comprising distinct grievances – rather than a single, coherent worldview. Such unity as they possess stems from a shared ambivalence about America, the sources and expressions of which differ according to time and location.

Explaining anti-Americanisms

Contrary to what critics of the Bush administration sometimes intimate, anti-Americanisms are not new phenomena. From the republic's founding, criticisms of American values, culture and influence were many, varied and forceful – long prior to 'America's (twentieth) century' and currently unprecedented and unrivalled global influence. What is distinctive about the current moment, however, is the breadth, scale and intensity of anti-Americanisms. Whilst analysts typically focus on America's international role – which must necessarily assume primacy in any explanation – the particular encounters with America that shape anti-Americanisms entail more dimensions of conflict than this factor alone, encompassing: clashes of rival and distinct nationalisms; the ideological transformations of the Left and Right wrought by the 'short' twentieth century (especially, but not exclusively, in Europe); and the continuing cultural clashes animated by 'Americanization'. Antipathy to US foreign policy in general, and that of Bush in particular, is therefore a necessary but insufficient explanation of the global spread of anti-Americanisms. Change in that foreign policy, equally, may mute but is unlikely to silence anti-Americanisms.

American power, principle and foreign policy: the cause of all mankind?

After 9/11, a nation that – according to President John Quincy Adams – 'does not go abroad in search of monsters' to destroy became occupied in precisely that venture. The manner by which it did so – from Guantanamo Bay and the 'axis of evil' to the 'Bush Doctrine' and preventive war in Iraq – compounded the international apprehension and aversion to the goals and instruments of US policy that attended Bush's victory in the 2000 presidential election regarding national missile defence and international treaties from the International Criminal Court and land mines to the ABM and Kyoto. For its many critics, hubris – rather than the humility that candidate Bush called for during the 2000 campaign – defined US foreign policy. If Benjamin Franklin was correct to note that America understands that its 'cause is the cause of all mankind', many non-Americans viewed America as more the cause of all mankind's ills. While Arthur Schlesinger, Jr. is surely right to observe that '[t]here is no older American tradition in the conduct of foreign affairs than unilateralism',[22] for observers less well-schooled in the republic's history and for whom the cold war provided the dominant template of analysis, Bush's approach was the rudest of awakenings.

But however much the unilateral tendencies and aggressive rhetoric of the Bush administration have aggravated international anxieties, as the world's 'hyperpower' – a sole superpower in the international order that is dominant in at least two of the four areas of national power (political, economic, military and cultural) – writers such as Laqueur are surely correct that America cannot but stoke opposition. Like previous imperial powers, the United States possesses disproportionate global power that simultaneously repels and attracts. As America rose to global dominance through the twentieth century, relations with Washington became central elements in most nations' fortunes and – hence – their domestic politics. If some hemispheres (notably Latin America) experienced American power in especially direct form, few have been insulated from oscillating patterns of dependence and independence with America. Moreover, the 'hard' power of military and economic instruments has been supplemented in many cases by increasing exposure to America's 'soft' cultural influence – the attractiveness of its values – as first Hollywood and popular music, and latterly television and the internet, brought the American nation and people, their fashions and foibles, directly to masses (as well as elites) around the world.

The empirical evidence here, however, is suggestive of mass publics outside America who can and do actively differentiate between US power, its foreign policy and Americans as people. Admittedly, a Pew Center survey in 2002 found that, despite an initial outpouring of public sympathy following 9/11, global discontent with America had grown. Images of America were tarnished among longtime NATO allies, developing countries, East European countries and, most dramatically, Muslim societies.[23] After 2000, favourable ratings for America declined in nineteen of the twenty-seven countries where trend benchmarks were available. In 2002, when asked if they thought that America listened to its allies, only Germany registered a positive response (53 per cent 'yes' to 45 per cent 'no') while Canadians (73 per cent 'no' v. 25 per cent 'yes'), the French (76 v. 21 per cent) and the British (52 v. 44 per cent) rejected the notion.[24] Moreover, in 2003, the Pew Center reported that non-Americans holding favourable views of America had declined sharply since 2002 (from 61 to 45 per cent in Germany, and from 63 to 43 per cent in France), while the notion that Europe should adopt a more independent approach to international matters had won the support of 76 per cent of the French, 62 per cent of Spaniards, 61 per cent of Italians and 57 per cent of Germans.

While criticism rose, however, impressive reserves of goodwill towards the United States remained. For example, the Pew Global Attitudes survey found that America and Americans continued to be rated positively by majorities in 35 of the 42 countries in which the question was asked. Among twenty-one nations polled in May 2003, most of them affirmed democratic ideals they generally associated with America. Respondents in no less than seventeen nations stated that the problem with America was 'mostly Bush' rather than 'Americans in general'.[25] Genuine dislike of America was confined to Islamic states in the Near East and Central Asia, for whom the abiding symbolism of the war in Iraq was less the fall of Saddam Hussein's statue than the graphic photos of abuse from the Abu Ghraib prison. (Even before the war, respondents to a Gallup survey of nine Muslim countries in 2001–2002 overwhelmingly described America as 'ruthless, aggressive, conceited, arrogant, easily provoked, and biased').[26]

Many mass publics recognize that, in resolving international problems, America remains the 'indispensable nation', one whose global commitments are maintained despite its people's impressively resilient insularity. But where US reluctance to intervene in international crises elicits charges of vacillation and timidity, US intervention invariably prompts accusations of 'Yankee imperialism'. As Samantha Power has recently documented, America's long-term dominance has left it open to criticisms – many justifiable, but some less so – for both action and inaction, sins of commission and omission.[27] But what is often missing in critiques of US policy is a positive and feasible – rather than a utopian – alternative. However vulnerable to criticism successive administrations have been, the reality remains that few serious critics of America wish it either to withdraw its military forces from around the world or abandon its security guarantees – the alternatives are, invariably, far less palatable.

Even the discussion of 'American imperialism' that now generates much scholarly attention points to the invidious position that America occupies. On the one hand, some analysts outside America encourage the United States to 'own up' to imperial status in order to discharge those onerous responsibilities from Latin America to the Middle East and Asia.[28] On the other hand, non-American critics frequently excoriate the United States either for admitting to 'imperial' designs or denying the obvious reality of *Pax Americana*.[29] That prior dilemmas over excessive interventionism (Iran in 1953, Vietnam, Chile in 1973) or insufficient interventionism (1920s and 1930s Europe, Rwanda in 1994–1995) are now refracted in the pressing issues of whether America should seek to promote democratization in the Middle East or accept theocratic and despotic regimes, confirms that since the end of the nineteenth century American power has been the central dynamic in generating international anti-Americanisms. But the exact nature of that dynamic is occluded by a concentration on mere power alone. The peculiar and unique nature of American nationalism powerfully shapes these encounters.

Rival nationalisms

Marked antipathy towards US foreign policy is a function of more than opposition to its goals, instruments, and effects. It also reflects an abiding concern for American hypocrisy in the international arena. If foreign policy presents a nation's face to the world, as Schlesinger once noted, America is 'two-faced'. Or, as the realist scholar, John Mearsheimer put it, '[i]t should be obvious to intelligent observers that the United States speaks one way and acts another'.[30] In this respect, anti-Americanisms gain especially strong purchase from the clash between 'conventional' nationalisms and the unique (and paradoxical) nature of American nationalism. Anti-Americanisms, in this sense, could not exist without Americanism that, in turn, reflects the continuing vitality of America's civic nationalism.

Although several scholars have rejected the notion of 'American exceptionalism' and sought to recast American civic nationalism as a self-serving myth – an ideological facade masking the ethno-racial, religious and gendered nationalism that has been America's truly dominant narrative – the popular hold that the normative rather than existential basis of American identity exerts remains tenacious.[31] Mass American conviction in America's essential innocence and goodness reflects and reinforces the historical fact that the nation was, and remains, the only nation state founded on a set of aspirational political values. As such, America's distinctive self-conception, comprising a normative discourse that is absent from comparable nationalisms, offers a powerful basis for anti-Americanisms. However discordant it sounds to non-American ears, habitual reference by US political leaders to 'American values' resonates with the majority of American people. If scholars on both the left and the right are correct about the ethno-racial sources of American identity, the self-perception of most Americans remains otherwise. As Peter McCartney compellingly argues, '[n]ational identity and foreign policy are intimately connected in the United States because the former rejects (formally, at least) ethnic or other ascriptive bases of national identity and relies instead on an ideological construction of the nation that insists on the global relevance of the American project'.[32]

Thus anti-Americanism represents in part merely the distaste of other nationalities for America's vibrant nationalism. Comparative surveys typically find Americans exhibiting the greatest national pride among Western nations. Prior to 9/11, for example, the University of Chicago reported that 90 per cent of Americans surveyed agreed with the statement 'I would rather be a citizen of America than of any other country in the world', while 38 per cent agreed with the statement that 'the world would be a better place if people from other countries were more like … Americans'. (Following 9/11 the respective figures rose to 97 and 49 per cent.) The World Values Survey reported that over 70 per cent of Americans declared themselves 'very proud' to be Americans, compared to fewer than half the peoples of other Western democracies expressing similar sentiments of pride (including the UK, France, Italy and Denmark). According to the Pew Global Attitudes survey, 79 per cent of Americans polled agreed that '[i]t's good that American ideas and customs are spreading around the world' and 70 per cent said that they 'like American ideas about democracy'. By comparison, fewer than 40 per cent of Western Europeans endorsed American ideas and customs and fewer than 50 per cent liked American ideas about democracy.[33]

But this clash of rival nationalisms is especially potent – and serves as one of the few unifying elements of ambivalence to anti-Americanisms – since it also reflects the uniquely paradoxical form of American nationalism.[34] Although a highly nationalistic people, most Americans do not view themselves as such. Despite its highly nationalistic character, American policy makers have hence rarely appreciated or dealt subtly with the remarkable and resilient power of nationalism abroad – in part, precisely because of the sincerely held belief that the values on which America is based are 'self-evident' universal truths of eternal veracity.

Moreover, American nationalism exhibits features that typically aggravate rather than ameliorate international antipathies: 'Americanism' is based on political ideals of universal application, not particularistic ethnicity; it is triumphant rather than aggrieved, deriving from successive victories rather than the humiliations of national defeat or conquest (hence the national trauma of Vietnam); and it is future- rather than backward-oriented, casting past glories merely as the prelude for future ones rather than nostalgic signposts in a narrative of national decline. Dynamism and universalism, celebratory through their maintaining a lasting popular hold via civic voluntarism rather than state-imposed coercion, provide a missionary zeal that can prove deeply disquieting to others. As Posner notes, many Americans live in happy ignorance of the apparent contradiction of being more pragmatic and more pietistic than other peoples, partly because historical experience has conferred partial confirmation of their idealistic self-conception:

> if the United States did not have constitutionalism, legality, democracy, religiosity, enormous wealth, a certain history, a special position in the world, and so forth, nationalistic slogans would fall flat. Because there is *some* truth to our hyperbolic, aspirational, self-congratulatory civic rhetoric, we would find total realism deflating and in a sense misleading.[35]

But the idealistic cast of America's self-conception also has the less congenial consequence of American bafflement at non-aligned, neutral or weaker nations during periods when US globalism is more characterized by what McCartney terms 'vindicationism' (the urge to change the world to render it, resemble and act more like America) than 'exemplarism' (the desire to stand apart from and serve as a model of political and social potential).[36] In the former case, during periods when 'universal' American truths are confronted by profound security threats, a Manichean worldview is invariably the result. What is self-evident to many Americans – you are either 'with us or against us' in confronting communism and terrorism – is simplistic to many non-Americans.

In this context it is unsurprising that nationalist movements throughout the non-American world have often experienced deep ambivalence towards America. On the one hand, America's own revolution against colonialism provides an inspirational legitimating example (Ho Chi Minh famously crafted the 1945 declaration of Vietnamese independence in Jeffersonian terms). Yet in many instances – especially during the cold war but also, for Islamist and Arab movements, then and thereafter – America often rebuffed insurgent nationalists as injurious to its interests or, more simply and mistakenly, as communists. Moreover, the particularistic, ethno-cultural nationalism that typifies contemporary nationalist movements often runs counter to America's 'universalist' civic nationalism. Particularly with their Islamic and Arab expressions, failure to guarantee voting rights and women's rights has proven a profound hindrance to their gaining American understanding, much less support. The inherent tension between promoting 'democracy' and tolerating the intolerant regimes that may result is one that no American administration has yet resolved.

The cumulative result is a demonstrable tension between American ideals and practice that applies both inside America and abroad. Mass publics outside the United States not only see an America whose substantive policies and actions they oppose, but experience these interventions being presented in an idealistic and moralistic terminology mostly alien to their own national traditions and their perceptions of the vital (self-) interests driving American policy. Simultaneously, Americans accustomed to moralistic public rhetoric regarding domestic and geopolitical concerns find it difficult (even when they oppose US policy) to do so in amoral terms; confirming still further the normative, aspirational cast of American nationalism. As McCartney argues, America's 'national interest will not – cannot – change unless and until the national identity upon which it rests also changes'.[37] Ironically, in an era of singular American power, the American 'Other' therefore provides a rich reference point by which rival nationalisms from France to Australia can recast their particular historical narratives and putative national identities. As Fareed Zakaria notes, 'nationalism in many countries is being defined in part as anti-Americanism: Can you stand up to the superpower?'[38] The European case, whilst distinctive, offers a particularly vivid window on this global phenomenon.

Mars and Venus? European anti-Americanisms

Anti-Americanisms can be divided into a three-fold typology: leftist criticisms based on the persistence and growth in socio-economic inequalities, within America and globally; rival nationalisms that abhor the idealistic basis of American identity, the heterogeneity of American society and the pretensions to universal truth of America's civic 'creed'; and 'cultural concerns' associated with the supposed threat posed to indigenous ways of life by 'Americanization' – the spread of American cultural products, norms and public policies. The rise of anti-Americanisms has rested heavily on the negative representation of America accompanying the projection of American military power outside its own hemisphere after 1898 and the remarkable popularity of and resentment towards American cultural exports.

Examined in this fashion it is possible to discern patterns of resemblance with prior phenomena, not least Anglophobia and anti-Semitism.[39] A core feature of each has been the externalizing of domestic problems: the projection onto the 'Other' of the main responsibility for problems whose origins are as much intra- as international. This is not for a moment to deny the enormous influence of America, benign and negative, but rather to qualify its status and to bring agency back into the frame for other actors. As such, no political tendency – left, right or otherwise – has possessed a monopoly on anti-Americanism. With the structure of the international system since 1991 so manifestly exhibiting unipolarity, the victory of market capitalism over its ideological foes has ensured that the only 'ideology of discontent' for those resistant to the status quo is anti-Americanism. Protesting the geometry of power is thus most easily expressed in a rough and ready anti-Americanism: an inchoate force but one no less powerful for that, in the absence of alternative compelling narratives of resistance.

The European case is especially illustrative. One might have expected that the intensity of anti-Americanism would be at its peak during periods of ideological confrontation. But the incidence and intensity of European anti-Americanism appears far greater today – after the defeat of Nazism, fascism, and communism, and the effective disappearance of socialist parties seeking to challenge rather than manage capitalism – than in prior eras. Moreover, the scale of anti-Americanism in Europe – a continent that has more reason than most not only to be positively disposed towards America but also anything but fearful of American power – is suggestive of a more multifaceted phenomenon than mere power projection alone: a cultural as well as political resistance to American influences.[40]

Europe provides a student of 'comparative anti-Americanisms' with a particularly telling case study, since it reveals that the phenomenon long predated America's dominant world-role and entails more than opposition to foreign policy. Europeans have been ambivalent about America since its founding,[41] treating Americans with bafflement and contempt from the nineteenth century.

> In the early nineteenth century, with optimism of the Enlightenment soured by years of war and revolution, critics were sceptical of America's naïve faith that it had reinvented politics. Later in the century, American economic power was the enemy, Yankee industrialism the behemoth against which the champions of social justice needed to take up arms. A third generation, itself imperialist, grumbled about the unfairness of a nation's rising to both continental and maritime ascendancy. And in the twentieth century, although the United States came to the rescue of Britain and France in two world wars, many Europeans were suspicious of its motives. A constant refrain throughout this long literature of complaint, and what European intellectuals even now find most repugnant, is American sanctimoniousness, the habit of dressing the business of power in the garb of piety.[42]

Prior to the twentieth century, however, European anti-Americanism was more cultural than political, with writers from Fichte and Baudelaire to Dickens and Waugh displaying a combination of snobbery and cynicism towards the vulgar and material 'New World'. The rise of a more political anti-Americanism resembled the trajectory of anti-Americanisms among Arab peoples in this regard, accompanying the development of – and fissures in – competing ideological tendencies. Whilst pockets of antipathy existed, America's image in the Arab provinces of the Ottoman Empire was generally positive, with those Arabs who knew of America viewing it as a great power unsullied by the imperialisms of Britain, France and Russia. Americans helped to pioneer higher education and liberal America was encountered as a reality in institutions such as the Syrian Protestant College (later the American University of Beirut). Only over the course of the twentieth century did hope in America cede successively into disillusionment in the post-1945 years and animus by its end – the product of successive US-supported interventions, coups, the dictates of its oil interests, support for Israel, the propping up of authoritarian regimes and two Gulf Wars.

Although marked cultural antipathy predated the twentieth century, the European encounter was not entirely dissimilar. The origins of anti-Americanism as an '*ism*' can be identified in the 1920s and 1930s and are found largely in the European right, which, after World War One and the Russian revolution, grew increasingly fearful of powerful threats to 'European' civilization. For the right, Jewish-driven international socialism inspired the European working classes and intensified class conflicts. But in the Anglo-Saxon/Anglo-American West, Jewish-controlled international capitalism was also alleged to have created the Depression and, through Hollywood and popular music, contaminated the purity and superiority of European civilization by encouraging an inferior, mongrelized and debased popular American culture. Socialists and communists meanwhile mixed admiration of America for its progressive achievements with condemnation of its political economy, racial segregation and imperialism (not least the abortive intervention in Russia following the Bolshevik coup). Both left and right drew on (selective) conceptions of the American 'Other' to anathematize and discredit their domestic political opponents.

But with anti-Semitism and the Nazi/fascist right discredited for most Europeans by the late 1940s, the primary exponents of anti-Americanism re-emerged in Europe on the left and – to a lesser extent – in the form of socialist and secular nationalist and pan-Arabist movements in the Middle East. One important distorting consequence of the cold war was therefore to cast European anti-Americanism as largely – even exclusively – a leftist syndrome. America's most notable failing, at home and abroad, was its injustice, a charge most vividly sustained at a mass level during the Vietnam War when – anticipating current anti-Americanisms – popular anti-American protests and elite critiques of 'AmeriKKKa' conjoined. To challenge America was to oppose a political economy unashamedly capitalist, exploitative and expansionist, sustained by a civic society wherein the mass opiates of religiosity and consumerism remained remarkably high in comparative terms and competed to dull American sensitivities to injustice either at home or abroad. Resentment at materialism, consumerism, and 'the military-industrial complex' complemented the criticisms of wealth and power inequalities for many on the European left not only during Vietnam but into the 1980s as President Reagan's actions – deploying Cruise and Pershing missiles in Western Europe – and rhetoric against the 'evil empire' caused 'progressives' to pour scorn on Washington's simplistic approach to international affairs.

That such critiques largely ignored this period as one of incredible energy on the progressive left in tackling inequalities of race, gender and sexual orientation, whose organization served as models for those in the rest of the developed world, need not unduly detain us here. More important for the broader analysis is the basic point that, whilst the existence of oppressive communist regimes in the Soviet Union, Eastern Europe and China assisted the ideological straitjacketing of anti-Americanism as a leftist preoccupation, communism's collapse in 1989–1991 deprived the left of its embarrassing 'city on a hill' but left intact – in America – its Sodom and Gomorrah. An important aspect underpinning the rise of post-1991 anti-Americanism has hence been the absence of a clear and comprehensive alternative programme to market democracy and/or an 'ideal' state that embodies such an alternative. The end of the cold war magnified rather than muted the non-communist left's opposition to democratic capitalism but this now assumed the guise of attacking 'globalization' rather than capitalism as such.

But the cold war context had also obscured important elements of overlap in antipathy towards America between the left and the traditionalist European right. European conservatives and nationalists were unsympathetic to a nation born in a revolution that was anti-colonial, republican and democratic. American egalitarianism, while self-consciously not one of results, was nonetheless a challenge to traditional hierarchies, undeferential to authority, individualistic, and irreverent towards the past. Unapologetically materialistic and lacking a clear ethnic/racial 'spirit', the fascist/Nazi right also shared with European conservatives a disdain for the unruly, democratic, mass society that rejected the *dirigiste* and statist culture of Europe. As Sergio Fabbrini has argued:

> … the left and right have found themselves united in their rejection of the United States, although the reason for the rejection on each side has been the opposite of that on the other. While both sides reject American democracy, the left does so for its (presumed) plebiscitarianism and the right for its (presumed) anarchism. While both reject American capitalism, the left does so because of the inequality that it produces and the right because of the egalitarian levelling that it encourages. But above all both left and right are united in their radical rejection of so-called 'American individualism', although the left has justified its rejection in the name of a social solidarity that individualism threatens, while the right has justified it in the name of an organic state that individualism undermines.[43]

Although European-American relations have ebbed and flowed for decades, at times – such as the early 1980s – witnessing expressions of anti-Americanism that resemble those of more recent vintage, the cold war's end had particularly profound consequences for European relations with America. Where Soviet-led communism more or less united the West (with the exception of European communist parties), the Middle East – in its various guises – currently divides it. Partly, this is based on genuine differences in diplomatic views. For Europe, the 'war on terror' is best won via an Israeli-Palestinian peace settlement rather than an Iraqi war or threats to Syria and Iran. Partly, though, the loosening of trans-Atlantic ties is based on mutual perceptions of more sinister intents. For many Americans, a once barely latent anti-Semitism is increasingly manifest in Europe, while for Europeans, American reluctance to pressure Israel is indicative of the malign power of the unholy alliance of the 'Jewish lobby' and the Christian right. The particular conflict thus serves not only as a source of divergence but also a catalyst for a further downward spiral of European anti-Americanism and American anti-Europeanism.

As the warm reception extended to Robert Kagan's *Paradise and Power* in European capitals and Washington alike suggested, policy makers on both sides of the Atlantic mostly accept the notion of an Atlantic drift even if they dispute his diagnosis. Americans – at least in the Bush circles – evidently rather like the idea of being martial warriors whose military might has neither peer nor precedent. Europeans, too, are increasingly seeking to define the EU against America as a method of forging a common identity and legitimating a unique experiment (an 'EU-topia') of transnational laws, economic integration, and democratic peace; a Kantian model, in short, at least as worthy of emulation as that of Hobbesian America, but based on different trade-offs between freedom and social solidarity, and between the market and the state. Many Europeans, especially in the continental political class, enthuse over this vision despite its chronic internal problems and meagre prospects for realization in other regions, and have sought actively to use opposition to US foreign policy to galvanize an otherwise dormant popular enthusiasm for a new European constitutional settlement.[44]

European concerns about US 'hard' power have also been compounded by the fear of America's 'soft' intrusion into Europe, as less the indispensable and more the inescapable nation. Cultural concerns informing anti-Americanism are ubiquitous but, again, not new, even if the national responses are decidedly varied (from resigned acceptance to various forms of 'cultural protectionism'). Despite the proliferation of universities, research institutes, libraries, museums and art galleries in America, the charge of American philistinism – what French president Jacques Chirac referred to on a visit to China in 2004 as the 'ecological disaster area' of American culture – remains potent. Hollywood movies, junk food and drink (though Muslim Cola represents an interesting attempt to claim the decadent Western product for Islam), cheap jeans (homogenizing through Gap), popular music and film have together served as the sites of profound concern over the putative erosion of national cultures. That competing political tendencies have selectively championed and censured such products is less significant than the shared resentment, fear and envy that have accompanied the general clamour against American 'culture' – invariably in quotation marks – as homogenizing, displacing and 'dumbing-down' the supposedly pristine high cultures of Germany, France and other European states. That ordinary Europeans should be so regularly complicit in the Americanization of their own nations makes the process at once poignant and galling for European elites to confront.

Yet the irony here is two-fold. First, such concerns seem to suggest a fragility and porousness to indigenous identities that belies their alleged greatness. If a centuries-old culture cannot withstand the onslaught of burgers, bluegrass and blue jeans, it was perhaps less securely embedded than its defenders imagined.

But second, there exists good reason to imagine that the encounters with America, far from threatening national identities, can reinforce them. It seems plausible to suggest that many individuals differentiate not only between the American administration, nation and people, but also its products. Indeed, a September 2004 study of 3,300 consumers in 41 countries published in the *Harvard Business Review* found that, despite widespread opposition to the Iraq war and Bush's foreign policy more generally, only a 'negligible' number boycotted the products of companies such as Coca-Cola or McDonalds merely because they were American. People typically purchase US brands for reasons other than a symbolic association with America. As one South African consumer pithily put it, 'I hate the country, but I love their products'.[45] That American products are hugely popular is undeniable.[46] That in consuming them distinct national identities hewn over decades, if not centuries, are thereby eroded is much less obvious.

'Americanization' and its discontents

The final factor that underpins anti-Americanism is 'Americanization': the set of cultural goods and political values with which Americans are commonly associated.[47] This is less in the sense of acceptance or resistance to American cultural products discussed above but more the transmission – through these products, the mass media, and educational systems – of substantive information about America. In consuming American products, non-Americans may plausibly resist a simultaneous challenge to their own identities – but the messages they receive about America and Americans may still be partial, parodic caricatures.

Few of us readily admit to lacking knowledge about America. For example, the British Council commissioned an extensive survey in 1999–2000, *Through Other Eyes*, of how the UK was viewed internationally by young people (aged 24–35, well educated with above average incomes) in twenty-eight countries.[48] The UK's reputation was, perhaps surprisingly, best among its former colonies but in all of the countries surveyed the view of America was consistently more favourable.[49] Of all the countries mentioned, respondents thought that they knew America best (69 per cent knew it 'very well' or 'a fair amount'), and the UK second best. 69 per cent also had a 'very' or 'mainly' favourable view of America, with 9 per cent mainly unfavourable and 4 per cent 'very unfavourable', 18 per cent saying 'neither/nor'. 97 per cent agreed that America has 'world beating companies' and 46 per cent chose the United States as the country of preference for study overseas (with the UK in second place at 26 per cent). But how well did these respondents in fact 'know' America?

Although the extent to which the mass media shapes rather than reflects public images is questionable, its role in the sociology of nationalism – in (re)creating national narratives and perceptions of 'the Other' – cannot be ignored. The sense of apparent familiarity that characterizes mass attitudes towards America relies most heavily on the dissemination of knowledge via film, television and music. It is hardly surprising, then, that the mundane and routine aspects of most Americans' lives are typically eclipsed for many non-Americans by sensationalism: mass shootings, executions, political scandals, violence, and celebrity culture. Rarely in the history of the world can its leading power have – intentionally and inadvertently – exported such a malign image. In particular, the tendency of such influences to embellish a basic sense that America is a primordial, dystopian force – violent, moralizing, incapable of acting with subtlety or from any motive higher than self-interest – is remarkably powerful. Since many, if not most, of those who write about America typically eschew the lurid programming that attracts millions of viewers, the corrosive impact of such media may not – even today – be fully appreciated by the commentariat.

Moreover, this is not just a matter of Europeans and others being exposed more to the world of Syracuse than Sydney, but also of non-Americans and Americans alike being presented with partial or distorted representations of both the sheer diversity and the predictable mundanity of much of American life. Almost one quarter of the US population is now non-white, for example, yet the programming of most network television – outside cop shows – barely reflects this demographic reality. Without wishing to over-emphasize the role of such products, the popularity of American film and television is undeniably conse-quential in presenting partial information not only to non-Americans but also to Americans themselves. Although exceptions exist, the logic of Hollywood block-buster production, combined with American global military and economic power has helped to 'dissemble at home and abroad' and thereby 'keep Americans in the dark'.[50] The oft-cited statistics about the number of murders witnessed by children on American television is only one, especially graphic, illustration of the partial picture accorded mass publics.

In addition, the personalization of politics that typically accompanies televi-sual coverage is especially distorting in the American case. Perhaps more than most Americans realize, there exists a pronounced tendency among non-Americans to associate – and judge – the nation according to the incumbent in the Oval Office. Already, therefore, the Clinton years have been partially re-written – even romanticized – as a benign period in which a cosmopolitan, urbane and intelligent Chief Executive sought to fulfil international demands in the face of implacable Republican opposition. The unilateral tendencies, mili-tary interventions, and non-UN sanctioned American wars in Bosnia and Kosovo and the attacks on Iraq, Afghanistan and Sudan recede in the public memory. Conversely, George W. Bush confirms the worst stereotypes harboured by non-Americans, whatever the actual actions at home and abroad of the administration and the role that a host of other actors contribute (from Democrats in Congress to state governments, courts and so on). Television coverage of the 2004 election was apt to imply that one man alone could either retard or reverse global development – never mind the domestic and interna-tional influences that conditioned his power to persuade at home and abroad. With movies and television frequently abetting the creation of a heroic style of political leadership, a Manichean view of presidents is not far away (JFK the idol, Nixon the villain) wherein the complexity and detail of particular historical eras, administrations and events is necessarily muted or even lost altogether.

If partiality in the sense of incompleteness represents one problem, partiality in the sense of deliberate distortion represents another. Not least, the re-writing of historical events from the struggle for independence (*The Patriot*) to World War Two (*Saving Private Ryan* – in which an all white, all American D-Day attack on Normandy's beaches neatly omits black Americans, the British and Canadians). This airbrushing out of other nations hardly endears Americans to those who fought alongside them for freedom from tyranny and other 'American' values. Hollywood projects a visual confirmation of John Locke's comment: 'In the beginning, all the world was America', thus compounding resentment abroad. Indeed, if 'American' values are genuinely universal, they are by definition not American. But once again the inability of Americans to abandon the discourse of ideals and values is matched by the inability of nations not founded on ideals fully to embrace it – or to treat with anything but suspicion and scepticism American motives – in at best a fitful fashion.

The 'Americanization' process would perhaps be less worrisome in this regard were its recipients also in receipt of dispassionate and balanced information about America. Despite the popularity of university courses on American politics outside the United States, however, only a paucity of dedicated American research specialists now hold tenure in British, European and Australian universities. Many US courses are taught by non-specialists. In some universities, students can even leave a four-year politics degree without having ever encountered American material. For those that do, in a profession where most teachers are themselves self-consciously progressive in their politics, the ease with which student prejudices can be confirmed rather than challenged can easily compound nascent anti-Americanisms gleaned from the mass media. Moreover, the relative lack of serious media discussion of American public life offers at best limited correctives (in the UK, for example, landmark BBC current affairs programmes from *Newsnight* to *Question Time* that once featured scholars now typically prefer celebrities to 'educate' the public on issues from climate change to war). That Americans may themselves be unaware of the skewed nature of American exports perhaps points to a dissonance that is wider than ever. In sum, it is not only in *madrasas* that anti-Americanism can – knowingly or otherwise – go unchallenged.

Conclusion

Just as most Americans can agree that 'un-American' activities exist while disagreeing about what constitutes such activity, so anti-Americanism is a heterogeneous construct that admits of starkly competing interpretations. It makes little sense to charge anti-Americanism as being a response either to what America does or to what America is. Elements of both are typically present, although in hybrid and often elliptical fashion. Anti-Americanism is neither a new nor an ideologically consistent discourse. Its intensity, coherence, and expressions vary tremendously across the non-American world. Although international crises in general and war in particular cause it to emerge with particular force, the sole unifying and main animating feature of anti-Americanism is ambivalence: admiration co-existing with disapproval and disappointment. To the extent that foreign policy represents the central focus for discontent, there is reason to view the phenomenon simply as a reaction to the dominant power of our time and a particularly unloved administration. As such, history – and the fluidity in international relations – might suggest that anti-Americanism can recede as rapidly as it has advanced. Were the United States to adopt a less self-consciously nationalist 'grand strategy' and instead embrace more internationalist elements – featuring economic development, multilateral engagement and a security strategy executed within existing alliances and institutions – the breadth and depth of anti-American sentiment might plausibly decline to a degree in the face of a United States evincing a more 'decent respect for the opinions of mankind'.

Although anti-Americanism is partly a response to international influences, it is sustained by factors that are unrelated to matters of 'hard' American power. These include the clash between American nationalism and that of other countries, resentment towards American insularity, Christian fundamentalism and the global dominance of American popular culture. But anti-Americanism is also a function of intra-national factors, especially since the end of the cold war. Politicians employ appeals against America for their own ends, as the presence of the United States – and resistance to it – in recent election campaigns in Brazil, Germany, Kuwait, Spain and Pakistan has well illustrated. As such, changes in both the style and the substance of US foreign policy under Bush and his successors can temporarily mute but are unlikely to silence the growing chorus that 'we are all anti-Americanisms now' that echoes throughout the non-American world.

Notes

1 See, for example: J-F. Revel, *Anti-Americanism*, San Francisco: Encounter Books, 2003; A. Ross and K. Ross (eds.), *Anti-Americanism*, New York: New York University Press, 2004; A. McPherson, *Yankee No! Anti-Americanism in US-Latin American Relations*, Cambridge, MA: Harvard University Press, 2003; R. Crockatt, *America Embattled: September 11, Anti-Americanism and the Global Order*, London: Routledge, 2003; I. Krastev, 'The anti-American century?', *Journal of Democracy*, vol. 15, no. 2, 2004, pp. 5–16; F. Ajami, 'The falseness of anti-Americanism', *Foreign Policy*, September/October 2003; and F. Zakaria, 'Hating America', *Foreign Policy*, September/October 2004.

2 W. R. Mead, 'Why do they hate US? Two books take aim at French anti-Americanism', *Foreign Affairs*, March/April 2003.

3 W. Laqueur, *No End to War: Terrorism in the Twenty-First Century*, London: Continuum, 2003, p. 161.

4 Z. Sardar and M. Wyn Davies, *Why Do People Hate America?*, Cambridge: Icon Books, 2002; M. Herstgaard, *The Eagle's Shadow: Why America Fascinates and Infuriates the World*, London: Bloomsbury, 2002; and G. Crister, *Fat Land: How Americans Became the Fattest People in the World*, London: Penguin Books, 2003.

5 Quoted in J. Glover, 'Blair attacks Europe's anti-Americanism', *The Guardian*, 21 May 2002.

6 The remarks were made on a BBC Radio 4 programme, 'Which way are we facing?', broadcast on 12 May 2003.

7 R. A. Posner, *Public Intellectuals*, Cambridge, MA: Harvard University Press, 2001, p. 260.

8 See, for example: Laqueur, *No End to War*; U. Makdisi, 'Anti-Americanism in the Arab world: an interpretation of a brief history', *The Journal of American History*, vol. 89, no. 2. Available <http://www.historycoop.org/journals/jah/89.2/makdisi.html> (accessed 26 May 2005).

9 C. Hitchens, *Regime Change*, London: Penguin, 2003, p. 27.

10 I should note that my discussion focuses on the international dimensions of the phenomenon, rather than the vexatious issue of un-/anti-Americanism within the United States tackled, for example, by P. Hollander, *Anti-Americanism: Critiques at Home and Abroad, 1965–1990*, New York: Oxford University Press, 1992.

11 P. Roger, *L'Ennemi americain: Genealogie de l'antiamericanisme français*, Paris: Seuil, 2002; J-F. Revel, *L'Obsession anti-americaine: Son fonctionnement, ses causes, ses inconsequences*, Paris: Plon, 2002.

12 S. Rushdie, 'Anti-Americanism has taken the world by storm', *The Guardian*, 6 February 2002.

13 J. Lloyd, 'How anti-Americanism betrays the left', *The Observer*, 17 March 2002.

14 C. Christie, 'US hate: a designer prejudice for our time', *The Times Higher Education Supplement*, 18 January 2002, p. 19.

15 Crockatt, *America Embattled*, p. 69.

16 A. Roy, 'Not again', *The Guardian*, 27 September 2002.

17 Hollander, *Anti-Americanism*, pp. 334–5.

18 M. Medved, 'World's most dangerous hatred'. Available <http://www.worldnet-daily.com/news/article.asp?ARTICLE_ID=25296> (accessed 26 May 2005).

19 Quoted in Glover, 'Blair attacks Europe's anti-Americanism'.

20 Mead, 'Why do they hate US?'.

21 P. B. Mehat, 'Anti-Americanism as an ideology', *The Hindu*, 21 September 2001.

22 A. M. Schlesinger, Jr., *War and the American Presidency*, New York: Norton, 2004, p. 3.

23 'What the world thinks in 2002'. Released: 4 December 2002. Available <http://people-press.org/reports/display.php3?ReportID=165> (accessed 26 May 2005).

24 See BBC News 7 January 2003. Available <http://newsvote.bbc.co.uk/1/hi/uk/2635419.stm?markResults=true> (accessed 26 May 2005).

25 Quoted in H. Meyerson, 'Reaping the world's disfavor', *The Washington Post*, 11 June 2003, p. A35.

26 See http://www.americans-world.org/digest/global_issues/terrorism/terrorism_summary.cfm (accessed 26 May 2005).

27 S. Power, *A Problem From Hell: America and the Age of Genocide*, London: Flamingo, 2003.

28 See, for example, M. Ignatieff, *Empire Lite: Nation-building in Bosnia, Kosovo and Afghanistan*, London: Vintage, 2003.

29 See A. J. Bacevich, *American Empire: The Realities and Consequences of US Diplomacy*, Cambridge, MA: Harvard University Press, 2002.

30 J. Mearsheimer, *The Tragedy of Great Power Politics*, New York: Norton, 2001, p. 26.

31 See D. King, *Making Americans: Immigration, Race and the Origins of the Diverse Democracy*, Cambridge, MA: Harvard University Press, 2000; G. Gerstle, *American Crucible: Race and Nation in the Twentieth Century*, Princeton, NJ: Princeton University Press, 2001; and R. Smith, *Civic Ideals: Conflicting Visions of Citizenship in US History*, New Haven, CT: Yale University Press, 1997.

32 P. McCartney, 'American nationalism and US foreign policy from September 11 to the Iraq war,' *Political Science Quarterly*, vol. 119, no. 3, 2004, pp. 399–423, at 400.

33 M. Pei, 'The paradoxes of American nationalism', *Foreign Policy*, May/June 2003.

34 Ibid.

35 R. A. Posner, *Law, Pragmatism, and Democracy*, Cambridge, MA: Harvard University Press, 2003, p. 54.

36 McCartney, 'American nationalism and US foreign policy from September 11 to the Iraq war', pp. 400–1.

37 Ibid., p. 423.

38 Zakaria, 'Hating America', p. 48.

39 In an otherwise excellent analysis, for example, it is strange that no reference is made by Richard Crockatt (*America Embattled*) to anti-Semitism.

40 See, for example: T. Judt, 'Anti-Americanism abroad', *The New York Review of Books*, 1 May 2003, pp. 24–7; C. Hudson, 'Uncle Sam is innocent', *The Times Higher Education Supplement*, 5 September 2003, p. 16.

41 Laqueur, *No End to War*, p. 166.

42 S. Schama, 'The unloved American: two centuries of alienating Europe', *The New Yorker*, 10 March 2003.

43 S. Fabbrini, 'The domestic sources of European anti-Americanism', *Government and Opposition*, vol. 37, no. 1, 2002, pp. 3–14.

44 As one British scholar of transatlantic relations notes, although Charles Kupchan (*The End of the American Era: US Foreign Policy and the Geopolitics of the Twenty-first Century*, New York: Knopf, 2002) sees Europe rather than China as the most likely rival to the United States, his is a decidedly isolated view. See T. Garton Ash, 'Anti-Europeanism in America', *The New York Review of Books*, 13 February 2003, pp. 32–4.

45 Cited in J. Gapper, 'A brand that does not work in every market', *Financial Times*, 4 November 2004, p. 19.

46 Although Michael Mann cites a 2001 survey of 60 nations that revealed that 7 of their top 10 television programmes were locally produced, not American imports. See his 'The first failed empire of the twenty-first century', in D. Held and M. Koenig-Archibugi, *American Power in the 21st Century*, Cambridge: Polity Press, 2004.

47 J. Davidson Hunter and J. Yates, 'In the vanguard of globalization: the world of American globalizers', in P. L. Berger and S. P. Huntington (eds.), *Many Globalizations*, New York: Oxford University Press, 2002.

48 The 1999 batch comprised Brazil, China, Egypt, France, Germany, India, Malaysia, Mexico, Poland, Russia, Saudi Arabia, South Africa and Turkey; the 2000 set included Argentina, Bangladesh, Czech Republic, Greece, Hong Kong, Hungary, Italy, Japan, Kenya, Korea, Nigeria, Pakistan, Singapore, Spain and Thailand.

49 *Through Other Eyes: How the World Sees The United Kingdom*, London: The British Council, 2000, p. 3.

50 D. King, 'America in the dark? – recent Hollywood representations of the nation's history', *Government and Opposition*, vol. 38, no. 2, 2003, pp. 163–80, at 164–5.

3 Ambivalent anti-Americanism

John Kane

Contemporary anti-Americanism is in part (but only in part) a natural reaction of foreign peoples to preponderant American power. It can therefore be expected to persist so long as the preponderance remains. Of course anti-Americanism wanes and waxes according to whether America's exercise of hegemonic power is perceived as more or less benign (as under Bill Clinton) or threatening (as under George W. Bush). Yet even the most virulent hatred of America is seldom without a touch of ambivalence. America and things American are frequently loved even as they are hated.

The attractive power America has by virtue of its democracy, its promise of individual liberty and opportunity, its immensely influential popular culture, is undeniable. Joseph Nye has labelled this America's 'soft' power and argues that it is just as significant a diplomatic resource as 'hard' power and often more useful.[1] Using this language, we could simply explain the ambivalence of anti-Americanism by noting that the attractions of soft power inevitably fall out of synch with American hard power when the latter is used in ways that the rest of the world finds offensive or threatening. This is quite true, but in this chapter I want to look a little more closely to discover the deeper roots of ambivalence.

I will argue that these are found in the success of the myth of America's peculiar role in history, and the consequent significance that America has for other countries and peoples. The myth succeeded in America, of course, but it is an important fact that it also succeeded internationally, giving every non-American a stake, if only a vicarious one, in America. America's belief in itself thus finds a mirror, often a distorting one, in the world's belief in America. No other great power in history has ever cared so much about whether it was loved, nor felt so deeply that it deserved to be. This is why Americans tend to nod complacently at signs of foreign love but to feel hurt and puzzled when they encounter hatred. It deserves to be loved because of the promise it holds for everyone.

But promise quickly turns to disappointment and even disillusionment when foreigners run up against tough American realities. Nor is the conflicted attitude that this collision produces found merely among foreigners, for ambivalent anti-Americanism begins at home, and for the same reason – the enduring distance between promise and reality. Ambivalence was inevitable given the expectations that the myth engendered and the sharp contradictions they were bound to meet in American society and history. Consider the following.

America is: a nation dedicated to liberty and equality, large sections of which were long addicted to slavery and segregation; an anti-imperialist nation that mythologized and glorified its conquest of an entire continent and the destruction of its original inhabitants; a nation that believed power inevitably corrupted virtue but also that American virtue would inevitably lead to wealth and power; a nation that valorized agrarian, republican simplicity while developing the world's most complex industrial civilization; a nation that strove to isolate itself politically from a wicked world while pursuing ever-deeper economic entanglement; a nation with an abiding puritanical streak but one that produced a profane culture based on pleasure and consumption; a nation that regarded its citizens as non-nationalistic examples of the universal humanity but which fostered a proudly parochial and loudly assertive patriotism; a nation founded in the secular values of the Enlightenment that remains one of the most religious of all developed countries; an optimistic nation dedicated to success and progress, yet harbouring millenarian expectations of Armageddon and the End of Days; a nation that combines firm conviction of its own innocence with an abiding belief in original sin; a nation that led the democratic Free World but supported and maintained vicious dictatorial regimes around the globe; an anti-militarist nation that developed the most powerful military machine the world has seen.

Some of these contradictions arise from the different motivations that prompted original settlement. The colony at Plymouth Rock sought religious purity and freedom, the one at Jamestown worldly profit. It is not entirely fanciful to say that America has been struggling to serve both God and Mammon ever since. Other contradictions plainly arose from the clash of attitudes one would expect in a broad continent marked by cultural, economic and regional diversity. But conflicting aims and interests are the stuff of political life everywhere, and the fact of them was less important than the effect they had on the myth that tried to contain and constrain them. At the founding of the United States, Americans struggled to harmonize regional differences and limit religious intolerances in order to preserve political unity and enable general economic progress. The elaboration of a unifying national myth (adopted originally to justify their revolution) was one important means to this end. Yet the myth – variously labelled the Myth of Mission, the Idea of America, the American Dream, American Exceptionalism, even the Mirage in the West – also sharpened contradictions by providing a high ideal against which lived realities were bound to appear divergent.

But why should the distance between mythical promise and mundane, often sordid reality have consequences abroad as well as at home? This was due to the fact that the American myth was not, originally, American at all, but European, a product of the Enlightenment's hope for a rational, more virtuous world. Europeans projected their hopes onto America and sometimes took the wish for reality. Americans, finding the mythical representation both flattering and useful, embraced it as their own. The result was that the United States at its formation felt itself to be deeply and morally implicated in the world, indeed the world's last best hope for free government, and the world (at least the European part of it) felt deeply implicated in America. The myth was perhaps too successful for America's own good. Transmitted via immigration policy and an exuberant popular culture to the whole globe, it inspired hope in places far distant from America's shores.

The national myth declared that the purpose for which Providence had called the United States into being was to reveal to all peoples of the world their own potential future, to show what Everyman could become under conditions of liberty and opportunity. It followed that the representative American was also the representative of ideal humanity. But basing a national identity on a supposedly universal character produced in Americans a permanent tendency to conflate their own values and interests with those of all humankind. With the growth of American economic and political power and the expansion of American foreign policy, real American interests were bound to clash with the particular interests and cultural sensitivities of others. When that happened, the hope that others had invested in America would turn to disappointment and criticism, and Americans, deeply imbued with the mythological sense of their own innocence and good intentions, would react to criticism with surprise, hurt and confusion.

Since I have explored some of the foreign policy manifestations of this elsewhere,[2] I will concentrate here mostly on the cultural and economic side of the American exemplary mission. I begin by exploring the European roots of the American mythology.

European foundations of the American myth

The Idea of America as an example to the whole world predates the birth of the United States. From the 1730s onward Voltaire and other *philosophes* had repeatedly drawn European attention to progressive aspects of America, particularly to Locke's *Constitutions of Carolina* and William Penn's legislation on religious toleration in Pennsylvania. European curiosity was quickened in 1767 when colonial Americans rose up against the Stamp Act imposed on them by the British government. Discerning Europeans, observing the escalating conflict, believed they saw a new nation emerging in the American wilderness. The colonists appeared ready to put to the practical test theories of politics, economics and morality that had hitherto been mere fancies of Enlightenment thought. It was this prospect that turned the arrival of Benjamin Franklin in France in 1767 into a sensation. Already well known for his experiments with electricity and now also the official representative of the colonies, recently famed as their great champion before the British parliament, Franklin sparked a fever of Americanism in France that proved a valuable political resource in the revolutionary years ahead. In the period between 1767 and 1775, according to one historian, 'the Americans had somehow come to symbolize the dream of a new order, in which men would escape from poverty, injustice, and corruption and dwell together in universal liberty, equality, and fraternity.'[3] Once the American Revolution began, French resentment of Great Britain encouraged a huge wave of sympathy for the colonists among all classes of society.

Every development in American politics was closely scrutinized for the meaning it held for France and Europe for several crucial decades. The significance of this attention for America itself, as both benefit and burden, can hardly be underestimated. The diplomatic value of a positive image of America among Europeans was undeniable, for the revolutionists were crucially dependent on foreign assistance, both financial and material. But to be entrusted with creating a model society and turning philosophical dreams into reality was a heavy responsibility indeed. Yet the United States, for reasons of its own, took up the dream and incorporated it into its own self-image, turning it into a founding myth of the new republic.

This was only partially due to the fact that Enlightenment values and philosophical optimism were deeply shared by influential members of the American elite, particularly by the circle around Thomas Jefferson that included Franklin, Benjamin Rush, Tom Paine, Joseph Priestley and David Rittenhouse. Jefferson's commitments could be plainly seen in the Declaration of Independence, yet it could hardly be said that the thirteen colonies had rebelled in order to realize such a philosophical ideal. Each had its own specific interests to protect and advance, and was but little concerned with asserting or fulfilling the abstract natural rights of humanity at large. If there was any general principle at work among the colonists it was one of defending their ancient rights and liberties as Britons under custom, law and charter against a tyrannous British parliament. This perspective inevitably altered as rebellion took a more radical turn, particularly once the decision had been made to assert independence. Independence made the appeal to English constitutional rights vain, and resort to the rhetoric of Lockean natural rights expedient (a transition made easier, however, given the assumption that these natural rights anyway formed the 'fundamental Law' underlying the British constitution).[4] But America's bold proclamation of Enlightenment ideals further encouraged already sympathetic Europeans to view the rebellion as a noble experiment in republican government, the inauguration of an age of universal liberty. Americans in their turn were increasingly encouraged to see themselves as they were refracted through the hopeful European gaze.

If this projection westward of the dreams of European *philosophes* was one stimulus for the American myth of mission, there was another in the colonists' inheritance of the English tradition of liberty. In fact these two strands were intertwined. Montesquieu and Voltaire had long ago made it a convention of Enlightenment thought that England was the great exemplar of civil and political liberty. French enmity with England, and defeat at her hands, had soured French Anglophilia, and the onset of hostilities in America provided an opportunity for French thinkers to transfer their affectionate hopes for political freedom to the fledgling nation. As colonial friction with England increased, many colonists became inclined to accept the grander version of their cause proffered by Europeans. It seemed that the break with the mother country did not have to mean a break with their English heritage insofar as the latter symbolized a strong connection to Liberty.

In the 1760s, the English constitutional balance seemed threatened by encroachments of the crown under George III. Old problems of standing armies, interference with judicial procedures and illegal taxation reappeared, and so-called 'Commonwealthmen' in both England and America grew alarmed at the perceived threat to their English rights and freedoms.[5] A host of English jeremiads, for which the colonists had long developed a hearty appetite, instructed them on the increasing corruption and immorality of English social and political life, as did the scandalized reports of colonial visitors to Britain, reinforcing the impression that the mother country had lost the virtue needed to sustain her own and her subjects' liberties.[6] Worse, English corruption, like a spreading cancer, seemed to be taking alarming hold in the colonies themselves. As revolutionary sentiment grew and more and more colonists exhibited a spirit of self-sacrifice and public service, the idea took root that a moral reformation might be possible, that republican virtue be reclaimed.[7] It seemed that America might be capable of rescuing the torch of liberty that was falling from the English grasp. Thus the English émigré Tom Paine declared in *Common Sense*, the pamphlet that galvanized popular revolutionary opinion in America, that Americans had it in their power to begin the world over again, freedom having been generally 'hunted from the globe': 'Europe regards her like a stranger, and England hath given her warning to depart. O! receive the fugitive and prepare in time an asylum for mankind.'[8] Convinced of the justice of their own cause, the rebel colonists believed that they were fighting for English principles that England had itself betrayed. It was therefore but a short imaginative step from the defence of their own particular liberties to the defence of Liberty in general.[9]

The thought of English religious dissenters, for long discriminated against in England, also encouraged Americans to see their own struggles, their own thought, and their own constitutional endeavours as evidence of their vanguard role in a progressive historical movement towards universal liberty. Here the opinions of the English theorist Richard Price, a friend of Benjamin Franklin's, were both representative and influential. Price's championship of the American revolution caused him to be widely read and appreciated in America, giving weight to his view that, next to the introduction of Christianity, the American revolution might be the most important step in the progressive course of human improvement. [It was a view that, seven decades later, William H. Seward would repeat almost exactly when he called the establishment of the United States government 'the most important secular event in the history of the human race'.][10] At the victorious conclusion of the revolution Price rejoiced:

> [I]n its termination, the war has done still greater good ... by providing, in a sequestered continent possessed of many singular advantages, a place of refuge for opprest [sic] men in every region of the world, and by laying the foundation there of an empire which may be the seat of liberty, science and

virtue, and from whence there is reason to hope these sacred blessings will spread till they become universal and the time arrives when kings and priests shall have no more power to oppress, and that ignominious slavery which has hitherto debased the world exterminated. I therefore think I see the hand of Providence in the late war working for the general good.[11]

We see here the essential features of the American myth. Whether many revolutionary Americans shared Price's apocalyptic religious views, the general idea was rhetorically useful and gave them a comforting sense that their bold enterprise was sanctioned by divine Providence.[12] Moreover, the religious interpretation conveniently mirrored and reinforced the secular Enlightenment view of human progress and of America's role in furthering it. The convergence of opinion between a man like Price and Frenchmen like A.-R.-J. Turgot and the Marquis de Condorcet (the great prophet of human progress who was averse to all religion, but especially Christianity) meant that Americans, whether conventionally religious or not, could find considerable intellectual support for a singular, appealing image of the national mission. Flattering Enlightenment views of America were in wide circulation both during and after the revolutionary war. In 1782, the year that peace was concluded, St John Crèvecoeur, a Frenchman who had farmed for some years in New York State, drew an idealized picture of the typical American. Crèvecoeur's 'new man' was an amalgam of all the hopes of the European Enlightenment: simplicity, virtue, equality, Rousseauean naturalness, tolerance, liberty, humanitarianism, a desire for political reform, and a symbol of unlimited individual opportunity. In 1786, the Marquis de Condorcet emphasized the promise of material progress, the inevitable result as he saw it of the enlightenment, equality and liberty that Americans enjoyed. 'It is not enough', he wrote, 'that the rights of man be written in the books of philosophers and inscribed in the hearts of virtuous men; the weak and ignorant must be able to read them in the example of a great nation. America has given us this example.'[13]

French praise of America was sometimes so extravagant as to embarrass the Americans themselves and draw forth appeals for moderation from Franklin, Paine and Jefferson. Nevertheless, the hopeful and flattering French projection inevitably made a deep impression on the American heart and soul. As Americans suffered the deprivations and injuries of revolutionary warfare, they could take comfort in the view of Europeans who argued that the colonists had acted on pure principle and not from motives of self-interest. The urgent and anxious inquiry into the nature of their society upon which Americans embarked at the start of their rebellion found aid and inspiration in the widely broadcast opinions of transatlantic sympathizers. As Gordon Wood concluded:

[Americans] could only be flattered by the portrait, 'so very flattering to us', that the Enlightenment had painted of them. Whatever the social reality may have been – and on examination it did not seem inconsistent – they could not help believing that America was what Europe said it was.

Everywhere they looked there was confirmation of what the Enlightenment and the English radicals had said about them.[14]

Once the common struggle had ended, however, there was more to divide the newly independent states than to bring them together in an ideal republic. The things they did share – language, law and institutions – recalled their now severed ties with Britain rather than suggested a brave new beginning. Moreover, the states were jealously determined to go their own way, opposed to the idea of any strong central power that might dominate them all. The principal worry that plagued European sympathizers in these early years was that such a loose federation would descend swiftly into anarchy, creating conditions conducive to the rise of dictatorship. Even after the Philadelphia delegates of 1787 had pursued their 'more perfect union', the new United States was a nation with no 'natural' sense of popular nationhood. Indeed it would not be until 1814, after success in another war against the might of Britain, that widespread popular nationalism would take significant hold there, and not till the end of the Civil War that the impediment presented by proponents of states' rights and strict constitutional construction would be swept away. American loyalties remained for a long time predominantly local. When Jefferson referred to 'my country', even as president, he meant Virginia. Moreover some of the revolutionists, like Paine and Joel Barlow, positively disavowed nationalism as a contemptibly parochial concept. They identified themselves as 'citizens of the world', the compatriots of anyone who believed in the principles of freedom, equality, reason, and human perfectibility. Yet the legal and political strands connecting Americans to one another would continue to be fragile unless reinforced by some positive popular attachment to the state they had created. The question was how a disparate and quarrelsome people, dangerously divided on sectional as well as ideological lines, could foster a popular national identity.

The nation eventually adopted as its own the European Enlightenment Idea of America. The new concept of nationalism was blended with the idea of individual rights to produce an innovative idea of national identity: unity was to be achieved, not through cultural homogeneity, but rather through the embrace of individual difference and belief in the possibility of individual advancement. To be an American was to be someone who exhibited the autonomy implied by natural rights doctrine, thus fulfilling the American mission by representing the virtuous future of all humankind. The issue was not, however, uncontested. During the presidencies of Washington and Adams, the elite was divided within itself as to what sort of nation America would be. Alexander Hamilton's wish, congenial to the mercantile oligarchs of the New England seaboard, was for a politically conservative, hierarchical nation focused on transatlantic commerce, with agriculture balanced by manufacture and trade defended by a modern professional navy. Jefferson's more expansive, agrarian vision, which appealed to farmers in the west and southwest, was continental rather than transatlantic in focus, and was adamantly opposed to central power and standing military forces that, he avowed, would inevitably lead to tyranny.

This ideological contest would play out in the divisions between Jefferson's Republicans and Hamilton's Federalists in the turbulent years after the start of the French Revolution of 1793. It was no accident that veterans of the American revolutionary war produced, during this period, a series of histories and memoirs that began to weave the diffuse strands of colonial history into a single compelling narrative, one that emphasized an American destiny underwritten by Providence.[15] The French revolutionary upheavals allowed Americans to revise their views of the significance of their own revolution, which could now be seen as the precursor of the French, the first stage in the progressive emancipation of all civilized humanity from the tyranny of rank, custom and prejudice. Americans had not fought just for their inherited liberties as Britons; they had fought for Liberty itself, a universal value that was the birthright of every human being.

Jefferson's version of the myth triumphed ideologically over Hamilton's more worldly vision though the nation that America became would much more closely resemble the latter. This produced a certain schizophrenic dividedness between ancient and modern forms of republican consciousness that was a source of much of America's own ambivalence about itself. Similar ambivalences were felt abroad. French infatuation with America faded when it ceased to be politically useful and particularly after hostile feelings, leading almost to war, broke out between the two revolutionary nations. But as a consequence of the initial exchange, Europeans, whether in hope or loathing, would ever after have some spiritual-psychological stake in the domestic politics of America, a stake the rest of the world would in time come to share. And Americans, by virtue of their mythology, would never be able to disconnect their own domestic progress from the fate of the whole world. Even their frequent insistence on the need for isolation from the world betrayed, paradoxically, this mythical connectedness since isolation was meant to preserve American virtue and thus the American example. Thus America was, at its foundation, deeply implicated in the world and the world in it. Yet there would always be ambivalence about what America really meant for the rest of the world.

Ambivalence about the American example

Right from the start, European opinion was divided about the nature and significance of the American experience, and whether the American example was for good or ill. The main doubt centred on whether the colonists, liberated from the constraints of Europe and facing the challenges of a new continent, would demonstrate at last the perfectibility of humankind or whether, on the contrary, they would be deformed and debased by their alien environment into a lower kind of European. This dispute was sharpened by the Dutchman, Cornelius de Pauw, who in 1768 argued that the climate of the New World, over generations, would inevitably cause the physical and mental degeneration of the colonists as it allegedly had of native American tribes and fauna. De Pauw aimed to prove the falsity of Rousseau's 'noble savage' theory by demonstrating the infinite superiority of European civilization, and thus to discourage the large-scale emigration to the New World that, he claimed, was sapping European strength to the point of catastrophe.[16] To support his theme of American degeneration, de Pauw had adduced as evidence the fact that American universities had not produced a single writer, teacher, scholar, philosopher, doctor or physicist of note. All America had to teach the world, he said, was the 'burning avarice' displayed by its merchants and adventurers. Ever after, the obverse view of corrupt Europe versus virtuous America would be Europe the sophisticate versus America the brash and greedy simpleton, a theme that plays down to the present day.

The American Revolution, too, produced a divided reaction: it infused French republican opinion with hope, but naturally filled the aristocracy with dread. Depending on who looked, America was either a magic mirror reflecting the future liberation of Europe or a horrible anticipation of the chaos to come. After they had undergone revolutionary changes of their own, Europeans began to think that American popular government really might be the crucial experiment that pointed the way the world would go, like it or not. '[I]n the beginning', John Locke had once written, referring to the alleged 'natural state' of American Indians, 'all the world was America, and more so than it is now.'[17] The American myth proclaimed that, one day all the world would once again be America in a new era of liberty.

In the first half of the nineteenth century, Europeans eager to observe the experiment at first hand flocked to the United States. Some were radicals hoping to see their democratic ideals in action, only to be appalled by the chaos, corruption and the 'howling wolves' of Congress. Others were conservatives, suspicious of the levelling effects of democratic government. Richard Cobden was very supportive of America's professed mission as 'civilizers and improvers of mankind' and hopeful that America's policy of avoiding wars and concentrating on their own business and industry would be emulated by Britain.[18] Many famous writers – including Harriet Martineau, Michel Chevalier, Charles Dickens, Captain Frederick Marryat, Fanny Trollope and her son Anthony Trollope – came with a pre-jaundiced eye and returned to deliver devastating commentaries to eager European audiences. John Bristed observed in 1818:

> The national vanity of the United States surpasses that of any other country, not even excepting France. It blazes out everywhere and on all occasions, in their conversation, newspapers, pamphlets, speeches and books. They assume it as a self-evident fact, that the Americans surpass all other nations in virtue, wisdom, valour, liberty, government and every other excellence. All Europeans they profess to despise as ignorant paupers and dastardly slaves.[19]

Shock was often expressed at the blatant hypocrisy of Anglo-Americans with regard to their own ideals of equality and the advancement of people of whatever gender, creed, colour or class. Mrs. Fanny Trollope declared that she might have respected Americans despite their rough manners and peculiar customs but:

> ... it is impossible for any mind of common honesty not to be revolted by the contradictions in their principles and practice... You will see them with one hand hoisting the cap of liberty and with the other flogging the slaves. You will see them one hour lecturing ... on the indefeasible rights of man, and the next driving from their homes the children of the soil [Indians], whom they have bound themselves to protect by the most solemn promises.[20]

The most brilliantly perceptive of visitors attempting to discern Europe's political future in the American experience was Alexis de Tocqueville. Tocqueville held to the common idea that an American was more 'natural' than a European, though he was ambivalent about whether this really implied Rousseauean virtue. Americans were individualistic, Tocqueville claimed, because they had stripped off, not just the European accretions of class or caste, but all forms of social distinction whatsoever including those of family and profession, and by repudiating the past had loosened even the bonds between generations. In the process they had come to approximate the basic constitution of man, 'which is everywhere the same'. It was for this reason that Americans were thrown back on conspicuous wealth as the only way of establishing social differentiation. Tocqueville recognized the restless energy that American individualism unleashed, but his view of natural man in a new democracy was not altogether flattering.[21]

The fate of the successive tides of new immigrants to America hardly supported this 'natural man' thesis. Many immigrants were non-Protestants who found it a challenge to adapt to and, in various ways, modify the already existing folk culture of the United States.[22] Though liable to be treated as unwelcome aliens and second- or third-class citizens, their journey to America and their struggles to gain a foothold nevertheless remained an authentic testament to the attractive power of the 'American dream'. Woodrow Wilson, indeed, said that these people, by harbouring the ideal in their hearts, had kept it alive at times when Americans themselves had forgotten it. They were thus a source of continuous renewal of the myth.[23]

The ambivalence of Europeans about America was evident again between 1861–1865, as they followed the progress of the devastating Civil War in horror and bewilderment. The upper classes, though generally anti-slavery, were stirred by the gallant South's defence of its right to self-determination. This seemed more comprehensible to them than the significance that Northerners placed on the defence of Union as the defence of the very possibility of free, democratic government on earth. Their opinion was important, too, since recognition of the Confederacy by Europe had the power to determine the outcome of the war in favour of secession. There was, perhaps, in Europe as in America, a certain class divide on this matter. Abraham Lincoln was vilified and ridiculed in the dominant European press, but when he sent a letter to the workingmen of Manchester, hurt by the Northern embargo on Southern cotton, thanking them for their forbearance and support, it was most enthusiastically received.[24]

In the latter half of the nineteenth century as Americans swept westward bent on the reckless, ruthless exploitation of the country's natural resources, America was, for European and particularly British financiers, a fruitful place for investment. It was the place where fortunes were made and lost, often repeatedly by the same person, and in which a clever upstart with a little luck, a bright idea, and raw determination could become very rich indeed. Swaggering American plutocrats of small learning and less cultivation began to invade Europe, set on finding history, plundering art works, and marrying their daughters into titled families in the hope of adding a patina of ancient respectability to gross new wealth. And polished aristocrats with ever-declining fortunes and expensive estates to maintain were frequently ready to oblige people whose manners they generally deplored. The palpable ambivalence of Europeans contemplating such sordid bargains was turned into literary art by an American of genius, Henry James, whose own ambivalence tipped over into loathing and rejection of his native land. For less elevated people both at home and abroad, America was mainly a place of curiosity, novelty and excitement. American popular culture began to take shape in the propagation of colourful stories of cowboys and Indians, a world of heightened frontier reality brought sensationally to life in a travelling American circus that frequently toured Europe in the late nineteenth century. The thrills and themes of Buffalo Bill's Wild West Show prefigured those of the cinematic western that would exert such a powerful appeal across the world in years to come.

Though an increasingly wealthy America was becoming more and more commercially and culturally entangled in the world, it held (apart from a brief burst of imperial adventure at the turn of the century) to an old dream of political non-entanglement aimed at preserving American virtue and thus the American mission. Political isolation became untenable, however, with the sudden acquisition of distant territories and novel interests, and given the imperial assertiveness of other nations. Most Americans were reluctant to accept this even when the European imperial powers became embroiled in a horrendous conflict of world reach. The American president, Woodrow Wilson, a great believer in the American mission and a man determined to expunge all selfishness from American foreign policy, tried to keep America out of the war but concluded at length that the mobilization of American military power was unavoidable. He decided, however, that American power would at least be purified by being used only for virtuous ends. Wilson attempted to use American power to end the war, and indeed to end all wars by establishing a league of equal, democratic nations, each lawfully obliged to respect and defend the security and independence of every other. Wilson's dream was of a Kantian society of nations existing in lawful, perpetual peace, instead of in the artificial and unreliable peace engineered by the old, discredited balance of power. It aroused enormous popular enthusiasm in Europe where Wilson was greeted as a saviour.

But American thought was obsessed by the idea of power and virtue as antithetical, and could not yet reach to prolonged commitment of American power to guarantee such an ideal order. The dream failed, dashing the exaggerated hopes that it had aroused among Europeans who now became deeply disappointed in America.

American diplomatic efforts to fulfil the same ideal during the 1920s, by means of universal treaties outlawing war, revived international hopes in the American example for a while, which again proved unrealistic. Yet American leadership had become important in other ways. The 1920s witnessed a truly enormous international dispersion of American mores, methods and entertainments.[25] The mythological hope that all the world would one day be America seemed about to become a reality, at least in a cultural sense. The Great War, its ancient mythos discredited and degraded to the point of extinction, had shattered Europe. European leadership in world affairs had perceptibly passed across the Atlantic, despite America's failure to join the League of Nations. American wealth and power commanded new prestige. American glamour incited infatuation and emulation. American music, dance, radio, movies, literature and style – whether of language, life or fashion – were everywhere the rage. A flood of American inventions and gadgets promised to make life easier or more entertaining. American popular and material culture began to exert on the world that intense attractive power that has distinguished it ever since. Such cultural attractiveness overlaid and reinforced the traditional mythological appeal of America as the place where anyone with native ability and determination could go to make good under conditions of political freedom and economic opportunity (though there was considerable irony in the fact that it was in these 1920s that Congress introduced drastically restrictive immigration laws). Viewed from abroad, the American dream seemed to have been positively realized in America.

It was notable that American business in this period acquired, with official encouragement, a self-consciously internationalizing mission. The war had materially strengthened America and turned it, for the first time, into a creditor rather than a debtor nation, so it was in a unique position to take over the central role formerly played by Great Britain in sustaining an international economy. Herbert Hoover, as secretary of commerce for eight years under President Coolidge and then as president himself, encouraged a massive expansion of American overseas investment.[26] He hoped that the organizational example of American business, as well as its hard capital, would lay the foundations of a global commercial civilization able to draw into its peaceful orbit all the nations of the world, including the Soviet Union. And indeed American industrial organization, efficiency and productivity were greatly admired everywhere, even by the likes of Josef Stalin. Nor did the gigantism and regimentation that characterized American industry dent the individualistic myth, but rather helped reinforce it, for efficient industry produced the material means for enriching individual life. Henry Ford's assembly line automobiles were manufactured at a price that the workers in his own factories could afford, thus granting them the freedom of the roads – at least on weekends. The American dream became universally visible, tangible, potentially achievable.

Yet, again, admiration for American industry was tinged with ambivalence (and sometimes outright hostility – two French writers denounced the cult of efficiency and productivity as 'the American cancer').[27] Many nations were dismayed by new restrictions on free immigration that had a clear racial bias and which sat in considerable tension with America's economic internationalism. They were even more upset by America's insistence on high tariffs. Nations wanting to access the American market in order to earn dollars to pay for American food and machinery to speed recovery and development after the war were bitterly resentful of the tariffs and accused the exemplary nation of setting a poor example. Hoover, however, thought that these countries should not complain but rather welcome this policy as being in their own long-term interests. He regarded protectionism as vital, and his reasoning revealed the strains between particularism and universalism that were embedded in the American mythology. America must not only survive but also thrive, and not just for its own sake but the world's. If it were now to be the essential driver of global economic development and the world's banker, it needed to stimulate its own domestic production, earn more revenue and strengthen the value of the dollar. Tariffs allegedly achieved these goals. Thus was genuine economic internationalism essentially linked to, while being arguably compromised by, economic nationalism.

The hope that America might lead the world to peace through commerce and industry was temporarily shattered by the Great Depression, as was the American dream itself. The evident failure of liberal democracy to deal effectively with depression caused profound distress, particularly when that failure was compared to the burgeoning success of powerful new rivals on the left and right. In Soviet communism America confronted a competing universalism whose mission, like America's own, was to transform the world and usher in an era of liberty and peace, but on assumptions quite incompatible with American understanding. Meanwhile many European nations, and also Japan, revealed a susceptibility to a very different, irrationalistic and aggressive ideology – fascism – that pointedly rejected both American liberalism and Soviet Marxism. Disillusioned and confused, Americans undertook a damaging withdrawal from world affairs until an unprovoked attack on Pearl Harbor forced engagement in another global war.

America would emerge from World War Two with its fortunes wholly revived. The American military machine was now the most powerful on earth and ready for the first time to put its might permanently at the service of global order. With the start of the cold war, the preservation of order became identical with defence of the Free World. America had concluded from its experiences with fascist aggression that it was not power itself that was the problem but whether the power-holder was good or evil. Since America was good, American power would be virtuous power arrayed against evil in the shape of communist aggression, and also acting in support of peacekeeping institutions like the new United

Nations. Yet once again, American ideals ran sharply up against American realities. Some Americans argued that international treaties like the UN Charter endangered American virtue through their potential impact on American law. In 1948 the president of the American Bar Association, Frank Holman, commenced a crusade to save American domestic law from subversion by 'internationalism'. Between 1952–1954 Senator Paul Bricker fought to get Congress to pass a Constitutional amendment that would meet Holman's aim, and introduced it by pointing to the dangers inherent in the United Nations Covenant on Human Rights.[28] This gained him significant support among Southerners who trembled to think of the impact that such rights would have, if enforced, upon their own peculiar social and legal arrangements. After all Congress had, in ratifying the UN Charter, pledged to promote respect for rights 'without distinction as to race'.

What was at stake here was not, of course, the preservation of American virtue but the preservation of conditions that constituted an enduring stain on virtue. In attempting to maintain racial segregation, Americans could not but feel the sharp inner-edge of the human rights sword. Segregation, standing as it did in permanent contradiction to America's vaunted ideals of liberty and equality, was much harder to explain away than other apparent anomalies. Most Americans, for example, preferred to believe that those who criticized America for imperialistic policies in the Third World were either straightforwardly un-American or communist dupes. Racial segregation, however, was too inconveniently near to home and too undeniable to allow so easy a gloss. It provided an inviting target for America's foes, doubly so since the charge of immorality was combined with one of egregious hypocrisy. As early as 1948, the National Association for the Advancement of Colored People (NAACP) had tried, unsuccessfully, to charge the US before the United Nations for violation of its Charter. The issue also proved a fruitful one for the communists, particularly in the ideological competition with America for the allegiance of Third World countries. It was difficult to spread the gospel of democracy among 'peoples of colour' while the American democracy accommodated so large and enduring an injustice against its own 'coloured' people.

In the ideological battle of the 1950s and 1960s, segregation was America's Achilles' heel. Any American criticism of communist regimes for violation of human rights was immediately countered with, 'Physician, heal thyself.' Nor was it just the legalized racism of the South that was at issue, for segregation was widespread throughout the nation. In 1960, Nikita Khrushchev cited the racism of New York City as one reason why the United Nations should be moved to another location. Many American leaders chafed under the realization that their nation's record on race relations put them at an ideological disadvantage, but domestic politics prevented effective action until a combination of legal activism and the Civil Rights Movement of the 1960s had decisively altered the political landscape.[29]

Despite this, American economic leadership after World War Two was unchallengeable. At the close of the war American capitalism stood strong and alone in a ruined world, ready to begin its surge into the long post-war boom that carried the non-communist industrial world along with it. And despite the economic ups and downs, the oil shocks of the 1970s, the relative decline over time against revitalized nations like Germany and Japan, the humiliating and expensive experience of Vietnam, America would, at the start of the twenty-first century, remain the leviathan economy at the heart of a booming international capitalist system. After the collapse of the Soviet system in 1989, it also stood triumphant as the world's only superpower, the centre of an informal empire of global reach. Even old enemies like Russia and China were now included in an international system and international economy dominated by the United States. Globalization was not *just* an American phenomenon but America lay at its heart, and the Americanization of the world seemed to gather more and more momentum. American materialist and popular culture became more pervasive in more countries than ever before.

Once again, however, there were voices of dissent. An inventive and tactically effective international anti-globalization movement took issue with the way the world was going, often arguing on behalf of threatened local cultures or against the unfairness of a system that excluded Third World producers from First World markets. Here again, as in the 1920s, the American example was found wanting, and the United States was accused of hypocrisy for crying 'free trade' while protecting its farmers and excluding cheaper products from poorer nations. Yet even nations thoroughly implicated in the new global culture often found cause for dissatisfaction with American cultural dominance. The distinctive American culture has always been resolutely popular and therefore generally obnoxious to non-populists. While to many ordinary people American fashions and products proved irresistible, sophisticated Europeans often reacted to America's 'cultural imperialism' with horror. French intellectuals, for example, expressed fury at the infiltration of American slang into their language, the construction of Disneyworld in Paris, and the appearance of KFC on the Champs Elysées.

Nor have Europeans been alone in feeling ambivalent about an acquisitive, consumerist culture whose pleasurable freedoms and material attractions can often seem more disturbing than comforting. Americans too, and not just the religious fundamentalists among them, often express distress over the fact that, accompanying the liberal freedoms that foster cornucopic material abundance, are rising crime, drug addition, divorce, abortion, environmental degradation and pornography. Even a staunch defender of America like Dinesh D'Souza, an immigrant who has made good on the American dream, wonders 'how we can love a society whose virtue loses all her loveliness?', and worries about shielding his daughter from 'the toxic influences in American culture that threaten to destroy her innocence'.[30] Islamic Iran once labelled America 'the Great Satan', fittingly enough given that Satan is the great tempter. If American wealth and American freedoms and American vices were not such a temptation, then those trying to defend a stricter and more ancient version of virtue would have no reason to hate America so deeply and so violently.

Conclusion

When, on 11 September 2001, dark reactionary forces struck at the central economic, political and military symbols of the world's only remaining empire to make a cruel point, horrified Americans wondered, 'Why do they hate us so?' Americans, after all, deserve to be loved. Even today, according to Daniel Flynn, when they look in the national mirror they see a flatteringly familiar vision:

> We see the country that serves as the model for many of the world's democ-racies. We see great freedom and, as a result, great wealth. We see unprecedented national generosity, the immigrant's most welcome destina-tion, and the primary defender of the freedom of other nations. The mirror's reflection reveals the nation most responsible for the world's advances in technology, medicine and scientific discoveries ... America is a force for good as no nation has been.[31]

This is, of course, to portray the traditional American myth as one already real-ized. Others are less sanguine and believe America is not there yet, and indeed that there is a need to 'remythologize the idea of America'. Jacob Needleman writes:

> America is ... a philosophical identity composed of ideas of freedom, liberty, independent thought, independent conscience, self-reliance, hard work, justice. That is both the weakness and strength of America. To love America is not to love one's roots – it is to love the flower that has not yet blossomed, the fruit as yet unripened.[32]

America remains in many ways a great enigma, a nation that has made grand promises to which it seldom fully lives up yet which are still always hopefully half-believed in. Part of the reason may be that universalistic ideals and values, even when they hypocritically obscure actual exclusions and inequalities, nevertheless remain available as rhetorical weapons for the excluded and unequal – and have been wielded as such in America by women, immigrant groups, gays and African-Americans, among others. As a general rule, criticism grounded in values upheld by the criticized carries more, and more painful, force than that which relies on opposing values. When Martin Luther King proclaimed that he had a dream, he was really articulating the hope that the great *American* dream would be at last properly fulfilled for all Americans, black and white. He was demanding, in effect, that America live up to its own ideals. If it is true that we commonly demand that people live up to their ideals, how much more should we expect of those who regard themselves as uniquely embodying those ideals?

This question has always been an uncomfortably loaded one for Americans, not least with respect to its relations with the rest of the world. Some have argued that the enduring problem of American foreign policy is a continual equivocation between realism and idealism. Unable decisively to choose between the two, Americans often seem to get the worst of both worlds. When they act idealistically they seem like innocents abroad and are condemned for their naïvety; when they act self-interestedly they are condemned as arrant hypocrites. More often, American idealism is perceived as little more than a self-deceiving cloak for determinedly selfish action, in which case Americans are condemned as simultaneously naïve *and* hypocritical. Not only that, but since Americans pride themselves on their innocent virtue, any instance of evil-doing – a My Lai or an Abu Ghraib – is not only unfortunate for their general enterprise but potentially catastrophic.

But why should the choice between realism and idealism be presented as peculiarly American? The trouble is that America *has* assumed that it is different in kind, and founded the mythological version of its nationalism precisely upon that assumption. It has also paradoxically presumed that the central point of difference is the fact that the true American represents the universal man or woman, who is, fundamentally, everywhere the same. This makes it difficult for Americans to distinguish between their own interests and those of other peoples. William Appleman Williams, who claimed that American diplomacy was driven principally by commercial interests, nevertheless pointed to the consequential and contradictory ideas that informed American foreign policy: a generous humanitarian impulse; a principle of individual and national self-determination; and a feeling that other people must necessarily, for their own good, adopt the American way.[33] Since American power has been assumed since World War Two to be virtuous by definition, any exertion of it must be presumed to be in the best interests of others. Thomas J. McCormick, who portrayed American hegemony as a systematic imperative of capitalistic expansion, noted that American arrogance after World War Two was an arrogance of righteousness as much as of power: 'American leaders assumed that American power was constructive simply because they believed American intentions self-evidently just and generous.'[34]

The frail ability to distinguish American interests from those of the rest of the world creates conundrums for hegemonic America as it blunders about seeking its true role in the world. This is partly because the American myth is not just American, but European in its foundations and ultimately global in its adherents. It has encouraged hopes and expectations in the world at large that were always unlikely to be consistently met if they could be met at all. Americans generally have not believed that their nation should act upon the same self-interested premises that allegedly motivate others and the world has taken them at their word. Consequently, whenever America's acts appear purely self-regarding, as is often the case, it is liable to be exposed to sharper criticism than other nations.

The Islamist adherents of al-Qaeda and its ilk want to defeat the American myth – which they see as the quintessential Western, infidel myth – and displace it with a religious one of their own, just as did communists and fascists before them. They are unlikely to succeed so long as the large numbers of Islamic people, however sharply divided within themselves, acknowledge the continuing attraction of the American dream. Samuel Huntington once wrote, 'America is not a lie: it is a disappointment. But it can be a disappointment only because it is also a hope.'[35] It is because America is always *both* disappointment and hope that anti-Americanism will always tend to be ambivalent anti-Americanism.

Notes

1 J. S. Nye Jr., *The Paradox of American Power: Why the World's Only Superpower Can't go it Alone*, Oxford: Oxford University Press, 2002, pp. 8–12.

2 J. Kane, 'American values or human rights? US foreign policy and the fractured myth of virtuous power', *Presidential Studies Quarterly*, 2002 vol. 33, no. 4, pp. 772–800.

3 D. Echeverria, *Mirage in the West: A History of the French Image of American Society to 1815*, Princeton, NJ: Princeton University Press, 1958, p. 38.

4 Famed revolutionary orator, Patrick Henry, had electrified a Virginian court as early as 1763 by invoking the doctrine of inalienable natural rights in a trial concerning the payment of clergymen with tobacco, a practice disallowed by King George III. The assumption was also explicit in the Massachusetts Circular Letter of 1768 and in many other colonial documents; see G. Stourzh, *Alexander Hamilton and the Idea of Republican Government*, Stanford, CA: Stanford University Press, 1970, p. 15. Stourzh notes John Adams's recollections of the argument in 1774 about whether to 'recur to the Law of Nature' which he strenuously urged. Hamilton was equally enthusiastic. Stourzh shows that, for support that the law of nature underlay the law, the colonists could turn to even the most conservative and famous of British constitutionalists, William Blackstone; see pp. 11–18.

5 C. Robbins, *The Eighteenth Century Commonwealthman*, Cambridge, MA: Harvard University Press, 1959.

6 B. Bailyn, *The Ideological Origins of the American Revolution*, Cambridge, MA: Harvard University Press, 1967, pp. 86–92.

7 This was an important addition made to Bailyn's republican thesis by Gordon Wood in *The Creation of the American Republic*, Chapel Hill, NC: University of North Carolina Press, 1969, Ch. 3. Wood argued that, rather than confidence in their special virtue, it was the colonists' fear that they may not inevitably be fit for republican government, and must therefore act before corruption had gone too far, that hurried them toward rebellion; p. 108.

8 P. S. Foner (ed.), *The Complete Writings of Thomas Paine, 1737–1809*, 2 vols, New York: Citadel Press, 1945, vol. 1, p. 32.

9 One of the leaders of the ensuing generation, Daniel Webster, would interpret Destiny so far as to suggest that England, in developing free institutions, had been unconsciously preparing herself 'under the Providence of God' for their transfer to the American colonies. 'England transplanted liberty to America; Spain transplanted power'. America could improve on that liberty because it did not receive from Britain its monarch, aristocracy, or church as an estate of the realm. [*The Works of Daniel Webster*, Boston: Little, Brown and Co, 1869, vol. 1, pp. 93, 97–8]. See E. McNall Burns, *The American Idea of Mission: Concepts of National Purpose and Destiny*, Westport, CT: Greenwood Press, 1957, p. 45.

10 G. Baker (ed.), *The Works of William H. Seward*, New York: Redfield, 1853–4, vol. 3, p. 78.

11 R. Price, 'Observations on the Importance of the American Revolution' [1785], in D. O. Thomas (ed.), *Richard Price: Political Writings*, Cambridge, Cambridge University Press, 1991, pp. 117–18. Price was a millennialist who held that the 1000 years preceding Christ's coming would be a time of gradual human improvement that would make the earth fit for Christ and saints. See Thomas, ibid., Introduction. This and other apocalyptic traditions served to give religious meaning to secular history; N. Cohn, *The Pursuit of the Millennium*, New York: Harper and Row, 1961. It was significant, too, that millennialism was often associated with the medieval doctrine of

'translation of empire', meaning the progressive transmission of imperial and ecclesiastical power (or Christian 'civilization') from east to west since the time of Christ. Protestants in sixteenth century Britain had designated England an 'elect nation' with a special role in sacred history, and it was tempting to imagine that role passing westward as England grew more corrupt. Certainly, America's western position in relation to Europe made it a plausible candidate for the final kingdom on earth; E. Tuveson, *Millennium and Utopia*, Berkeley, CA: University of California Press, 1949.

12 Margaret C. Jacob reveals precedents for this view among Anglican 'latitudinarians', including Newton, in seventeenth century England, who interpreted the English revolution, the Restoration and then the Glorious Revolution in terms of divine providence and 'election'. Newton and his friends believed that his science, with its emphasis on design, order and simplicity, were incontrovertible proof of God's providential design in human as well as natural affairs. It is surely no accident that Newton was one of Jefferson's great heroes. M. C. Jacob, *The Newtonians and the English Revolution, 1689–1720*, Ithaca, NY: Cornell University Press, 1976, p. 137.

13 Quoted in Echeverria, *Mirage in the West*, p. 153.

14 Wood, *The Creation of the American Republic*, pp. 99–100. The title of a book by Henry Steele Commager says it all: *The Empire of Reason: How Europe Imagined and America Realized the Enlightenment*, Garden City: NY, Anchor Press/Doubleday, 1977.

15 J. Appleby, L. Hunt and M. Jacob, *Telling the Truth About History*, New York: Norton, 1994, pp. 101–4.

16 Franklin was well aware how deeply this theme had penetrated French consciousness and was tireless in his efforts to counter it, both by his own brilliant example and through tales that caused his French hosts to think that, in America, every citizen must be a philosopher. He astutely linked the cause of America with the Philosophes' dream of a new Heavenly City of Men that was to replace the outmoded City of God. De Pauw's views, however, were further popularized (and vulgarized) by the Abbé Raynal in the 1770s, and remained in wide circulation (perhaps never quite to fade from the Gallic mind); Echeveria, *Mirage in the West*, pp. 28–36.

17 J. Locke, *Second Treatise on Civil Government*, Ch. V, para. 49.

18 See E. Hoon Cawley (ed.), *The American Diaries of Richard Cobden*, New York: Greenwood Press, 1952, pp. 34–6.

19 Quoted in J. Louise Mesick, *The English Traveller in America, 1785–1835*, New York: Columbia University Press, 1922, p. 304.

20 F. Trollope, *Domestic Manners of the Americans*, edited by Donald Smalley, Gloucester, MA: Peter Smith, 1974 [originally 1832], pp. 221–2.

21 A. de Tocqueville, *Democracy in America*, New York: Vintage Books, 1945 [1835–40], vol. 2, Ch. 2. It could be argued that Tocqueville saw the creation of a democratic culture and democratic institutions as devices for maintaining this naturalness, especially natural equality, and thus for preventing the emergence of distinctions based on aristocratic excellence and merit that were essential to high civilization.

22 On the existence of a singular, genuine American nation, see M. Lind, *Next American Nation: The New Nationalism and the Fourth American Revolution*, New York: Free Press, 1995.

23 'Address to Newly Naturalized American Citizens,' Philadelphia, May 10, 1915, in J. Brown Scott (ed.), *President Wilson's Foreign Policy: Messages, Addresses, Papers*, New York: Oxford University Press, 1918, pp. 94–5.

24 See J. Kane, *The Politics of Moral Capital*, Cambridge: Cambridge University Press, 2001, Ch. 3.

25 See E. Rosenberg, *Spreading the American Dream: American Economic and Cultural Expansion, 1890–1945*, New York: Hill and Wang, 1982. Rosenberg argues that an informal collaboration between government and business – producing domestic institutional reform, improved efficiency and new opportunities for expansion at home and abroad – underlay American cultural expansion.

26 J. Brandes, *Herbert Hoover and Economic Diplomacy: Department of Commerce Policy, 1921–1928*, Westport, CT: Greenwood Press, 1975 [1962].
27 They were R. Aron and A. Dandieu and their book, *The American Cancer*, was published in Paris in 1931.
28 In its original form, the Bricker amendment would have left decisions on the enforceability of international obligations to the political discretion of Congress or the state legislatures, a reversion to conditions under the Articles of Confederation in the eighteenth century. Faced with this acute challenge to its authority over foreign affairs, the executive branch naturally resisted. Despite the opposition of the Eisenhower administration, however, the amendment gained significant support in Congress and among particular sections of the public. In the end it was only narrowly defeated in the Senate. See H. S. Parmet, *Eisenhower and the American Crusades*, New York: Macmillan, 1972, Ch. 28.
29 Lyndon Johnson's 1964 Civil Rights Act was the most far-reaching civil rights bill in US history. It forbade discrimination in public accommodations and threatened to withhold federal funds from communities that maintained segregated schools. The Voting Rights Act of 1965 eradicated the tactics used in the South to disenfranchise black voters and permitted blacks to attain political office in record numbers.
30 D. D'Souza, *What's So Great About America?*, New York: Penguin, 2002, pp. 25, 34.
31 D. Flynn, *Why the Left Hates America: Exposing the Lies that have Obscured our Nation's Greatness*, Roseville, CA: Forum, 2002, p. 10.
32 J. Needleman, *The American Soul: Rediscovering the Wisdom of the Founders*, New York: Tarcher Putnam, 2002, p. 3.
33 W. Appleman Williams, *The Tragedy of American Diplomacy*, 2nd edn., New York: Delta, 1978, p. 13.
34 T. J. McCormick, *America's Half-Century: United States Foreign Policy in the Cold War and After*, 2nd edn., Baltimore, MD: Johns Hopkins University Press, 1995, p. 48.
35 S. Huntington, *American Politics: The Promise of Disharmony*, Cambridge, MA: Belknap Press, 1981, p. 262.

4 Anti-Americanism in the Muslim world

A sceptic's guide

Iyanatul Islam[1]

'The twentieth century', proclaims Ivor Krastev, 'was the "American century"', but after the terrorist attack of September 11, 2001, '... the era we are now entering may well come to be called the "anti-American century"'.[2] Stryker McGuire, *Newsweek*'s London Bureau Chief, concurs: 'If the twentieth century was the American century, the struggle between America and anti-Americanism will help to shape the twenty-first [century].'[3] Despite such apocalyptic announcements, the literature on anti-Americanism is noted more for its partisan nature than its ability to promote a deeper understanding of such a disturbing global phenomenon. One gets the impression that some critics – usually with conservative proclivities – of the critics of America are consumed by the ideological compulsion to denigrate and delegitimize their adversaries.[4] It seems to be a case of confronting those who 'blame America first' by arguing that 'America can do no wrong'. Victor Hanson claims that 'hating America' is best interpreted as a display of 'primordial emotions such as envy, resentment and self-loathing'.[5] He is convinced that the 'world's elite damn Americans for who they are and what they represent rather than what they actually do', while conveniently overlooking the fact that millions of ordinary citizens across the world, rather than just 'elites', harbour anti-American sentiments.

Some commentators see the Muslim world as a particularly egregious case of anti-Americanism. The Claim that the United States is an ardent advocate of a Zionist project is noteworthy because it is the principal theme in the analysis of Muslim anti-Americanism proffered by some scholars. Thus, Paul Johnson concludes that 'anti-Semitism and anti-Americanism are now intertwined in the minds of many Arabs. This is the poisoned soil from which suicide bombers and al-Qaeda have sprung'.[6] Josef Joffe, like Johnson, opines that 'anti-Israelism and anti-Americanism travel together', but notes that while in the 'Arab Middle East, the link is standard fare', it is also evident in Europe. Joffe argues, in the same vein as others, that primitive emotions of envy and resentment bind the ties between 'anti-Americanism and anti-Israelism'. Thus, 'Israel and the United States are the most successful states in their respective neighbourhoods: Israel in the regional arena, the United States on the global beat ... [m]oreover, both are stable and vibrant democracies'. To Joffe, 'the United States and Israel may not be unique, but they stand out because of their strong senses of national identity ... [t]hey know who they are and what they want to be'.[7]

Others interpret anti-Americanism in the Arab-Muslim world as a case of cynical manipulation of popular opinion by political and civic leaders in order to deflect attention from the internal inadequacies of Muslim societies. As Barry Rubin puts it: 'The United States is blamed for much that is bad in the Arab world, and is used as an excuse for political and social oppression and economic stagnation. By assigning responsibility for their own shortcomings to Washington, Arab leaders distract their subjects' attention from the internal weaknesses that are their real problems'.[8] The conclusions of Salman Rushdie are remarkably similar. Anti-Americanism 'has become too useful a smokescreen for Muslim nations' many defects – their corruption, their incompetence, the oppression of their own citizens, their economic, scientific and cultural stagnation'. To the Muslim world, 'America-hating has become a badge of identity ... [i]t contains a strong streak of hypocrisy, hating most what it desires most'.[9]

Merv Wurmser joins the chorus of those who claim to know the roots of Muslim anti-Americanism. In her view, 'Islamic fundamentalists and Arab nationalists hate America because it stands for democracy, freedom, and human rights. America's free and democratic culture made it not only the world's most prosperous land but also the world's most dominant power ... [f]or many in the Middle East, our success is a constant and sad reminder of their failure'.[10] Fareed Zakaria is emphatic in his conclusion that hatred of America culminating in the murderous nature of anti-American terrorism is simply the 'product of failed societies'.[11]

The hypothesis that anti-Americanism in the Muslim world is either a case of primordial envy and rage or a cynical ploy used by Muslim political leaders to distract attention from the fatal deficiencies of failed societies cannot be easily reconciled with the available evidence. If the hypotheses were valid, anti-Americanism would be largely confined to so-called failed societies. This is not the case, as anti-Americanism is evident even in such successful societies as South Korea and predates 9/11.[12] Furthermore, Israel and the United States are not the only exemplars of 'stable and vibrant democracies' whose success incurs the wrath of Muslim societies. Canada and Norway, to take two examples, are equally 'stable and vibrant democracies'. Indeed, in terms of social statistics and broad-based measures of well-being, they rank above the United States and Israel.[13] Yet, Canadian and Norwegian successes have not attracted the hostility of Muslims. Furthermore, there are a total of 88 'free' countries in the world based on the annual survey of political rights and civil liberties by *Freedom House*.[14] Hence, neither the United States nor Israel is unique in that respect. What distinguishes the United States is its undisputed status as the supreme global military power and Israel, aided and abetted by the United States, as an unassailable regional military power. Hence, it is possible to suggest that Muslim hostility towards America and Israel has a lot to do with the use and abuse of power rather than envy incited by stable and vibrant democracies.

If resentment of the United States represents an integral and innate aspect of Muslim societies, then one would expect it to be constant over time and across different groups in the Muslim world. This is not the case. The incidence of Muslim anti-Americanism seems to fluctuate sharply over time. Fawaz Gerges notes that the 1950s was the golden age of pro-Americanism in Muslim societies when the United States was widely admired. In recent years, the reversal in positive opinion of the United States held by various Muslim countries has been quite dramatic.[15] Thus, in Indonesia, in 2002, more than 60 per cent had a favourable opinion of the United States; it fell to just 15 per cent by 2003. In Turkey, over 50 per cent of the population in 1999–2000 claimed that they liked the United States; the proportion fell to 15 per cent by 2003.[16] The case of Iraq – the central object of US attention these days – is even more intriguing. In February 2004, 48 per cent of Iraqis expressed confidence in the United States; by May 2004, the incidence dropped to 20 per cent.[17]

As an affirmation of the point that reaction to the United States is a consequence of events and policies, it is worth pointing out that there are still distinct enclaves of pro-Americanism in the pan-Islamic community, including Albanian Muslims in Kosovo, Kuwaitis in the Middle East and Kurds in Iraq. All of these communities and countries have been the direct beneficiaries of US-led action to protect them from their adversaries.[18]

Not all commentators who have sought to examine anti-Americanism in the world at large and the Muslim world in particular condemn it either as an irrational creed or as a cynical exercise to find a convenient external target for dealing with domestic discontent. Joseph Nye is concerned that anti-Americanism signals the decline of America's 'soft power', that is, 'its ability to attract others by the legitimacy of US policies and the values that underlie them'. The author recognizes that some resentment of the United States is unavoidable because of its unique status as the world's lone superpower, but he is optimistic that 'wise policies can reduce the antagonisms that the unassailable status of the United States inevitably engenders'.[19]

Nye draws attention to recent history when the United States, after World War Two, played a pivotal role in developing multilateral institutions that restrained America's unilateralist impulse and allowed other nations, most notably those in Europe, to participate with the United States in shaping a global agenda of multilateralism. Unfortunately, the tone and rhetoric of the Bush administration after 9/11 has angered its allies, created justifiable fears of unrestrained US unilateralism and diluted its 'soft power'. This has been particularly evident in the case of the Muslim world that sees current US policy as an attack on the world of Islam. Nye's point is that the essentially benevolent role that the US plays in world affairs is being misconstrued and misunderstood in Muslim societies. The US government needs to effectively communicate its values and virtues to the pan-Islamic community rather than being preoccupied with projecting US military power. This requires, the author suggests, a much more enhanced role for public diplomacy to mitigate anti-Americanism.

The 'soft power' framework in interpreting Muslim anti-Americanism is an improvement over the strident 'America can do no wrong' mindset of some conservative commentators, but it shares with them the basic premise that places faith in the view of an essentially benevolent American power. The issue is the ineffective communication of American values and virtues to the Muslim world. Thus, America is a misunderstood, but not a misguided and malicious, power. The message seems to be that America does not harbour imperial ambitions to dominate the Middle East for the sake of securing oil supplies and/or enhancing the security of Israel. Muslim societies need to understand America's beneficent intent and the US government needs to creatively and relentlessly communicate that message. As Peter Peterson, Chairman of the Council of Foreign Relations Taskforce on Public Diplomacy puts it: 'The America much of the Muslim world hates is largely a concocted fiction. It's time to tell our story'.[20] Unfortunately, in 'telling our story' Petersen and others are not really prepared to listen to 'their' story. One can avoid unpleasant discussions of America's interventions in the Middle East – most notably the unresolved issue of Palestinian nationhood and the mess created by the singularly ill-judged invasion of Iraq – even as one professes to engage in public diplomacy. Not surprisingly, as the subsequent discussion on public diplomacy and the ambitious agenda of democratizing of the Middle East will show, the current US strategy of winning the hearts and minds of Muslims has turned out to be ineffective.

In light of the paucity of prevailing interpretations of anti-Americanism in the Muslim world, this chapter offers an account that is quite different from the standard fare. The various hypotheses of the roots of Muslim anti-Americanism – irrational rage and resentment, cynical attempts to deflect attention from internal problems, failure of the United States to effectively communicate its values and virtues – approach the issue from the perspective of the American policy elite with an unshakeable belief in the benevolence of American power. Hardly anything is said about the epistemological stance of this elite in terms of their willingness and capacity to understand the complexities of the Muslim world. It is taken as axiomatic that Muslims display envy and resentment because of the failures of their society. This is a particular manifestation of 'American orientalism' where some influential groups within America interpret Muslim societies as a means of re-affirming US power and cultural primacy.[21] The result is a selective – and, at times, Islamophobic – view of the Muslim world. Furthermore, although the ascendancy of American orientalism becomes evident after the end of the cold war, it is unable to escape the legacy of the cold war. Thus, the Islamic world is perceived as a threat to America in much the same way that global communism before the fall of the Berlin Wall was. Indeed, some observers see it as an even greater danger.

American orientalists differ on the methods for dealing with this post-cold war threat. Some advocate the notion of strategic containment but others opt for an ambitious strategy to transform the Muslim world by using force if necessary because of the conviction that the silent majority in the pan-Islamic community are keen to embrace American values and virtues. Strategic containment advocates are realists who seek to preserve the status quo in which existing non-democratic regimes in Muslim societies are sustained as pro-American allies. The neoconservatives and liberal hawks seek to create pro-American democracies. Both approaches, however, fuel the forces of anti-Americanism in the Muslim world because both are seen as attempts to sustain American hegemony and power.

One of the fatal legacies of 9/11 is that influential members of the current Bush administration and their loyalists are unwilling or unable to move beyond American orientalism and consider the rich scholarship on Islam that resides within the broader American and non-American academic community. Such a community recognizes the past and current inadequacies of US policy towards the Muslim world and appreciates the capability of Muslim societies to bring about an internally generated Islamic reformation. This important message is currently marginalized as the advocates of orthodoxy seek to sustain the dominance of their paradigm by subverting the marketplace of ideas.

Why do they hate us? The ascendancy of American orientalism after 9/11

In the aftermath of the tragedy of the 9/11 terrorist attacks, a central question emerged. As President Bush put it: 'Why do they hate us'? The answer was readily given. America's success and prosperity – and the values of freedom and democracy that America embodies – engenders primordial rage among Islamic terrorists who come from so-called 'failed' states and societies. Such a view did not suddenly materialize in the wake of the tragedy of 9/11. It can be traced to the work of two conservative American scholars. The discussion commences with Harvard don Samuel Huntington's thesis of a 'clash of civilizations' and proceeds to the so-called Lewis doctrine associated with Princeton historian Bernard Lewis.

Samuel Huntington's thesis of the 'clash of civilizations' came to global attention after the publication of an article on this theme in the summer of 1993 in *Foreign Affairs*, the journal of the foreign policy elite in the United States. The *Foreign Affairs* article provided the basis for a book in 1996. This work was revitalized after the terrorist attacks on America and became a bestseller.

The author seeks to offer '... an interpretation of the evolution of global politics after the cold war. It aspires to present a framework, a paradigm, for viewing global politics that will be meaningful to scholars and useful to policymakers'.[22] Huntington posits 'seven or eight' civilizations that make up the post-cold war era, but focuses on the implications of the interactions of the West with Islam and China. The cultural determinism of Huntington's framework stems from the view that 'efforts to shift society from one civilization to another are unsuccessful'. In a multicivilizational world, the West should give up 'universalist pretensions'. Modernization is distinct from 'Westernization' and is not producing a universal civilization in any meaningful sense. Western universalism, if left unchecked, will find itself '... in conflict with other civilizations, most seriously Islam and China'.[23]

While Huntington posits dual challenges to the West – Sinic assertion and Islamic militancy – there is a crucial difference between the two challenges. In the case of China, the assertiveness is primarily expressed in terms of acquiring economic, political and military strength. In the case of Islam, however, the militancy is ideological in nature and entails an aggressive reaffirmation of its non-Western cultural values.

Huntington has two concerns, how to preserve the survival of the West and how to avoid a global war of civilizations. This will entail a reaffirmation of Western identity by America as a 'core state' of the Western civilization and 'Westerners accepting their civilization as unique, not universal, and uniting to renew and preserve it against challenges from non-Western societies'. It will also entail 'world leaders accepting and cooperating to maintain the multiciviliza-tional character of global politics'.[24]

It is clear that Huntington ultimately subscribes to the conventional notion of 'strategic containment' that was the hallmark of US foreign policy since the end of World War Two. Instead of containing the 'old' threat of the Soviet Union, the author urges American policy makers and their Western allies to contain the 'new' threats of Sinic assertiveness and Islamic militancy. Huntington clearly advises against the much more ambitious idea of seeking to shift non-Western societies to a Western civilizational mode because it will trigger a 'clash of civilizations'.

In retrospect, US policy makers appear to have followed Huntington's advice with respect to China, accepting its economic and political clout, and legitimizing its global role through supporting China's membership of the WTO and the UN's Security Council. It seems that the Bush doctrine and its attempt to democratize the Muslim world through regime change in Iraq and through the subsequent promulgation of the 'Greater Middle East initiative' is very much at odds with Huntington's notion of maintaining the 'multicivilizational character of global politics'.[25]

It is important to emphasize that Huntington's model of a post-cold war world of multiple civilizations does not necessarily stem from a respect for diversity. The author accepts diversity on a global scale as inevitable. This is the logic of cultural determinism. One cannot – and should not – remake the world in the American/Western image, but one should seek to re-assert the Western identity of American society.[26]

Huntington's cultural determinism is reflected in the view that 'in the modern world, religion is a central, *the* central, force that motivates and mobilizes people in the world'.[27] It is perhaps not surprising, given such a view, that the author is driven, as if by default, to adopt a model of the collective behaviour of Muslims that ignores debates and diversity within the Islamic faith as well as the possibility of shared values with the West. The author draws attention to an 'Islamic Resurgence' that has swept the Muslim world over the last twenty years, but he is generally pessimistic that it will yield a democratic dividend. Thus '[t]he general failure of liberal democracy to take hold of Muslim societies is a continuing and repeated phenomenon for an entire century beginning in the late 1800s. This failure has its source at least in part in the inhospitable nature of Islamic culture and society to Western liberal concepts'.[28]

Huntington is pessimistic about the relationship between Islam and the West. His pessimism stems from his belief that it is difficult, if not impossible, to break the shackles of history.

> Some Westerners, including President Bill Clinton, have argued that the West does not have problems with Islam but only with violent Islamist extremists. Fourteen hundred years of history demonstrate otherwise. The relations between Islam and Christianity ... have often been stormy. Each has been the other's Other. The twentieth-century conflict between liberal democracy and Marxist-Leninism is only a fleeting and superficial historical phenomenon compared to continuing and deeply conflictual relation between Islam and the West.[29]

Drawing attention to the link between the Islamic faith and terrorism, which is described as a 'quasi-war', Huntington notes:

> American leaders allege that Muslims involved in the quasi-war are a small minority, whose use of violence is rejected by the great majority of moderate Muslims. This may be true, but evidence to support it is lacking. Protests against anti-Western violence have been totally absent in Muslim countries. Muslim governments, even the bunker governments friendly to and dependent on the West, have been strikingly reticent when it comes to condemning terrorist acts against the West.[30]

The author is emphatic that '[the] underlying problem for the West is not Islamic fundamentalism. It is Islam, a different civilization whose people are convinced of the superiority of their culture and are obsessed with the inferiority of their power'.[31]

A major influence on Samuel Huntington's interpretation of the relationship between Islam and the West [and hence America] is the work of Bernard Lewis, Professor Emeritus of Middle Eastern Studies at Princeton University.[32] Huntington notes that Lewis highlighted the issue of 'clash of civilizations' in an influential 1990 article in the *Atlantic Monthly*, although Charles Glass points out that Lewis first referred to the 'clash of civilizations' in a 1957 seminar at Johns Hopkins University.[33] In the much-noted 1990 piece, Lewis dissects the 'roots of Muslim rage' and observes that '[i]t should by now be clear that we are facing ... no less than a clash of civilizations – that perhaps irrational but surely historic reaction of an ancient rival against our Judeo-Christian heritage, our secular present and the worldwide expansion of both'. As in the case of Huntington, Lewis is quick to point out that the confrontation with this 'ancient rival' could indeed provoke a clash of civilizations. The author warns: 'It is crucially important that we on our side should not be provoked into an equally historic but also equally irrational reaction against that rival.'[34]

The 'roots of Muslim rage' is a theory of the terminal decline of Islam both as a civilization and an imperial power that coincided with the decline of the Ottoman Empire and ultimately the dissolution of the caliphate. This looms large, claims Lewis, in the Muslim consciousness. 'During its nearly thirteen centuries, the caliphate … remained a potent symbol of Muslim unity, even identity; its disappearance … was felt throughout the Muslim world … Many Muslims are still painfully conscious of this void'.[35] Using this perspective, Lewis paints a picture of Muslim peoples trapped in the ruins of their history and unable to adapt to modernity, with some among them consumed by nihilistic rage against the West.

The 1990 piece by Lewis urged caution and restraint in dealing with the Muslim world, lest it provoke a clash of civilizations. After 9/11, he shed such inhibitions. Peter Waldman offers a flattering account of the so-called Lewis doctrine as Bernard Lewis resurrects the thesis of the historic 'roots of Muslim rage' and conveys it to the key planners who eventually carve out a strategy for invading Iraq. Lewis wastes no time in media interviews to embellish his long-held beliefs.[36] 'The question people are asking is why they hate us. That's the wrong question', Lewis opined after the 9/11 attacks.

> In a sense, they've been hating us for centuries, and it's very natural that they should. You have this millennial rivalry between two world religions, and now, from their point of view, the wrong one seems to be winning. More generally … you can't be rich, strong, successful and loved, particularly by those who are not rich, not strong, and not successful. So the hatred is something almost axiomatic. The question which we should be asking is why do they neither fear nor respect us?[37]

Waldman notes that after 9/11 Lewis advocated the need to confront an implacable and irrational foe to instil 'fear and respect' through a combination of American military might and benevolence. The author appears to suggest that the Lewis doctrine was shaped under the trauma of 9/11, but Robert Blecher suggests that the genesis of the so-called Lewis doctrine can be found in 1998 when Lewis (and others) urged President Bill Clinton to use military intervention to topple Saddam Hussein.[38] In any case, Michael Hirsh is convinced that Lewis exercised inordinate influence on key members of the Bush administration that led them to 'misread' the Arab world. This, Hirsh maintains, ultimately paved the way for the current misadventure in Iraq.[39] For example, Paul Wolfowitz is on record as claiming that 'Bernard has taught us how to understand the complex and important history of the Middle East, and use it to guide us where we will go next to build a better world for generations to come.' Dick Cheney referred to Lewis as 'one of the great students' of the Muslim world.[40]

In the post 9/11 era, the 'why do they hate us?' movement has also spawned an attempt among its adherents to show a formal link between Islamic extremism and the threat of communism during the cold war. In July 2004, two influential American politicians – Democrat Senator Joe Lieberman and

Republican Senator Jon Kyl – announced that they had embarked on a bipartisan enterprise to resurrect the 'Committee on the Present Danger' [CPD], first set up in the 1950s to deal with the global threat of communism. Now, argued the midwives who saw the re-birth of the CPD, it was necessary to deal with the global threat of Islamic fundamentalism.[41]

Going beyond 'why do they hate us?' – alternatives to American orientalism

The fundamental lacuna in Huntington's version of the 'clash of civilizations' as well as the Lewis doctrine is the lack of consideration given to the role that contextual variables play in shaping the collective behaviour of people. Huntington starts from the premise that the post-cold war era has moved from a secular contest between Western liberalism and communism to a multicivilizational contest based on religious and cultural identity. The author then proceeds to analyse the implications for global politics that follow from such a transition without satisfactorily explaining why such a monumental transition has come about. To Lewis, only history matters. Hence, ancient animosities shape contemporary conflicts where the followers of the vanquished [Islam] are consumed with nihilistic rage against the adherents of the victors [the West]. Both authors conveniently overlook the fact that the ancient rivalries between Islam and Christendom were also marked by productive collaboration between two cultures.[42]

Huntington and Lewis realize that alternative interpretations of the relationship between Islam and the West can be – and have been – readily constructed. Consider, for example, the relationship between Islamic values and Western liberalism. Huntington argues that the failure of democracy to take root in the Muslim world is due to the incompatibility between Islamic values and the ethos of Western liberal democracy, although he concedes that other non-cultural factors may be more important as explanatory variables.[43] During the cold war, the United States and its Western allies often embraced 'friendly tyrants' in the Muslim world and were rather wary of 'unfriendly democracies' because their primary concern was to find allies in the Western world that could act as a bulwark against the global spread of communism. Thus, the US-led West was reluctant to encourage democracy in Muslim societies. At the same time, the 'friendly tyrants' suppressed the development of a secular opposition and even courted Islamists to offset such opposition. Thus, it is possible to argue that the rise of radical Islamists can at least partly be attributed to the nature of cold war politics.[44]

Lewis recognizes alternative paradigms but disparages their credibility. The author rejects the view that the so-called 'Muslim rage' could in any way be connected to '… all the dreadful things that we of the West have done to them'. While Islam needs an enemy, the West does not need 'an enemy to replace the defunct Soviet Union'.[45] Despite such denials, other scholars have assembled evidence to show that a culture of fear pervades the United States and the West in modern times, where the Muslims are once again the enemy in the 'new crusades'.[46]

Mahmud Mamdani offers perhaps the most forthright argument rejecting the notion that Islamic fundamentalism or even Islam is a threat to America because of immutable religious beliefs and deeply entrenched historical circumstances. In Mamdani's framework, contextual variables play the primary role in understanding the rise of radical Islamism. It is a very modern and secular phenomenon and is the product of cold war politics.[47] The author suggests that the 'bad' Muslims of today were, in fact, the 'good' Muslims of yesterday. In order to appreciate this point, it is necessary to trace the evolution of cold war politics and how it eventually deviated from the traditional doctrine of strategic containment of global communism.

After defeat in the Vietnam War, US administrations resorted to 'proxy wars' to contain the threat of global communism. This entailed the active, but indirect, support by the CIA of violent new right wing groups that were essentially terrorist and proto-terrorist organizations. These proxy wars erupted across a wide front including Indo-China, Latin America, Africa and Afghanistan with the aim of rolling back nationalist movements fuelled by Marxist-Leninist principles. These proxy wars can be traced to the Nixon administration under the guidance of Henry Kissinger. Such wars became an ideology under the Reagan administration that was committed to delivering the fatal blow to the 'evil empire' of the Soviet Union. It is in such an environment that a pan-Islamic front was created to repel the Soviet invasion.[48] Members of this front were even hailed by Reagan as the 'moral equivalents' of America's founding fathers.

For the first time, religiously inspired Islamists had a clearly defined enemy and became part of a global network of uprooted and stateless individuals. The defeat of the Soviet Union in Afghanistan emboldened this group of *Mujahedeen* – the predecessor of al-Qaeda and its affiliates – in their capacity to defeat superpowers. Thus was born the creed of global Jihadism that fused religious fervour and the use of violence into a murderous mix.

In trying to demonstrate that Islamic fundamentalism is essentially a secular movement, Mamdani compares and contrasts it with Christian fundamentalism.[49] The latter entails the entry of religious clergy into secular politics best exemplified by such 'televangelists' as Billy Graham and Jerry Falwell in the United States. Islamic fundamentalism was a movement to 'Islamize' politics led by intellectuals who were not part of the clergy. Iconic figures include Maududi, a Pakistani journalist, Syed Qutb, an 'Egyptian literary and educational scholar' and Ali Shariati, an Iranian 'humanist intellectual'.[50] Both the state and the clergy in Muslim societies then had to respond to this movement.

As Hugh Eakin notes, Mamdani's thesis will inevitably engender controversy given that it deliberately seeks to overturn the dominant paradigm on Islamic fundamentalism.[51] Its detractors predictably belong to the Huntington/Lewis camp. Its supporters, who see the thesis that Islam is an existential threat to the West as a self-serving paradigm, feel vindicated. Others, such as John Esposito, seek a middle ground in which both religious identity and international politics interact to create the current global discourse on Islam.

One could argue that Esposito and like-minded colleagues – such as John Voll and Charles Kurzman – primarily object to the 'clash of civilizations' hypothesis and the caricature of Muslims in the work of Lewis because it offers a rather partial and misleading picture of developments in the Muslim world. The Islamic Resurgence underway over the last two decades may be seen as the basis of both a 'quiet revolution' and a 'reformation'. Educated middle class Muslims rather than obscurantist mullahs lead the Resurgence. Such groups are interested in political and social change through 'ballots rather than bullets'. One should take account of 'Islam's democratic essence' and the emergence of 'Islamic democrats'. The contemporary intellectual debates among Muslim scholars resonate with the modernist movement between 1840 and 1940. Such debates, both then and now, show remarkable similarities with the values of Western liberalism pertaining to religious pluralism, equality and human rights.[52]

There is a growing conviction by some scholars that radical Islamism was, by the mid 1990s, a spent political force.[53] Indeed, Sadik Al-Azm makes the provocative claim that 9/11, far from signifying the resurgence of militant Islam, represents its 'last gasp'.[54] The thesis of the rise and decline of militant Islam draws attention to its failure to engender mass support. Islamic states from Pakistan to Sudan turned out to be bitter disappointments. Pro-Western and secular regimes in much of the Middle East and North Africa remained firmly in power as they defeated the militants with the backing of US power by the late 1990s. The failure of the Islamic Revolution in Iran was a particularly hard blow to the Islamists who saw it as a model worthy of emulation. Wahhabist Saudi Arabia is now under a great deal of global scrutiny for seeking to export a puritanical brand of Islam to the rest of the Muslim world.

There is a conscious effort by Muslim intellectuals and others to seek a more peaceful and democratic process of change in the Muslim heartland. Ziauddin Sardar claims that in the post-9/11 era, countries ranging from Morocco to Indonesia may be in the throes of an early 'reformation'.[55] These developments, if sustained, suggest a complex evolution in the Muslim world that cannot be captured in the 'closed' view of Islam embedded in the work of Huntington and Lewis. Indeed, one could make the argument that the Huntington/Lewis framework and its adherents revived the waning political fortunes of radical Islam by granting it global publicity.

American orientalism and its alternatives

Given that there are alternative theories of the rise of Islamic fundamentalism in the post-cold war era, why is a particular version given primacy over others today by the United States and its 'coalition of the willing'? A plausible explanation is that a powerful lobby can sustain the dominance of a paradigm by subverting the marketplace of ideas. Such a lobby reflects the premise that the principal function of scholars is to produce policy relevant knowledge that responds to the imperatives of the state, especially in the area of foreign policy and national security.

The marketplace of ideas may be regarded as a collection of stakeholders – universities, think tanks, media, business, government, civil society associations, the broader community – who interact to create and use ideas. There is a specialist segment of this market that entails substantial investments of intellectual capital by individuals, usually residing within the academic community, who produce ideas through their acts of research and scholarship. In an ideal world, the creation of ideas is likely to proceed in a neutral and rational fashion through empirical investigations and verifications of competing theories and paradigms undertaken within a framework of transparent and accountable peer review. Robust ideas that have withstood rigorous scrutiny dominate those that cannot meet this test.

Unfortunately, the marketplace of ideas in the real world may be afflicted by a number of imperfections. These imperfections in turn may lead to 'market failure', that is the persistence of particular ideas of dubious empirical validity. In analysing the marketplace of ideas, one should take account of the problem of scientific uncertainty, the difficulty of insulating dispassionate scholarship from ideological proclivities and the information asymmetries that afflict both the willingness and ability of ordinary citizens to form an informed opinion. Such features of the marketplace of ideas create a fertile environment for the exercise of 'market power' by an agenda-driven group of public intellectuals and opinion makers with close ties to the policy and political elite. The exercise of 'market power' can in turn be used to temper the emergence of rival ideas to contest a dominant paradigm.

Consider first the implications that flow from the incidence of scientific uncertainty.[56] Although the notion that paradigms rise and decline within a neutral, rational framework is attractive, in practice expert opinion is often divided over various issues because of the inherent difficulty of 'proving' beyond any reasonable doubt that theory X is superior to theory Y. While some extreme positions may become untenable, genuine disagreements may persist over issues such as the effects of global warming, whether or not globalization has increased or reduced inequality, the role of religious beliefs in fuelling terrorism and so forth. Furthermore, controversies cannot be unambiguously resolved in the presence of scientific uncertainty. Politicians, however, have to reach decisions on a wide spectrum of issues even in the presence of scientific uncertainty. They are also beholden to specific political agendas. This yields the incentive – and at times the compulsion – to create an artificial consensus even in a democracy that simultaneously nurtures the belief in the diversity of views.[57]

In understanding the particular nature of the marketplace of ideas, it is necessary to take account of the multiple identities that shape the intellectual disposition of the scholarly community as producers of knowledge. The view that scholars are engaged in a dispassionate and relentless quest for knowledge strains reality. They are actors in a political and social space and have to juggle multiple identities that shape their personal views independently of their professional experiences. They are citizens; they are members of a community; they may have particular political and ideological proclivities. Research also requires external funding and patronage that may create conflicts of interest between the personal convictions of the scholar and the agenda of the patrons. While concern about professional reputation is a powerful motive for insulating personal beliefs and the agenda of external actors from influencing the integrity of the scholarly community, it is not always possible to maintain such independence. This leads to a situation where members of the scholarly community may cross the line from being independent thinkers to partisan activists seeking to influence public opinion. They can form strategic alliances with powerful elites in the media and in the political community who in turn require intellectual legitimacy for their agendas. This creates a utilitarian relationship between the scholar and the state. The former produces policy relevant knowledge that serves the political imperatives of the latter. A typical strategy, that is now quite common in the United States, is to set up think tanks with preferential access to influential outlets in the media and thereby circumvent the peer review process that typifies traditional research.[58] This works to the detriment of a well-functioning marketplace of ideas as individual scholars are then pitted against an influential lobby seeking to mould civic opinion in favour of its agenda.

Informational asymmetries between producers and consumers of knowledge also need to be taken into account in analysing the marketplace of ideas. Given the complexities of many social and political issues, it is usually not possible for ordinary citizens to be armed with sufficient information to make considered judgements on a variety of issues. They may rely on media reports and expert commentary offered through the media to enunciate an opinion or reinforce their views on particular issues. They may rely on mere 'sound bites' and interactions with their peers either to form a view on a political or social issue or to reinforce their prior convictions. Such an environment of collective ignorance is particularly conducive for motivated and agenda-setting public intellectuals and opinion makers to either co-opt or delegitimize producers of rival ideas. The effect in, essence, is to construct collusive arrangements that aim to sustain a dominant paradigm. Thus, the marketplace of ideas is unable to work in a contestable fashion.

Of course, forces of competition in the marketplace of ideas, as in other markets, cannot be forestalled forever. Rival ideas are always jostling to overturn the prevalence of existing ones. The power structure may shift, causing the political patrons to lose their capacity to support a process of manufacturing consent. Global events may change in such a way that it thoroughly discredits a dominant view. The spread of modernization itself has been antithetical to the prevalence of orthodoxies. Examples of such developments are not hard to find. Thus, widely held views about slavery, colonization, gender discrimination, racial discrimination and anti-Semitism have, at various points, been supported and sanctioned by intellectuals. Yet, their ethical and intellectual legitimacy has crumbled under the influence of modernity and the unpredictable onslaught of global events, such as the American civil war, the two World Wars and the horrors of the Holocaust.

To what extent will external developments today impinge on the marketplace of ideas? Will the war in Iraq and its aftermath change the nature of the global debate on the role of Islam in contemporary international relations, especially in the United States? There are grounds for optimism as well as reasons for being circumspect.

To the obvious discomfort of the Bush administration and its loyal band of public intellectuals and opinion-makers, the war in Iraq has turned out to be a highly hazardous enterprise. The initial rationale for regime change in Iraq pertaining to Saddam Hussein's alleged links to al-Qaeda and the possession of weapons of mass destruction can no longer be sustained. It is, by now, public knowledge that virtually no credible evidence exists to support the thesis that the invasion of Iraq was undertaken as a central element in a US-led 'war on terror' on al-Qaeda and its affiliates. In such circumstances, the ability of a dominant paradigm to be sustained becomes progressively difficult.

On the other hand, defenders of orthodoxy who claim that Islamic fundamentalism is the biggest threat to an American-led global order that has emerged after the cold war era are unlikely to cede their ideological terrain to their critics easily. It is always possible for highly motivated political actors to defend their views even in the presence of seemingly overwhelming empirical evidence that undercuts the affirmation of such views. Consider how the Bush administration has reacted to the latest finding confirming the absence of WMDs in Iraq prior to its invasion. An ex-post rationale has been constructed in which lack of possession of WMDs does not 'prove' that Saddam Hussein did not intend to acquire them if he was given an opportunity to do so. Unfortunately, the latest report on WMDs in Iraq encourages such a position. It explicitly states that Saddam Hussein harboured ambitions to reconstitute WMDs. Opinion polls in the United States suggest that 59 per cent of Americans endorse the Bush administration's position that Saddam Hussein intended to produce WMDs.[59] Such evidence illustrates how political elites can sustain a plausible position that resonates with the broader community.

One could argue that while Bush's victory in the November 2004 elections will sustain the 'market power' of the American orientalists in Washington and its close allies, it does not necessarily follow that the electoral demise of the Bush administration would have fatally impaired its legacy. William Tabb has proposed the thesis of 'the two wings of the eagle' in which there is an enduring elite consensus in the United States that cuts across political boundaries.[60] Mainstream Republicans and Democrats share the paradigm of the benevolence of American power and the sheer malevolence of its enemies. Of course, millions of Americans oppose such an elite consensus, but it is also true that '[t]ens of millions of Americans ... accept unquestionably the bright, positive image of America and its unique goodness'.[61] Surveys apparently show Americans to be among the most patriotic and religious nations in the world.[62] Such a combination of patriotism and religiosity makes it difficult for dissidents to effectively challenge the durability of elite consensus in the United States.

One should not also underestimate the ability of those who support a particular view of Islam to use aggressive tactics to intimidate their ideological adversaries. Such tactics go beyond the use of think tanks and media commentary to create a counterweight to the ideas about Islam emanating from traditional research. They entail what might be called a 'new American McCarthyism' as it parallels the fear and intimidation that the late Senator McCarthy used to suppress dissenting views about the threat of global communism during the early years of the cold war. There is a systematic campaign in the United States by the American Right and the Bush administration to undermine critical thought about the Middle East, Islam and the Arab world.[63] The 'new' McCarthyism starts from the premise that the external threat of radical Islamism is matched by the internal threat of those 'who blame America first'. This group of 'un-American' voices includes American scholars of the Middle East – and of Islam – in general. They failed, so the argument goes, to alert US policy makers to the existential threat posed by Islamic fundamentalism and, even worse, end up being an apologist for it. Proponents of the 'new' McCarthyism see themselves as defenders of civilization against pre-modern, fanatical forces. They are strong supporters of the American invasion of Iraq and adopt, given their links with the right wing, pro-Israeli lobby, an uncompromising attitude towards the Israeli-Palestinian conflict. In this worldview, both Israel and the United States are engaged in a 'war on terror' against a common foe. Israel deserves unconditional support as a close US ally in its fight against Palestinian terrorism.

Activists in this campaign to marginalize dissenting voices within the American scholarly community on the Middle East include Daniel Pipes, Michael Kramer and Stanley Kurtz. Pipes, who runs the *Middle East Forum*, is responsible for setting up *Campus Watch* to monitor the activities of the Professoriate engaged in the study of the Middle East in the United States.[64] The aim is to intimidate scholars who question the view of Islam advanced by the American orientalists. A salient target of attack appears to be the Middle East Studies Association [MESA], the peak body in the United States bringing together scholars, students and others interested in the Middle East.

The right wing critique of the perceived ideological orthodoxy of the academic community in the United States as it pertains to the Middle East resonates with the sentiments expressed by politically well connected bodies that are concerned about an alleged culture of 'blaming America first'. These include organizations such as the American Victory over Terrorism [AVOT], a subsidiary of the Project for the New American Century [PNAC]. The latter – which has been advocating regime change in Iraq since 1998 – came to public attention because it included in its list of membership key members of the current Bush administration. William Bennet, a former Secretary of State for Education, runs AVOT. Also noteworthy is the American Council of Trustees and Alumni (ACTA) that published in November 2001 a treatise entitled *Defending Civilization: How Our Universities are Failing America and What can be Done about it*. ACTA is chaired by the wife of Dick Cheney, the current American Vice President.

The latest phase in the 'new McCarthyism' to suppress open debate on the Middle East is the attempt by the right wing lobby to influence funding policies of the US government that directly impinge on the study of Islam and its role in current world affairs. The aim is to promote 'ideological diversity' in the academic community by seeking to ensure, through legislative initiatives, that funding supports work that can ameliorate the alleged ideological bias inherent in the study of the Middle East and promote the notion of American benevolence. Whether this ambitious strategy will succeed remains to be seen, but the case study presented here is a good illustration of the various ways in which a powerful lobby seeks to subvert a well functioning marketplace of ideas.

Dealing with anti-Americanism in the Muslim world

Anti-Americanism – both in the Muslim world and the world at large – represents a global challenge. It impedes international cooperation and thus impairs the capacity of the international community to cope with common concerns and challenges. Current efforts at explaining Muslim anti-Americanism either focus on notions of primordial envy and rage or interpret it as a cynical strategy used by Muslim political leaders to distract attention from the glaring inadequacies of failed societies. This reflects the ideological presumption of the critics of anti-Americanism that 'America can do no wrong'. This faith in the benevolence of American power is also reflected in the more nuanced 'soft power' theorists who posit anti-Americanism as the insufficient ability of American policy makers to effectively project American values and virtues to the Muslim world.

Unfortunately, such a premise of 'America can do no wrong' or that it is a misunderstood benevolent power robs the current explanations of Muslim anti-Americanism of their analytical vitality, empirical credibility and policy relevance. Thus, treating anti-Americanism in Muslim societies as an irrational creed and/or the product of failed societies leaves its advocates without any practical agenda for dealing with this global problem. All that the United States can do 'is show the world that [it] is steadfast in support of its interests and allies'.[65]

The 'soft power theorists' of anti-Americanism do not fare much better other than advancing the modest proposal that American policy makers should invest more in public diplomacy in order to win the hearts and minds of Muslims across the world. Unfortunately, efforts at public diplomacy have borne little fruit because they stem from the inability to concede that current events in the Middle East in which the United States is a principal actor – most notably the unresolved Israeli-Palestinian conflict and the mess in post-Saddam Iraq – shape public opinion in that part of the world. In any case, 'the budget for the State Department's public diplomacy programs worldwide for 2004 is $685 million – the majority of which does not go to the Muslim world'. Furthermore, 'the numbers of people reached directly by key US programs are extremely small'.[66]

The US government has launched a major broadcasting initiative with *Radio Sawa* in Arabic, *Radio Farda* in Farsi and *Al Hurra*, an Arab language television station, to respond to what it sees as anti-American propaganda fomented by *Al Jazeera* and its prototypes. The verdict on the effectiveness of such a strategy is disappointing. As Telhami concludes, 'the media's role in shaping anti-Americanism is modest and ... the most important factors are policies and events on the ground, not strategies pursued by the media as such'.[67]

In late 2003, President Bush announced that his Presidency would be dedicated to the promotion of democracy in the Middle East and that Iraq would become a showcase model of this noble enterprise.[68] This was seen as the best long-term solution to both anti-Americanism and anti-Israelism. It was also claimed to be a central plank in the 'war on terrorism'. This subsequently evolved into the so-called 'Greater Middle East Initiative' [GMEI]. Unfortunately, GMEI received a frosty reception in the Arab-Muslim world.[69] The US State Department's own evaluation showed that, while some backed the 'vast plan to democratize the Muslim world', the mainstream view was that the Arab world must adopt its 'own model of democracy', not one that is externally imposed. Critics also warned that US policy towards Iraq, Israel and Arab allies lessened its credibility in the region, while more hardline critics dismissed the initiative and its 'hidden American intentions for hegemony'. There has, since then, been a quiet retreat on the ambitious agenda of transforming the Middle East into vibrant democracies. So-called 'realist' impulses seem to be creeping back as security and stability re-emerge as primary concerns in shaping America's relations with the Middle East. This has led Moses Naím to lament that the bloody aftermath of the Iraq war has led to the ignoble death of the idea of promoting democracy in the Arab-Muslim world.[70]

In retrospect, it is perhaps not surprising that democracy-building in the Muslim world as a means of mitigating anti-Americanism would turn out to be a rather hazardous terrain for the Bush administration. To start with, if history is any guide, of the fifteen interventions by the United States to bring about democratic transformation in various parts of the world since 1898, only four may be regarded as success stories. None of them entailed Muslim societies.[71] More importantly, the current US administration, as in the case of past administrations, has not resolved the fundamental tension that exists between sustaining pro-American governments and helping to create democracies. Genuinely democratic governments in the Middle East – as elsewhere – reflect national aspirations that may or may not be aligned with America's political and strategic interests. Democratic transitions happen most effectively when the process is nationally owned and led. The successful transition to a democratic government in Indonesia [the world's most populous Muslim country] after thirty years of autocratic rule under a pro-American dictator is a robust affirmation of this thesis.

In the past, the strategic imperatives of cold war politics led American administrations to embrace 'friendly tyrants' in the Muslim world rather than courting 'unfriendly democracies'. With the Iraq war – as well as the Afghan war – the Bush administration appeared to focus on creating pro-American democracies. The cruel irony is that it now faces the unpleasant option of either allowing an anti-American and Islamic government in Iraq to emerge or continuing with the highly dubious quest of sustaining a pro-American puppet regime.

In any attempt to rethink the rather troubled relationship between America and the Muslim world, US policy makers and strategic planners would need to reflect on the heavy price that they have paid by falling so readily under the influence of American orientalism. The 'clash of civilization' hypothesis and the 'Lewis doctrine' represent flawed interpretations of the collective behaviour of a faith-based community. These theories focus exclusively on cultural and historical parameters and ignore the geopolitical context that shapes Muslim perceptions of the use and abuse of American power. It is unfortunate that the political appeal of American orientalism – exemplified by simplistic answers to the profound question of 'why do they hate us?' – increased dramatically after 9/11. The US administration appeared too keen to capitalize on a national tragedy by endorsing a tendentious narrative in which self-proclaimed American heroes were committed to vanquishing Muslim villains while rescuing the silent majority of Muslim victims. It was simply assumed that such victims were keen to embrace American notions of freedom and democracy. The dangerously flawed idea that ballots can be engendered in the Middle East through bombs and bullets took hold. Unfortunately, what America seems to have reaped is the bitter harvest of animosity in Iraq and beyond. More importantly, US policy makers have allowed America's vibrant marketplace of ideas to malfunction. The Bush regime listened to one theory of the Muslim world rather than carefully reflecting on the implications of competing ideas.

It thus seems appropriate that one should urge the US government to re-engage with the diverse community of both American and non-American scholars for a deeper understanding of the evolution of Islam in the post-cold war era. Such scholars – most notably those based in the United States – emphasize the 'quiet revolution' that is underway in the Muslim world, and highlight Islam's 'democratic essence' and the early, but promising signs of a reformation in the post-9/11 period. Such scholars will help the US administration to appreciate the folly of reducing Muslims to one-dimensional entities. In the popular imagination, they are merely theocratic creatures trapped in the ruins of their history and hostage to their beliefs. An overarching religious identity has effectively suppressed the multiple and essentially secular identities of Muslims as citizens of nation states and members of a global community. Reversing this regressive narrative will require an affirmation of our common heritage and values that many scholars – both American and non-American – have so eloquently argued.[72] Recognizing our shared heritage, while respecting diversity, is the only sustainable way to build an inclusive, multi-faith global community. The alternative is the bleak status quo in which an embattled superpower reigns alone in the anti-American century.

Notes

1 The author is grateful for helpful comments received from Brendon O'Connor, Michael Heazle, Mary Farquhar, John Butcher, Maureen Todhunter, Michael Wesley, Nancy Viviani and Anis Chowdhury. The standard *caveat* applies: remaining errors and omissions represent the author's sole responsibility.

2 I. Krastev, 'The anti-American century', *Journal of Democracy*, 2004, vol. 15, no. 2, pp. 5–16.

3 S. McGuire, 'The anti-American century', *New Statesman*, 25 October 2004, p. 19.

4 As Caeser puts it 'much recent conservative commentary has been quick to dismiss challenges to current American strategic thinking and immediately attribute them, without sufficient analysis, to the worst elements found in the historical sack of anti-Americanism'. J. Caeser, 'A genealogy of Anti-Americanism', *Public Interest*, 2001, vol. 152, pp. 3–17.

5 V. Hanson, 'Fear and Loathing', *National Review*, 25 October 2004, pp. 54–8, in a review of a collection of essays edited by P. Hollander, *Understanding Anti-Americanism: Its Origins and Impacts at Home and Abroad*, New York: Ivan R. Dee, 2004.

6 P. Johnson, 'Ridding the Arab world of intellectual poison', *Forbes*, 25 November 2002, p. 45.

7 J. Joffe, 'The axis of envy', *Foreign Policy*, September/October 2002, pp. 68–9.

8 B. Rubin, 'The real roots of Arab anti-Americanism', *Foreign Affairs*, November/December 2002, pp. 73–83.

9 S. Rushdie, 'Anti-Americanism has taken the world by storm', *The Guardian*, 6 February 2002.

10 M. Wurmser, 'Why does the world hate America? A symposium of views', *The International Economy*, 2001, vol. 17, no. 1, pp. 27–8.

11 F. Zakaria, 'The politics of rage: why do they hate us?', *Newsweek*, 15 October 2001.

12 For an update on anti-Americanism in South Korea, see S. Kim, 'Anti-Americanism in Korea', *The Washington Quarterly*, 2002, vol. 26, no. 1, p. 109. He claims that, in the post 9/11 era, anti-Americanism is rising at an alarming rate that will imperil the US-Korea alliance. South Korea is, of course, one of the few examples in recent decades of a rags-to-riches story. In the mid 1960s, South Korea's per capita income was roughly similar to that of Pakistan. By 1996, South Korea became the second Asian country [after Japan] to become a member of the OECD.

13 See UNDP, *Human Development Report 2004*, New York: Oxford University Press, 2004 [Statistical appendix]. The measure is known as the *Human Development Index* and combines information on per capita income, life expectancy and education. Norway is ranked 1st, Canada is ranked 4th, the United States is ranked 8th and Israel is ranked 22nd.

14 The United States receives a score of 1.0, but Israel receives a score of 2.5, with 1.0 being the 'best' and 7.0 being the 'worst' in the scale of 'freedom'. See Freedom House, *Freedom in the World 2004: The Annual Survey of Political Rights and Civil Liberties*, Lanham, MD: Rowman & Littlefield, 2004.

15 F. Gerges, *America and Political Islam: Clash of Cultures or Clash of Interests?*, New York: Carnegie Council on Ethics and International Affairs, 2001.

16 These statistics are cited in 'United States: the world out there', *The Economist*, 7 June 2003, that in turn draws on the Global Attitudes Survey conducted by the US-based Pew Research Center.

17 The polls refer to the opinions about the US-led Constitutional Provisional Authority [CPA] that came into being after the invasion of Iraq and was terminated in mid 2004 with the installation of the interim Iraqi government. For the first poll, see G.

Langer, 'Poll: most Iraqis ambivalent about the war, but not its results', *ABC News*, 15 March 2004; for the second, see T. Ricks, '80 per cent in Iraq distrust occupation authority: results of poll, taken before prison scandal came to light, worry US officials', *Washington Post*, 13 May 2004.

18 The case of Albanian Muslims is discussed in *The Australian*, 23–24 October 2004 that draws on a report in *Der Spiegel* to suggest that the Albanians 'have a soft spot for America'. Surveys show that, at a time when anti-Americanism is rife in the Muslim world, 63 per cent of Kuwaitis declare themselves to be pro-American ['United States: the world out there', *The Economist*, 7 June 2003, p. 46]. The initial opinion polls that were conducted in Iraq after the fall of Saddam Hussein show that nearly 90 per cent of Kurds approved US-British military intervention to oust Saddam Hussein vis-à-vis roughly 47 per cent of all Iraqis. See Langer, 'Poll: most Iraqis ambivalent about the war'.

19 J. Nye Jr, 'The decline of America's soft power', *Foreign Affairs*, May/June 2004, pp. 16–22.

20 P. Peterson, 'Why does the world hate America? A symposium of views', *The International Economy*, 2001, vol. 17, no. 1, pp. 26–7.

21 This view resonates with the late Edward Said's seminal work on orientalism.

22 S. Huntington, *The Clash of Civilizations and the Remaking of World Order*, New York: Simon & Schuster, 1996, p. 14.

23 Ibid., p. 20.

24 Ibid.

25 Huntington reconfirms this position in a recent interview with a *New York Times* correspondent where he describes himself as an 'old-fashioned Democrat' who was 'dead-set against us going into Iraq'. See D. Solomon, 'Three cheers for assimilation', *The New York Times*, 2 May 2004.

26 This emphasis on reaffirming the Western identity of American society has recently become the subject of heated debate. Huntington's latest work, warning of the dangers that America's 'Anglo-Protestant' culture faces from a 'Hispanic challenge' is, like his preceding work, once again at the centre of controversy. Even conservatives offered a gentle rebuke. See S. Huntington, *Who Are We: The Challenges to America's National Identity*, New York: Simon & Schuster, 2004; D. Brooks, 'The Americano dream', *New York Times*, 24 February 2004.

27 S. Huntington, *The Clash of Civilizations*, p. 66.

28 Ibid., p. 114.

29 Ibid., p. 209.

30 Ibid., p. 217.

31 Ibid.

32 As in the case of Huntington, Lewis has his band of admirers but faces an army of detractors.

33 C. Glass, 'Lewis of Arabia', *The Nation*, 13 September 2004.

34 As cited in Huntington, *The Clash of Civilizations*, p. 213.

35 B. Lewis, *The Crisis of Islam: Holy War and Unholy Terror*, London: Phoenix, 2003, p. 5.

36 P. Waldman, 'Bernard Lewis blueprint: sowing Arab democracy', *Wall Street Journal*, 3 February 2004. The citations attributed to Lewis are culled from this source.

37 As cited in Waldman.

38 R. Blecher, 'Free people will set the course of history', *Middle East Report Online*, March (2003). Available <http://www.merip.org/mero/interventions/blecher_interv.html> (accessed 28 May 2005).

39 M. Hirsh, 'Bernard Lewis revisited', *The Washington Monthly*, November 2004.

40 Waldman highlights these remarks by Wolfowitz and Cheney.

41 See J. Lieberman and J. Kyl, 'The present danger', *The Washington Post*, 20 July 2004, p. 17.

42 Such an omission is particularly unfortunate in the case of Lewis who has drawn attention to Islam's contribution to the West and its shared heritage with both Judaism and Christianity. See Lewis, *The Crisis of Islam*, pp. 4–5.

43 Huntington, *The Clash of Civilizations*, pp. 114–15.

44 Huntington himself is clearly worried that a project of supporting democracy in the Muslim world will simply allow the 'fundamentalists' to assume power. See S. Huntington, 'Two Wests', *New Perspectives Quarterly*, 2003, vol. 20, no. 4, p. 3.

45 Lewis, *The Crisis of Islam*, p. 23.

46 E. Qureshi and M. Sells (eds.), *The New Crusades: Constructing the New Enemy*, New York: Columbia University Press, 2003.

47 M. Mamdani, *Good Muslim, Bad Muslim: America, the Cold War and the Roots of Terrorism*, New York: Pantheon, 2004. Mamdani's thesis is part of a growing literature that seeks to interpret Islamic fundamentalism as a secular and modern movement that cannot be isolated from the arena of international politics. Representative examples of work in this genre include: S. Kinzer, *All the Shah's Men: An American Coup and the Roots of Middle East Terror*, New York: Wiley, 2003; L. Pintak, *Seeds of Hate: How America's Flawed Middle East Policy Ignited the Jihad*, London: Pluto Press, 2003; A. Saikal, *Islam and the West: Conflict or Cooperation?*, Basingstoke: Palgrave Macmillan, 2003; S. Telhami, *Stakes: America in the Middle East*, Boulder, CO: Westview, 2002; and the collection of essays in A. Karam (ed.), *Transnational Political Islam: Religion, Ideology and Power*, London: Pluto Press, 2004. See M. Malik, 'Seeds of hate', *Middle East Policy*, 2004, vol. 11, no. 2, pp. 180–3, for an insightful review of this literature. See also M. Ibrahim, 'Mohammad Ayoob on political Islam: political image and reality', *The Washington Report on Middle East Affairs*, 2004, vol. 23, no. 7, p. 77. Ibrahim draws attention to the work of Mohammad Ayoob, a US-based scholar of political Islam. Of course, the various scholars cited here vary in terms of their arguments, but international politics as a key variable permeates such work. R. Khalidi [*Resurrecting Empire: Western Footprints and America's Perilous Path in the Middle East*, Boston: Beacon Press, 2004] maintains that the troubled relationship between the United States and the Muslim world, especially after the Iraq War, reflects a lamentable lack of appreciation among US policy makers of the historical knowledge of the Middle East. The region has seen protracted periods of colonization and occupation in the past that has bred a culture of resistance and rebellion against external powers. The United States may thus be the latest victim of ignoring history as it resurrects the imperial tradition of the past with tragic consequences.

48 J. Pilger, *The New Rulers of the World*, London: Verso, 2003, pp. 155–6, highlights the pivotal role that Zbigniew Brzezinksi, President Carter's National Security Advisor, played in supporting the *Mujahedeens* as the foot soldiers employed to defeat the Soviet Union in Afghanistan. See also S. Coll, *Ghost Wars: The Secret History of CIA, Afghanistan and Bin Laden*, New York: Penguin, 2004.

49 M. Mamdani, 'Shattering myths on the roots of extremist Islam', *African Perspectives*, 20 March 2003.

50 The work of some of these iconic figures and their impact on Islamic fundamentalism is subject to a variety of interpretations. For example, P. Berman, 'The philosopher of Islamic terror', *New York Times Magazine*, March, 2003, regards Qutb as a 'philosopher of terror', but Khan portrays Qutb in a much more sympathetic light, highlighting his passion for social justice. See M. Khan, 'Liberal Islam, radical Islam and American foreign policy', *Current History*, 2003, vol. 102, no. 668, pp. 417–21.

51 H. Eakin, 'When US aided insurgents, did it breed future terrorists?', *New York Times*, 12 April 2004.

52 Excellent examples of scholarship in this genre include: J. Esposito, 'Behind the headlines: changing perceptions of Islamic movements', *Harvard International Review*,

2003, vol. 25, no. 2, pp. 16–20; J. Esposito and F. Burgat (eds.), *Modernizing Islam: Religion in the Public Sphere in Europe and the Middle East*, London: Hurst, 2003; M. Browers and C. Kurzman (eds.), *An Islamic Reformation?*, Lanham, MD: Lexington Books, 2003.

53 G. Keppel, *Jihad: The Trail of Political Islam*, London: I. B.Tauris, 2003; N. Gvosdev and R. Takeyeh, *The Receding Shadow of the Prophet: The Rise and Fall of Radical Political Islam*, Westport, CT: Praeger, 2004.

54 S. Al-Azm, 'Time out of joint: Western dominance, Islamist terror, and the Arab imagination', *Boston Review*, October/November, 2004. Available <http://bostonreview.net/BR29.5/alazm.html> (accessed 28 May 2005).

55 Z. Sardar, 'Can Islam change?', *New Statesman*, September 13, 2004. See also A. Sabir, 'New liberties for Moroccan women', *The Humanist*, 2004, vol. 35, who documents the significant changes to the family code in Morocco that seek to ensure gender equality for the first time in Moroccan history.

56 M. Heazle, 'Scientific uncertainty and the International Whaling Commission: an alternative perspective on the use of Science in policy making', *Marine Policy*, 2004, vol. 28, pp. 361–74, is among the few authors who discuss the implications of scientific uncertainty for policymaking.

57 This resonates with the thesis of 'manufacturing consent' in democracies. See E. Herman and N. Chomsky, *Manufacturing Consent*, New York: Pantheon, 1988.

58 Z. Lockman ('Behind the Battles over Middle East Studies', *Middle East Report Online*, January 2004) highlights the ascendancy of the think tanks in the United States, especially in the area of foreign policy and national security. To prominent economist Paul Krugman (*The Great Unravelling: From Boom to Bust in Three Scandalous Years*, Camberwell, Victoria: Penguin Australia, 2003, p. 3), such ascendancy is part of an attempt by the 'radical right wing movement' in the United States to usurp political power.

59 The latest report confirming the absence of WMDs in Iraq is known as the Duelfer report that nevertheless claimed that Saddam Hussein had the 'intention' to pursue a programme of reconstituting WMDs. The opinion poll is based on a CNN survey. For details, see R. Eccleston, 'No WMD but our invasion was right: Bush', *The Australian*, October 9–10 2004.

60 W. Tabb, 'Two wings of the eagle', *Monthly Review*, July-August (2003). See also M. Leffler, 'Bush's foreign policy', *Foreign Policy*, July/August 2004, who highlights the continuity between elements of Bush's foreign policy and his predecessors, both Republican and Democrat.

61 P. Singer, *The President of Good and Evil: The Ethics of George Bush*, Melbourne: The Text Publishing Company, 2004.

62 L. Menand, 'The new nativism of Samuel P. Huntington', *New Yorker*, 17 May 2004.

63 The discussion in this section draws on: J. Beinin, 'The new American McCarthyism: policing thought about the Middle East', *Race and Class*, 2004, vol. 46, pp. 101–16, and his article *Thought Control in the Middle East*. Available <http://www.antiwar.com/article.php?articleid=2236> (accessed 28 May 2005); J. Zogby, 'Silencing debate', *Washington Watch*, 23 February 2004; Z. Lockman, 'Behind the battles over Middle East studies', *Middle East Report Online*, January 2004; M. Dobbs, 'Middle East under scrutiny in the US', *Washington Post*, 13 January 2004. It is important to emphasize that one should not conflate the right wing movement discussed here with the American conservative movement in general. There are many distinguished conservative critics of the Bush administration.

64 See S. Goldenberg, 'Bush appoints anti-Muslim to peace role', *The Guardian*, 23 August 2004, on Pipes and his hostility to the Islamic faith as well as to Muslims.

65 B. Rubin, 'The real roots of Arab anti-Americanism', *Foreign Affairs*, Nov/Dec 2002, p. 83.

66 R. Wright, 'US struggles to win hearts, minds in the Muslim world', *The Washington Post*, 20 August 2004.

67 S. Telhami, 'Hearing on the Broadcasting Board of Governors: Finding the Right Media for the Message in the Middle East', *United States Senate Committee on Foreign Relations*, 2004, p. 6. The author was an advocate of the 'need for public diplomacy' but appears to have become disillusioned with this enterprise [S. Telhami, 'US policy and the Arab and Muslim world', *The Brookings Review*, 2002, vol. 20, pp. 47–8]. See also M. Deeb, 'A new kind of war: communicating with the Muslim mind', *The World & I*, 2004, vol. 17, no. 3, pp. 26–32, for a critique of US efforts at communicating with the Muslim world.

68 Office of the Press Secretary, The White House, 6 November 2003.

69 See G. Achcar, 'Greater Middle East: The US plan', *Le Monde Diplomatique*, April 2004. Available <http://mondediplo.com/2004/04/04world> (accessed 28 May 2005).

70 M. Naím, 'Casualties of war', *Foreign Policy*, September /October 2004, pp. 95–6.

71 M. Pei, 'Lessons of the Past', *Foreign Policy*, July/August 2003.

72 See K. Armstrong, *A History of God*, New York: Ballantine Books, 1994, who provides a magisterial history of the world's three great religions demonstrating their commonalities and differences. F. Peters, *The Children of Abraham: Judaism, Christianity, Islam*, Princeton, NJ: Princeton University Press, 2004, is another classic study of the three Abrahamic faiths. R. Bulliet, *The Case for Islamo-Christian Civilization*, New York: Columbia University Press, 2004, makes the case for an 'Islamo-Christian civilization'. He predicts that in about two decades the Muslim world will have active democracies led by a new generation of leaders who are currently at the periphery. See also I. Rouf, *What's Right with Islam: A New Vision for Muslims and the West*, San Francisco, CA: HarperCollins, 2004, who advocates a new vision for Islam and the West based on a shared understanding of Judaism, Christianity and Islam. In this framework, all stakeholders – politicians, civil society, members of the religious communities and business – will have to play a key role.

5 America, Israel and anti-Americanism in the Middle East

John Chiddick

The nature and sources of anti-American sentiment in the Middle East constituted a contentious topic before the events of 11 September 2001, and have become even more so since. On the one hand, President Bush and his supporters maintain that America's opponents in the region are inspired by a visceral hatred of Western freedoms, and of what America is rather than what it does. On this view, the answer to the problems posed by anti-Americanism is to achieve a political and ideological transformation of the region, thus creating a political culture more amenable to Western purposes through the putatively pacifying effects of democratization.[1] On the other hand, critics of American policy argue that the extreme anti-American rhetoric associated with groups like al-Qaeda acquires wider credibility among Arab and other Muslim populations in the Middle East because American policies and actions render it plausible even to those who do not espouse Islamist or other radical ideologies. If this view is correct, democratization would not necessarily mitigate America's difficulties, but might even worsen them, and the United States would be well advised to refashion its regional policies, especially in relation to Palestine.

This chapter takes issue with those writers, such as Bernard Lewis and Barry Rubin, who have questioned or played down the causal link between Middle Eastern anti-Americanism and America's relationship with Israel. It does so by reference to current evidence about the motivation of America's Middle Eastern critics, as well as the evolution of American policy itself, to determine the extent to which the latter affords an explanation for the former. It concludes with some observations about the relationship between US policy and any democratization process that may occur in the future.

A preliminary point about nomenclature is worth noting. The very term 'anti-Americanism' has about it a pejorative tone, suggesting a pathological hostility rather than a rationally based critique. Critics of America, whether in the Middle East or elsewhere, do not on the whole readily designate themselves 'anti-American', but insist that their objections are to specific policies, actions or leaders of the United States. Our current usage, however, does not provide a shorthand means of distinguishing 'anti-Americanism as pathology' from 'anti-Americanism as rational critique'. Rather than invent a clumsy neologism, this chapter will use the term 'anti-Americanism' in a fashion that presupposes no conclusion about the rationality of the attitudes referred to. Nobody old enough to recall the ideological atmosphere of the late 1960s and 1970s, or even later, will doubt the existence of a rancorous and emotional anti-Americanism, marked by loose analogies between the United States and Nazi Germany, and similar extravagances. The question to be examined here is whether current attitudes in the Middle East are of this type, or have some more solid basis, in particular one connected with the Arab-Zionist confrontation.

America, Israel and the Arabs: the era of ambivalence

Bernard Lewis and Barry Rubin have expounded the view that the American relationship with Israel does little to explain the extent of anti-American sentiment in the Middle East. In his article 'The Roots of Muslim Rage',[2] which appeared against the backdrop of the crisis produced by the Iraqi invasion of Kuwait, Lewis revived his notion of the 'clash of civilizations', originally adumbrated in the 1950s. While acknowledging that American support for Israel was 'a factor of importance', he suggested that there were 'some oddities, difficult to explain in terms of a single, simple cause'. For in the early days of Israel's formation and existence the Soviet Union accorded swift *de jure* recognition to the new state, together with material support in the form of arms sent via Czechoslovakia, while the United States 'maintained a certain distance'. Furthermore, during the Suez crisis of 1956 it was American pressure that compelled the Israeli and Anglo-French invading forces to desist, and subsequently withdraw from Egypt. Nonetheless, argues Lewis, the USSR met with 'no great ill will' as a result of its stand in 1948, and in the late 1950s and 1960s it was to Moscow, not Washington, that the rulers of Egypt, Syria and Iraq turned for arms, and the Soviet bloc with which they formed 'bonds of solidarity'.[3] In a more recent article, Lewis has reiterated these points, adding the claim that the strategic relationship between the United States and Israel was a 'consequence, not a cause of Soviet penetration' in the region, being part of the American response to Egypt's 1955 arms deal with the Soviet bloc.[4]

Barry Rubin, more briefly, maintains that the American-Israeli relationship was 'quite ambivalent' for the first twenty-five years of Israel's existence, intensifying only in the face of hostility from Arab states which aligned themselves with Moscow, and that American policy has been based on the twin principles of assuring Israel's survival and promoting a peace settlement acceptable to both sides.[5]

While the empirical claims embodied in these accounts, as opposed to attributions of motive, are largely uncontentious, they omit so much else as to amount to *suggestio falsi*. In the first place, Lewis's account of Soviet policy overlooks the fact that Stalin's flirtation with Israel was short-lived indeed. As early as 1949 a full-throated 'anti-Zionist' campaign was once more under way in the Soviet bloc, culminating in the Slansky trial in Prague in November 1952, and the 'doctors' plot' affair in the Soviet Union itself early the following year. These developments doubtless owed more to internal pressures in the Soviet bloc and

Stalin's personal obsessions than to a considered revision of Moscow's Middle Eastern policy, and were in any case brought to a halt after Stalin's death in March 1953.[6] Nonetheless the post-Stalin leadership did not restore the pro-Israel position of 1948, and from the mid 1950s Nikita Khrushchev embarked on a systematic wooing of non-aligned countries previously disregarded in Soviet diplomacy, which in the case of the Middle East took the form of an *entente* with Egypt. In these circumstances it is not surprising that Arab nationalists found it possible to overlook Moscow's earlier behaviour.

Secondly, it is misleading to imply that Nasser's Egypt and other Arab states turned to Moscow for military aid out of ideological hostility to the United States, thus driving America into a strategic alignment with Israel. It should be remembered that the Egyptian Free Officers' regime, in which Abdul Nasser became the dominant figure by 1954, was initially well regarded by the West and correspondingly disparaged by the Soviet Union. The deterioration in Nasser's relations with the West, especially the United States and Britain, initially sprang from two contemporaneous developments in 1955. One was the dispute over the Baghdad Pact, an alliance comprising Iraq, Turkey, Iran, Pakistan and Britain, which Egypt, Syria and Arab nationalists elsewhere wished to exclude from the Arab world. The other was indeed the Egyptian-Czech arms agreement announced in September, which was effected against the background of a serious increase in tension along the Egyptian border with Israel. In February 1955 Israeli paratroopers led by Ariel Sharon attacked an Egyptian military headquarters in Gaza, costing the lives of 37 Egyptian soldiers as well as eight Israelis. This episode was the handiwork of David Ben-Gurion, Israel's Defence Minister, and one of its effects was to undermine the behind-the-scenes peace discussions that Nasser had been conducting through intermediaries with Moshe Sharett, Prime Minister of Israel and Ben-Gurion's rival. Faced with Ben-Gurion's aggressive stance and French arms supplies to Israel, Nasser initially sought weapons from the West, including the United States, before turning to Moscow.[7]

It is nonetheless true, as Lewis and Rubin suggest, that America was not invariably committed to a partisan pro-Israeli position at this early stage. Indeed, the Eisenhower Administration (1953–1961) displayed a readiness to censure, and even impose sanctions on, Israel to a degree that would be unimaginable in more recent decades. The United States supported United Nations Security Council resolutions condemning Israel for its raid on Qibya, in Jordan, in October 1953, and on Syrian positions near Lake Tiberias in December 1955. Above all, as Lewis notes, the United States was instrumental in compelling the withdrawal of the invading forces in the aftermath of the 1956 Suez war. Precisely because of Eisenhower's position on such issues, the relationship between Washington and the Arab nationalist forces then represented by Nasser was an ambivalent one, displaying an oscillation between periods of antagonism and periods of *rapprochement*. Nasser publicly thanked the Americans for their stand over Suez, but was soon at odds with them again over the Jordan and Turco-Syrian crises of 1957. The Iraqi Revolution of July 1958 then produced an unexpected upturn in Cairo's relations with Washington. Although the overthrow of the Hashemite monarchy was initially assumed to be a triumph for Nasserism, it soon became clear that the new regime of Abdul Karim Kassem embodied a prickly form of Iraqi nationalism, and for a time seemed susceptible to Communist influence. Pro-Nasser and Baathist groups were suppressed, and the basis was created for a measure of American-Egyptian common purpose, even as Nasser and Khrushchev publicly disagreed over the Iraqi events. In his study of America's Middle East policy in the Truman and Eisenhower years, Peter L. Hahn tells us that American diplomats encouraged Nasser to 'mobilize Arab nationalism as a counter-weight to Iraqi communism', in the hope that the Iraqi army would move against Kassem. Israeli protests against this policy were brushed aside.[8]

Kassem was indeed overthrown and killed in the military coup of February 1963, by which time John F. Kennedy was in the White House. Evidence of CIA involvement in the coup, which was carried out by an alliance of Nasserist and Baathist officers, is fragmentary and inconclusive,[9] but there is no doubt that the outcome was welcome in Washington. One consequence was the destruction of the Iraqi Communist Party, hitherto the most influential in the Arab world.

In sum, the period from Israel's foundation to the mid 1960s saw the emergence of forms of Arab nationalism which were at odds with American policy across a range of issues, but not on all. The Iraqi events demonstrated that Arab radicals did not necessarily see the Soviet Union and its acolytes as their allies, and this might have created the basis for a more lasting accommodation between America and Arab nationalism of the kind which some believe President Kennedy aspired to.[10] The relative quiescence on the Arab-Israeli front in the early 1960s perhaps encouraged such hopes. In the event, the revival of military confrontation between Israel and its neighbours in the middle of the decade produced consequences of a wholly different kind.

The estrangement takes root

The assassination of Kennedy in November 1963 has left us free to speculate as to how he might have handled relations with the Middle East had he lived longer, just as similar speculation flourishes about his likely course of action in Vietnam. One view can point to the fact that he was generally inclined to see advantages for America's global standing in a more sympathetic approach to Third World nationalists, even when they were determined to maintain their non-alignment. On the other hand, he did agree in 1962 to the supply of Hawk missiles to Israel. Moreover, to press for a Palestine settlement acceptable to Arab opinion would have entailed domestic political risks, especially for a Democrat.

No such uncertainty surrounds the position of Kennedy's successor. For it was during Lyndon Johnson's incumbency that a decisive shift in the American relationship with Israel occurred. Johnson was a long-standing champion of Israel, and had criticized the Eisenhower Administration for the pressure it exerted on Ben-Gurion in the aftermath of the Suez conflict. An early sign of a shift in policy came in 1966, when there was a sevenfold increase in American military aid to Israel compared with the previous year.[11] But the clearest evidence of the tilt towards Israel was afforded by Washington's response to the June 1967 Arab-Israeli war, the outcome of which was Israeli occupation of the West Bank and Gaza Strip, East Jerusalem, the Golan Heights and the Sinai Peninsula. Although the Johnson Administration made mild appeals for restraint in the days before Israel's purportedly pre-emptive attack on Egyptian and Syrian targets, its conduct before, during and after the conflict showed a clear disposition to assist in the achievement of Israeli goals. Nearly two weeks before the outbreak of war, Johnson secretly authorized the despatch of military equipment and weapons systems to Israel.[12] In the United Nations Security Council debates during the war, the American delegation thwarted moves to call for the return of armed forces to pre-war lines, endorsing a ceasefire that allowed Israel to retain its conquests. After the war the United States abstained from supporting an overwhelming United Nations General Assembly resolution condemning the Israeli annexation of East Jerusalem.[13]

The Johnson Administration's stance has been variously explained as reflecting the growing power of the Israel lobby in American politics, the belief that Israel was the most reliable ally in the region at a time when the anti-communist containment policy was being sorely tested in Vietnam, and the influence of the President's pro-Israeli advisers. Its consequences may be stated with more certainty. One was that the Arab-Israeli confrontation assumed, to a greater extent than before, a cold war dimension. The two superpowers were arrayed on opposing sides, whereas in 1948 and 1956 they had, in an accidental fashion, been on the same side. A second, related, result was the strengthened position of the Soviet Union, which was able to benefit both from heightened anti-American sentiment in the region and from its ability to resupply the shattered armed forces of Egypt and Syria, whose dependence on Moscow, like that of Iraq and Algeria, was at least temporarily reinforced. One indication of Moscow's enhanced status came a year later, when the official media in a number of Arab countries either endorsed or refrained from criticism of the Warsaw Pact's overthrow of the Dubcek regime in Czechoslovakia in August 1968.

Yet another consequence of the June War, though not directly of the American response to it, was the stimulus provided to Palestinian nationalism by the Israeli occupation. The Palestine Liberation Organization (PLO), previously little more than a creature of the Arab League, became increasingly a political actor in its own right, commanding sympathy around the Arab and Islamic lands and elsewhere in the Third World. The Arab-Israeli conflict, which had hitherto been primarily an inter-state one, with the 'refugee problem' a largely neglected aspect of it, came to encompass a national liberation struggle, in a fashion unhelpful to America's image in the region. A symbolic expression of the emerging gap between the United States and much of the world was the invitation to Yasser Arafat to address the United Nations General Assembly in November 1974, and the ovation he received on that occasion.

The pattern established in the Johnson years was sustained by his successors, whether Republican or Democrat, with the partial and arguable exceptions of President Carter and the first President Bush. This was true even of Richard Nixon, who had been Vice-President under Eisenhower and at first showed some inclination to revert to the more even-handed posture of the 1950s.[14] Any such inclination was undermined by a variety of factors, including the growing conviction that Israel constituted a 'strategic asset' for the West in the global confrontation with the Soviet bloc, and the influence of the strongly pro-Israeli Henry Kissinger. Even if Nixon had seriously wished to take a different path in the Middle East, the weakening of his personal authority through the Watergate affair would have rendered such a venture extraordinarily difficult, if not impossible.

A key episode in confirming the Nixon Administration in a partisan stance was the Jordan crisis of September 1970, in which King Hussein's regime battled the PLO. Faced with Syrian intervention on the side of the PLO, and believing that the Soviet Union was behind an attempt to bring down the Hashemite monarchy, Washington sought an indication of Israeli willingness to intervene against the Syrians. In the event, Hussein's forces drove out the Syrians and suppressed the PLO without any such intervention, and the evidence suggests that the Soviet role was a moderating one. Nonetheless the outcome was regarded by the administration as a demonstration of Israel's strategic value.[15]

In the next major Middle East conflict, the October 1973 war, the United States assisted Israel both militarily and diplomatically. In addition to a substantial arms airlift, Nixon secured from Congress an appropriation of US$2.2 billion in emergency aid to Israel, put American forces on a high state of global alert to counter a threatened Soviet intervention on behalf of the trapped Egyptian Third Army, and conducted the ceasefire diplomacy at the United Nations in a fashion generally, though not in every detail, convergent with Israeli purposes. One notable feature of this conflict was that it displayed a growing gap between America's attitude to Arab-Israeli issues and that of its West European allies, most of whom, including Britain, adopted a neutral position.

President Jimmy Carter in the early months of his term showed signs of taking a more sympathetic view of the Palestinian case. In particular, a joint Soviet-American statement on the Middle East, issued on 1 October 1977, referred to the 'legitimate rights' of the Palestinians. This form of words was unprecedented in official American pronouncements, and, taken together with Carter's moves to convene an international conference on the Middle East which would have included the Soviet Union, aroused vehement opposition both from the Israeli Government and from its vocal lobby in the United States.[16] The Israeli Prime Minister, Menachem Begin, was averse to the prospect of such a conference, especially with Moscow's participation, and moves in this direction were undercut by the bilateral communications between Begin and President Sadat of Egypt that began in 1977. Faced with these obstacles, Carter effectively abandoned the quest for a comprehensive Middle East settlement in favour of the more readily attainable separate peace between Israel and Egypt.[17]

Under Ronald Reagan in the 1980s the alignment with Israel was further reinforced. The main task that his administration set itself in its early years was to reassert American global power and reverse the West's strategic setbacks of the 1970s. It was by no means self-evident that this purpose was served by a pro-Israeli policy rather than by one closer to Eisenhower's, but the view that it was clearly prevailed with the main figures in the administration, including the President himself. The United States came closer than ever before to a formal alliance with Israel in November 1981, when Caspar Weinberger, the American Secretary of Defense, and his Israeli equivalent, Ariel Sharon, signed a Memorandum of Strategic Cooperation. This committed the two parties to joint efforts to contain threats posed by the Soviet Union or 'Soviet-controlled forces'.[18] Israeli cooperation with the United States in this phase of the cold war was not limited to the Middle East, but was extended to the conflicts in Central America, then a major focus of the Reagan Administration's concern.[19] The limitations of the usefulness of so close an identification with Israel were, however, illustrated by the debacle of the American 'peacekeeping' operation in Lebanon in the aftermath of Israel's 1982 invasion of that country. Following deadly suicide attacks on American targets, including one in which 241 marines died in the bombing of their headquarters, US forces were withdrawn from the country in a severe blow to an administration whose foreign policy in other respects could claim substantial successes.

After the cold war: a new beginning?

If America's alignment with Israel had indeed been primarily the product of the latter's supposed usefulness in the cold war, one would have expected the collapse of the Soviet bloc to have resulted in a return to a more even-handed American stance on Middle Eastern issues. In the early 1990s many predictions were ventured that precisely this would occur, but from the vantage point of a decade and a half later they look a little threadbare. In fact, under two of the three post-cold war presidents, Bill Clinton and George W. Bush, American policy on some key questions has moved further away from the international consensus and towards acceptance of Israeli positions previously rejected, however perfunctorily, in Washington.

In the aftermath of the 1991 Gulf War, in which the United States received the support of a number of leading Arab countries, the first Bush Administration did attempt to promote a general settlement of the Arab-Israeli disputes, even exercising a degree of coercion on the obdurate Israeli Government of Yitzhak Shamir. Although Bush had dismissed Saddam Hussein's attempt to link an Iraqi withdrawal from Kuwait to an Israeli with-drawal from the occupied territories, he was aware that a link between the two issues existed nonetheless in the minds of Arabs. The contrast between the speedy and forceful American response to the Iraqi invasion of Kuwait and the decades-long tolerance of Israeli behaviour became a standard topic of Arab and Muslim commentary on the Gulf crisis, by no means limited to those who

had some sympathy for Saddam Hussein.[20] A successful 'peace process' would
have deprived Saddam, or other hostile figures, of an effective propaganda tool.
So it was that in 1991 Bush threatened to deny Israel US$10 billion in loan guar-
antees unless it desisted from expanding Jewish settlements in the occupied
territories. The Shamir Government had been rapidly expanding the settlements, with the result that the number of settlers reached 225,000 by September
1991.[21] This was the first time since Eisenhower that an American administration had used its muscle to compel a change in Israeli policy, and seemed to
some to constitute a major breakthrough. Bush's pressure may have been a
factor in the defeat of Shamir in the June 1992 Israeli election, which brought to
power the more accommodating government of Yitzhak Rabin. But the agreement ultimately arrived at by the two governments fell short of a total halt to the
settlement process. In August 1992 Rabin agreed to stop what he called 'political' settlements, but not 'security' settlements, and made it clear that he would
proceed with the construction of thousands of housing units on which work was
already in progress.[22]

Under the Clinton Administration there was a further retreat in the American
position. In the course of the 1992 presidential election campaign Clinton had
criticized Bush's pressure on Israel, and during his term official spokespersons
displayed unwillingness to characterize the settlements as illegal, preferring the
locution 'a complicating factor'. When the Israeli-Palestinian peace negotiations
at Camp David broke down in July 2000, Clinton shared the Israeli interpretation of the outcome, namely that a generous offer from the Israeli Prime
Minister, Ehud Barak, was rejected by an intransigent Arafat.[23]

President George W. Bush, after initially displaying little interest in the
Israel-Palestinian impasse, presented a 'road map' to peace in April 2003. One
of its proposals was the establishment of a Palestinian state. The credit that
Bush might have hoped to secure from this commitment was, however, dimin-
ished by his conspicuous expressions of sympathy for the hard-line policies and
tactics of Israel's new Prime Minister, Ariel Sharon. In April 2002 Bush antago-
nized Arab opinion by praising Sharon as a 'man of peace' during the Israeli
military operation in the Jenin refugee camp. Two years later, in April 2004, he
appeared to acquiesce in the Israeli intention to retain large portions of occupied Palestinian land under any future peace agreement, referring to the West
Bank settlements as 'new realities on the ground', which a final agreement
should reflect. These remarks came after a meeting with Sharon, who had
announced a plan to close all the Jewish settlements in the Gaza Strip, but only
four of the 140 settlements on the West Bank.[24] In July 2004 the United States
delegation at the United Nations maintained a long tradition by voting against
a General Assembly resolution, overwhelmingly passed, which called on Israel
to heed the advisory opinion of the International Court of Justice that it should
halt construction of the barrier being built on the West Bank. The resolution
was approved by 150 votes to six, with 10 abstentions, the opponents being,
apart from Israel and the United States, Australia and three Pacific
microstates.[25]

All
down Sad
mass destruc
military charact
not fail to notice t
Israel's nuclear arma
Muslim states, has not s
America would show simil

Public opinion and the im
democratization

The discussion so far has sought to est
decades has indeed shown a distinct bias
exceptions, mainly in the 1950s. But the star
question whether this predilection and its ass
source, or at least one major source, of anti-Ameri
East. Is it the case, as the Secretary of the Arab Lea
tains, that America's 'flagrant bias' explains this phene
evidence now available suggests that, to a large degree, it is.

A poll conducted by Zogby International in 2002 surv
Lebanon, Jordan, Kuwait, Saudi Arabia, the United Arab Emir
and Egypt, as well as among Israeli Arabs. In all eight countri
unfavourable majority opinions of the United States and Britain, bu
France, Germany and Canada, suggesting that the antagonism is not to W
societies *per se*. Asked how America could improve its standing, responde
specifically mentioned the Israeli-Arab conflict in the context of criticism o
inequitable American conduct.[27]

Two years later another poll, conducted in the same countries except for
Kuwait and Israel, showed an even less favourable result for the United States,
evidently because of the Iraq war. In Egypt, 98 per cent now had a negative
view of America, compared with 76 per cent in 2002. In the United Arab
Emirates the unfavourable figure was 73 per cent, and in Jordan 78 per cent.
The most favourable result for America was in Lebanon, but even there 69 per
cent expressed a negative view. When asked how America could improve its
standing, the respondents most frequently replied that it should change its
Middle East policy, stop supporting Israel, and get out of Iraq. (The first two
suggestions, we may assume, largely overlap.)[28]

The conclusion which emerges most clearly from this evidence, if it is reliable,
is that it is American foreign policy, especially in relation to Palestine and Iraq,
which makes America unpopular, not American values or way of life. This has
implications for the relationship between democratization in the Middle East
and American interest in the region. So long as American policies antagonize
such large sections of the populations in the area, any democratizing process
which may occur could well obstruct rather than facilitate the achievement of

this happened against the backdrop of the American campaign to bring
dam Hussein, partly on the ground that he was developing weapons of
tion, and the subsequent pressure on Iran to demonstrate the non-
er of its nuclear development. Arab and Muslim onlookers could
he contrast between this stance and the tolerance afforded to
ment. While it is true that Israel, unlike the two targeted
gned the Non-Proliferation Treaty, it strains belief that
forbearance to Iran if it were not a signatory.

lications of

blish that American policy over many
in favour of Israel, with occasional
ing point of the chapter was the
ociated policies constitute the
an sentiment in the Middle
ue, Amr Moussa, main-
menon?[26] A body of

yed opinion in
ates, Morocco
s it found
t not of
estern
nts

C. A. Rubenberg, *Israel and the American National Interest: A Critical Examination*, Urbana and Chicago, IL: University of Illinois Press, 1986, pp. 211–12.

17 K. Christison, 'Bound by a frame of reference, Part II: US policy and the Palestinians, 1948–88', *Journal of Palestine Studies*, vol. 27, no. 3, Spring 1988, p. 29.

18 Rubenberg, *Israel and the American National Interest*, p. 267.

19 Ibid., pp. 268–9.

20 For one example, see H. Ashwari, 'The other occupation: the Palestinian response', in P. Bennis and M. Moushabeck, *Beyond the Storm: A Gulf Crisis Reader*, Edinburgh: Canongate Press, 1992, pp. 193–4.

21 D. Neff, *Fallen Pillars: US Policy Towards Palestine and Israel Since 1945*, Washington, DC: Institute for Palestine Studies, 1995, p. 161.

22 Ibid., pp. 163–4.

23 For an alternative view, see J. Slater, 'What went wrong? The collapse of the Israeli-Palestinian peace process', *Political Science Quarterly*, vol. 116, no. 2, Summer 2001, pp. 171–99.

24 *The Times* (London), 15 April 2004.

25 *U.N. Press Release GA/10248*. Available <www.un.org/News/Press/docs/2004/ga10248.doc.htm> (accessed 29 May 2005).
26 *Christian Science Monitor*, 6 November 2003.
27 *Washington Post*, 7 October 2002.
28 These poll findings are available at <www.aaiusa.org/PDF/Impressions_of_America04.pdf> (accessed 29 May 2005).

Part II

Sources of anti-Americanism

6 American power

Martin Griffiths

If it all works out, Iraq will be a capitalist's dream.

(*The Economist*, 27 September 2003, p. 62)

In this chapter I examine the global power of the United States as a source of anti-Americanism. At first sight, it may seem obvious to suppose that there is a direct link between them. The powerful are always resented by the weak. Why should the United States, whose economic, military and political powers surpass that of any other country since the collapse of the Roman Empire, be any different? I will argue that the rise of anti-Americanism cannot be explained by American power considered in isolation from how that power is employed – what might be called US 'grand strategy' whose military dimensions are explored by Andrew O'Neil in chapter eight – and the global context in which it is used to shape outcomes. Contemporary manifestations of anti-Americanism are in part a substitute for the old balance of power in world politics. In the past, the response of weak states in the face of the strong was to fashion countervailing alliances against them. This is no longer possible, or even desirable except as a rhetorical strategy to appease popular feelings of anti-Americanism. If anti-Americanism is in part a symptom of impotence rather than mere weakness, one could argue that it does not matter very much. Unfortunately for the United States, it matters a great deal because of the goals that the United States has set out as central to its prospects for winning the 'war on terror'. As I shall argue, these goals are mutually contradictory.

The nature of US power

The American empire differs in many ways from empires of the past. It is based not on territorial acquisition or colonization but on the maintenance of a particular international strategic and economic order. Today, military and economic might are the main determinants of US 'hard' power, supported by its technological dominance. The United States has a unique capacity to project power internationally. It has a global reach of nuclear weapons and conventional forces, a military expenditure greater than those of the next nine states combined, and is the world's clear leader in military research and development. In economic terms, American share of world GDP is equal to the next five countries combined (Japan, China, Germany, Britain, France), and it leads the world in science and technology. US 'hard' power, defined in military terms, is complemented by what Joseph Nye calls 'soft' power, namely the ability to attract and persuade rather than coerce.[1] This includes American values (political and economic freedom) and American cultural influence (language, film, television, music, popular culture). The apparent enormity of American power is demonstrated by the fact that no other state has ever managed to dominate in all these areas so decisively across the globe.[2] However, it is the way in which US hard and soft power is exercised in the form of grand strategy that distinguishes the American Empire from previous empires.

Grand strategies combine elements of security, political and economic policy for the purpose of advancing national security and building international order. US grand strategy has traditionally combined hard and soft components. In the second half of the twentieth century the 'hard' component was designed to counter Soviet power, and was based on cold war concepts of containment, deterrence and the maintenance of a bipolar global balance of power. The 'soft' or more liberal component was designed to address the lessons of the two World Wars and the 1930s Great Depression, and was based on the building of multilateral institutions, market democracies, open economies and a rule-based international order. As Ikenberry argues, this order was based on two historic bargains, at least between the United States and other industrial countries. The United States provided for both international security and prosperity, and other states accepted US leadership and bound themselves to cooperate through multilateral institutions. Thus the United States made its power 'safe for the world' and produced the most stable and prosperous international system in world history.

Since the end of the cold war, many scholars have argued that the nature and exercise of US power will cause other states to balance against it, as has happened to other empires throughout history. However, the nature of US power suggests that there is little prospect of power balancing in the foreseeable future because of the considerable economic and strategic benefits of US hegemony and because of the absence of any rivals for power.

Traditional theories of power balancing do not apply in the contemporary strategic environment because of the economic benefits rather than the costs of US hegemony. The international system is characterized by US military and political power combined with global economic interdependence. The interdependence of economic interests diffuses the unipolar nature of US power. States today determine their national interests based on the perceived benefits and costs of participation in the US hegemonic system. In the case of those states that might wish to balance against US power, the benefits of economic cooperation with the United States far outweigh the benefits of balancing against it.

For example, in the Asia Pacific, the United States provides strategic and economic stability and prospects for greater prosperity. Other states have far more to gain from trade and economic and technological cooperation with the United States than from military competition, as the Soviet Union learned rather late in the day. Others have also learned from the Soviet experience the folly of attempting to engage in an arms race with the United States. Thus China – the greatest potential competitor for the United States – has struck a Faustian bargain with the hegemon, designed to underpin the political stability of its communist system with economic growth based on a partial liberalization of the economy and its partial integration into the global economy, including membership of the World Trade Organization (WTO). China cooperates with the United States to facilitate its economic modernization, and the United States acts as China's patron for its integration into the global economy.

In short, the United States is widely accepted (at least by other governments) as a more benign and desirable hegemonic power today than any other potential contenders, through the benefits it provides in terms of international and regional strategic stability. As a predominantly maritime power, the United States has no territorial ambitions, which means that other states – other than specific 'rogue states' – have no cause to fear US military aggression, and can focus instead on economic rather than military rivalry with the world's greatest economic power. Furthermore, all potential aspirants to global hegemony would be unacceptable to other states. China is perceived as dominant and potentially expansionist in East Asia, Russia is weak and distracted by its own 'war on terror', while Japan's pretensions are constrained not just by its faltering economy but also by its historically imperialist and militaristic role in the Asia-Pacific. Europe is politically divided, has no common foreign policy and no public support for hegemonic aspirations.

While there is no need for other industrialized states to fear (even if they may resent) US hegemony, there is much to gain from it. Despite their inevitable resentment of US power, that power serves the security interests of all other major states in relation to regional threats far more than any alternative arrangements.

Claims that widespread resentment of unilateral US behaviour will undermine US soft power also miss a crucial point. There has been a tendency to confuse the reaction to US power at the state or elite level with the reaction at the public level. At the state level, decisions about whether or not to support the American-led invasion of Iraq in 2003 were based on hard-nosed assessments of national strategic and economic interests in relation to the US, Iraq and the Middle East. Some states, such as Pakistan, even seized the opportunity to improve relations and win benefits from the United States despite considerable anti-American public sentiment. Thus, while most states would have preferred the United States to work within the UN framework, few were prepared to actively oppose the exercise of US power. As always in international politics, pragmatism and self-interest were the guiding principles on Iraq, not idealism.

The United States faces no potential rivals for power for some decades, as no other state is likely to approach US economic and military might in the foreseeable future. The sources of US power are so pervasive, resilient and renewable that it can be expected to retain its dominance until at least the middle of the twenty-first century, based on anticipated continuity in its technological superiority, economic productivity, positive demographic trends, national unity, individual creativity, market flexibility, and enduring political ideals of liberty and democracy.

The continuing positive and benign contribution of the US to global security and prosperity explains an important but much overlooked phenomenon. Aside from a few rogue states and some petulant Europeans, most states today maintain good relations with the United States. It can be expected that some of them will resent American lecturing on human rights (China) or economic management (Indonesia), and that others will object to US unilateralism on a variety of issues, not just Iraq. But such resentment takes a distant second place to the most important international public goods that the United States provides – peace, stability and economic opportunity. This explains why the governments of most states today nurture their relations with the United States carefully and do not allow domestic manifestations of anti-Americanism to inhibit their crucial interests.

If anti-Americanism is a phenomenon that is more evident in popular attitudes to the United States rather than the behaviour of governing elites, and if (as I have argued to this point) the United States is fundamentally a benign hegemon, it may be tempting to dismiss much anti-Americanism as the resentment of the impotent. Unfortunately, it cannot be dismissed that easily. Anti-Americanism is in part a manifestation of the failure of the United States under the Bush Administration to adapt its grand strategy for a post-cold war world and to reconcile two dimensions of American foreign policy (the economic and the political) that are fundamentally at odds with each other. The events of 9/11 provided the United States, and indeed the international community as a whole, with a unique opportunity to begin to shape a new world order to enhance global security in addition to the American 'homeland' and other 'core' states. What had been framed (in the 1990s) as a moral problem within a discourse of humanitarian intervention to deal with a growing list of 'failed states', was now a strategic issue in which the security of the 'core' was linked with that of the 'periphery' via the demonstrated ability of al-Qaeda to establish a foothold in Afghanistan and elsewhere. Unfortunately, the Bush Administration has not taken that opportunity. Whether it still exists remains an open question, but there is little doubt that the window is closing fast. The next section of this chapter elaborates the distinction between core and periphery that was a central metaphor for the post-cold war period among many commentators. In this context, I suggest that the key failing of American grand strategy post-9/11 is not, as is sometimes claimed, the substitution of multilateralism and containment by allegedly novel forms of unilateralism and military pre-emption, but rather the United States' simultaneous support for nation building and a neoliberal foreign economic policy designed explicitly to weaken the state in the periphery.[3]

Core/periphery: two worlds of security/insecurity

In the 1990s there was a distinct trend in the study of international relations to replace the terms 'First World' and 'Third World' with the terms 'core' and 'periphery'.[4] Following the demise of the Second World, the terms First and Third World lacked descriptive value. While the Third World referred to a group of countries commonly associated by their underdevelopment, the term was primarily political in origin, referring to an ideological alternative between the First and Second Worlds.[5] Without recourse to ideology or misleading geographical metaphors of global inequality, a number of scholars argued that the terms core and periphery were analytically more useful in describing the differential impact of the end of the cold war, at least on patterns of peace and war.[6] Economically, the core refers to the industrialized states of Western Europe, North America, and Japan, whereas the periphery refers to agriculturally based states in the developing world, especially sub-Saharan Africa.

Among core states, many observers noted that war has become obsolete, the result of changes in society, economics, and politics since 1945.[7] National prosperity is the key goal, and the primary objective of diplomacy is the realization of economic and social well-being. As Japan and Germany have so clearly demonstrated, wealth and security are no longer clearly linked to territorial sovereignty and military power. The relationship between the costs of war and the benefits of conquest has also changed. Costs have risen exponentially among all nuclear powers. So too, the benefits of conquest have declined to the point where it is doubtful whether there would be any gain sufficient to warrant war. The pursuit of wealth, once a major consideration in the waging of war, is now considered by core states to be better realized through other means.[8] Economic growth in the core is primarily dependent on knowledge-based forms of production that in turn require a skilled, free population, and on the unencumbered movement of trade and investment.[9] As the national economies of core states have become increasingly interdependent, mutual economic interests serve as a powerful deterrent against the use of force. Complex interdependence serves as both cause and effect in the obsolescence of war. Although globalization enhances economic competition within the core, economic issues tend to be susceptible to non-zero sum solutions, to be determined in boardrooms and courts rather than on the battlefield.

Finally, many commentators noted the development of a set of shared values within the core. Unlike the 1970s, it is no longer an ideologically divided world which is becoming increasingly interdependent but one in which the norms of economic liberalism and political democracy are widely shared and where the domestic characteristics of core states have a remarkably similar hue. As Buzan points out, 'liberal capitalism, despite its faults … now commands a broad consensus as the most effective and desirable form of political economy available. The difficult formula of political pluralism and market economics has many critics, but no serious rivals'.[10] The absence of war between democratic states since 1945 indicates that there are features inherent in democratic societies that militate against them using force against one another.[11] Where conflict does exist, it is bounded by these shared norms. Deepening ties of interdependence and the emergence of mutual empathy and even common identity, in turn facilitate the orderly transaction of exchanges and the peaceful resolution of disputes.

During the cold war, international security was dominated by the highly militarized and highly polarized ideological confrontation between the superpowers. The dominant feature of the post-cold war era was a security community among the major centres of power.[12] They formed a relatively cohesive bloc for whom security was inseparable from its political and economic environment.

In the periphery, however, things were different. War, conflict, and instability are as characteristic of the periphery as interdependence and stability are of the core. It is now a commonplace to point out that during the cold war analyses of conflict in the periphery tended to focus not on the local roots of instability but on the great game being played out by the superpowers.[13] This disguised the possibility that with the lifting of ideological overlay, conflict could increase. A range of problems was identified as potential sources of violent conflict in the periphery. Historical mistrust, territorial disputes, ethnic heterogeneity, regional hegemonic ambitions, and religious and nationalist rivalries have long been features of the periphery, and have all, at one time or another, been the cause of interstate and intrastate war. The changes in society, economics, and politics that have led to the creation of a zone of peace characterized by economic interdependence and liberal democratic norms have not taken place in much of the periphery. Similarly, the change in the cost/benefit equation that has served to make war less likely in the core has, in the periphery, been far less pronounced.[14]

More importantly, the dynamics of conflict in the periphery are to be found primarily in the political, economic, and social conditions of periphery states themselves.[15] The state tends to be weak and fragile, characterized by domestic instability, and subsequently vulnerable to internal in addition to external threats. Such threats constitute the most potent challenge to the security of a periphery state. Many of the recent conflicts in the periphery have been the result of a disintegration of domestic political order rather than external aggression.[16] National security has traditionally been conceived in terms of a cohesive state defending its territorial boundaries and protecting its core values from external threats. In the periphery, security must be defined in relation to vulnerabilities that threaten or have the potential to bring down or significantly weaken state structures, both territorial and institutional, as well as the regimes that preside over these structures and profess to represent them internationally.[17]

Indeed, the status of the nation-state is itself uncertain and insecure. Where the very idea of the nation-state is in question, and its basic structures contested or simply not accepted, the potential for violent conflict remains high. If we take Seton-Watson's definition of a nation as 'a community of people, whose members are bound together by a sense of solidarity, a common culture, a national consciousness', and the state as 'a legal and political organization with the power to require obedience and loyalty from its citizens', then it is clear that many of the political entities of the periphery are neither nations nor effective states.[18]

Here a comparison with the core proves useful. The processes of state making and nation building in the core European countries have taken place over a period of three to four centuries, with central power and legitimacy being arrived at only after long periods of violence, coercion, threat and resistance.[19] European state makers sought for centuries to monopolize the means of violence and establish territorial control and the institutions of the state. The competitive pressures and dynamics of the international system compelled national governments to consolidate their political and economic position domestically for not to do so risked being swallowed up by stronger neighbours.[20] The struggle for national existence and the drive for political and economic development became inextricably linked. Sovereignty, or independence, in the classic European experience, reflected an internal reality; the existence of a political structure with sufficient authority and power to govern a defined territory and its population. Over time these conditions have developed to the point where the core states are characterized by an internal cohesion, rational bureaucratic structures, and a high level of consensus on fundamental issues of political, economic, and social organization.

In contrast, most periphery states came into being virtually overnight. With statehood bestowed on them by retiring colonial powers and through the United Nations, peripheral states had, and continue to have, few of the empirical features of statehood associated with the European model.[21] The infrastructural penetration and administrative capacity that is expressed in the notion of sovereignty is absent in much of the periphery. Creating states where previously there had been none, the European powers determined the parameters within which the new states embarked on the initial and crucial stages of state making and nation building. Many of the territorial units within which nationalist movements sought to win independence were overwhelmingly creations of imperial conquest, often no older than a few decades and encompassing diverse ethnic, cultural, and linguistic groups. Nationalist movements were composed of a number of these different elements, representing sometimes convergent, sometimes divergent, economic and political interests, temporarily pulled together in an anti-colonial struggle. With the dissipation of anti-colonial sentiment the task of creating a sense of national identity fell to the new state. As Seton-Watson notes, 'if national consciousness based on religion, language, and deeply rooted historical mythologies were not available, then the agent of continuity could only be the central power'.[22]

The task of state consolidation and the creation of a national identity and common purpose proved difficult for a number of reasons, not least of which is the relative youth of most periphery states, and their peripheral status in the global economy. Compared to the European experience most periphery states have had little time to consolidate their position and authority. As Ayoob notes, the 'drastic shortening of the timeframe and the telescoping of the various phases of state making, combined with the initially low level of state power from which state making takes place' provides an important explanation for the continuing instability that has characterized the periphery.[23] Another factor complicating the task of state consolidation in the periphery has been the colonial legacy of arbitrarily imposed borders that often bore little resemblance to the boundary lines of indigenous societies.[24] Here the political legacy of a state without a nation has often been joined by an even more difficult reality: a state with many nations.[25]

Perhaps the most significant factor in the range of difficulties confronting state making and nation building in the periphery has been the economic under-development that has provided the context in which political development must take place. Integrated into the world economy as suppliers of raw materials and as markets for manufactured goods and the capital equipment for basic infra-structure, much of the periphery has remained dependent upon core economic activities.[26] Often reliant on a small range of export commodities with a high degree of external vulnerability, periphery states have had to undertake the diffi-cult tasks of state making and nation building in a context of economic and financial insecurity. The conditions of under and uneven development continue to determine the conditions of stability and legitimacy, for without a sufficient level of economic development together with some form of equitable distribu-tion, the terms of a societal consensus on the contract between ruler and ruled will prove elusive. The allocation of scarce resources is, of course, a source of conflict in any society. In the periphery, however, domestic patterns of uneven economic growth have militated against national unity, 'as the benefits, such as they are, are often differentially enjoyed by particular regions, ethnic groups, political party members, and government officials'.[27] The process of economic change and development thus tends to become a major cause of domestic insta-bility as governments, unable to meet the aggregate demands of their rapidly increasing populations, attempt to mediate between competing groups. In many cases 'governments will further exacerbate and deepen [existing] cleavages through purposeful efforts to promote one group over another in order to fortify their political base'.[28] One expression of this form of favouritism is the tendency in much of the periphery for governments to favour urban populations and development over rural investment.[29] This in turn complicates the task of nation building and provides a source of domestic friction, increasing the 'alienation of large sections of society both from their ruling elites and quite often from the state structures over which these elites preside'.[30]

Alienation is most immediately expressed in the weakness of legitimacy. Legitimacy is at the core of the state making problem for it relates to whether the citizens of a state accept the authority of the state and believe the existing insti-tutions of the state to be 'functionally competent, legally right, and morally proper'.[31] A public commitment to the state and the institutions of government, lacking in so much of the periphery, derives not only from the public's estimation of state competency in meeting their basic material needs, but also from the psycho-political need for the state to be an expression of common identity, of shared values and shared culture. Where states in the periphery lack legitimacy they are ruled by regimes with narrow support bases, sustained more through patronage and coercion than by ability or mandate. Rather than rendering the citizens secure, such states may directly violate the security of their own popula-tions and create the conditions for powerful resentments and oppositional forces to emerge.[32] Authoritarian rule merely serves to exacerbate and focus the conflicts that arise in the domestic context. Where legitimacy is weak, the state is constantly under threat as any number of problems can escalate to threaten the very existence of the state. In most cases, however, it is the institutions of the state itself that are the site of conflict as oppositional forces do not wish to do away with the state, but rather to control it. Since independence, the struggle for state power has become virtually the only issue of politics in the periphery for the state 'provides a source of power and wealth entirely disproportionate to that available from any other organised force within society'.[33] Whereas the state in the core is essentially a bureaucratic body providing political goods such as law and order, security, justice, and welfare, the state in the periphery is 'more a fountain of privilege, wealth and power for those who control it'.[34] Consequently, those who control the state will not relinquish their hold lightly. As incumbents and rivals resort to varying degrees of political violence, and as weapons have become more readily available for purchase by both governments and dissidents, intrastate political violence has increased dramatically.

Thus it has tended to be the case in the periphery that political competition has been dominated by a 'winner takes all' struggle in which all of the institutions of the state are implicated. The characteristic features of immediate post-independence politics – corruption, repression, violence, and factionalism – have, in many periphery states, attained extreme forms. While the authority of the state has been repeatedly challenged, on occasion, its very survival has been threatened. In such cases the state begins to disintegrate, producing either populist revolt or uncontrolled political violence and civil war.

The central feature of the political landscape in the periphery is the continuing challenge, faced by state makers, to consolidate state structures.[35] The unfinished processes of state making have been responsible for much of the domestic conflict and political instability that has beset the periphery. Hence one of the primary security challenges for periphery states is to overcome the crises of political and economic development that so often end in violent conflict and war. More than ever, the security agenda of the core must address the problem of how periphery states can meet the political, cultural, and economic needs of their constituents.[36]

Prior to 9/11, and despite some optimism that the post-cold war era would usher in a 'new world order' after the 1991 Gulf War, the pattern of international relations in the core did not translate into stronger collective security and regional management regimes, nor did the liberation of periphery states from superpower rivalry result in the strengthening of linkages to the systemic security of the core.[37] By and large, core security interests in the periphery were insignificant. Most regional conflicts remained at a sufficiently low level of intensity ensuring the relative indifference of the core states. Of course there were exceptions. The decisive action taken against Iraq in 1991 reflected the particular importance of the balance of power in the Middle East, the supply of oil, and the unambiguous nature of Iraq's invasion of Kuwait. That special combination of features was not replicated elsewhere. Despite calls for the core to throw its weight behind an array of UN initiatives and deal decisively with conflict and instability besetting the periphery, strategic and commercial interests continued to dominate the foreign policy of core states.

State building/state busting: the paradox of American foreign policy

Since 9/11, the most consistent critique against the Bush administration revolves around its substitution of containment and multilateralism by allegedly novel strategies of unilateralism and military pre-emption.[38] However, even if the United States adopts a more cooperative stance towards other states in its attempt to escape from the quagmire that Iraq has become, a deeper problem must be confronted. This is the fundamental contradiction between its rhetorical commitment to state building *via* the spread of electoral democracy, and its ongoing support for neoliberal restructuring at a global level.[39] In this context, what is happening today in Iraq is symptomatic of a broader contradiction in core/periphery relations.[40] Since the 1980s, the United States has advocated a development model based on the primacy of individualism, market liberalism, outward-orientation, and state contraction. The organizing principle of what become known as the Washington Consensus was the notion of a minimal state whose principal role was confined to that of securing law and order, macroeconomic stability and the provision of physical infrastructure.[41] The new orthodoxy identified widespread and excessive state interventionism as the primary cause of weak economic progress. The natural implication of this diagnosis was to liberate the market from the distorting influences of large public sectors, pervasive controls and interventionism. Such thinking, in turn, exercised a key practical influence on the policy discourse of key Bretton Woods institutions such as the IMF and the World Bank.[42] The state itself was conceived as the problem rather than the solution to 'good governance' in the periphery. The universal policy proposal was to pursue a systematic programme of decreasing state involvement in the economy through trade liberalization, privatization and reduced public spending, freeing key relative prices such as interest rates and exchange rates and lifting exchange controls. Efficient allocation of resources would be guaranteed by relative prices determined through the impersonal forces of the free market.

The logical corollary of this line of thinking was that the cost of 'government failures' arising from rent-seeking and price distortions associated with excessive protectionism would always outweigh 'market failures' associated with imperfect competition and the under-provision of public goods. Unfortunately, overall growth in the world economy has been strikingly lower and more unstable during the neoliberal era compared to earlier periods. Not only has overall growth been lower but also the degree of inequality in the global economy appears to have increased during the era of neoliberal restructuring. Even those who claim that the poverty rate has fallen over the past decade concede that this record was due mostly to good performance in Asia, particularly China.[43] The experience of many countries under neoliberal reforms, notably the cases of

Argentina and Turkey, has clearly demonstrated that economic growth *per se* was insufficient to deal with the problem of endemic poverty. Premature exposure to the vagaries of financial globalization has been costly for many economies in the periphery that found themselves trapped on a highly fragile growth path based on short-term and highly speculative inflows of capital. Reliance on debt-led growth, without paying sufficient attention to the need to increase domestic savings and the long-term competitiveness of the real economy and the need to establish an adequate regulatory framework for their financial sectors, rendered such economies increasingly vulnerable to speculative attacks and frequent financial crises. Indeed, the very frequency of financial crises primarily, if not exclusively, in the periphery has been one of the most striking features of the global economic environment in the post-1990 era.

What is also striking is that such crises have not been confined to certain regions of the periphery, such as Latin America. Crises also occurred in Eastern Europe, as well as in East and South-East Asia, semi-peripheral regions that were successful in avoiding financial crises in the past. In many cases, a disproportionate impact of such crises has fallen on the poor and the middle strata of society, with highly negative social consequences. The liberalization process itself helped to undermine the effectiveness and legitimacy of state institutions.[44] Thus the reform of the international economic system is still necessary to promote an international environment more conducive to development.[45] In particular, there is an urgent need to democratize international financial institutions to give them a developmental orientation and to regulate the massive short-term capital flows that promote instability in developing countries. The very foundations of the neoliberal orthodoxy that has informed the thinking of the key Bretton Woods institutions have been dramatically shaken in the context of the 1990s. The process of neoliberal restructuring has been associated with a weak growth performance, persistent poverty, rising inequality and endemic crises with costly ramifications. Countries that have been performing better than average have typically been those (such as China and Malaysia) that have managed to deviate from rigid neoliberal norms.

Clearly, there is a fundamental tension between American support for neoliberal forms of economic globalization and its war on terror. There is compelling evidence that although inequality and poverty do not in themselves cause terrorism, when combined with the absence of what Michael Mousseau calls 'market civilization' in many developing countries, they feed much of the anti-American resentment that sustains sympathy for, if not participation in, terrorist organizations such as al-Qaeda.[46] The consequences of neoliberal policies at the global level have been the subject of much academic debate in recent years, but it is clear that the benefits of globalization are distributed in an extremely uneven fashion. Large parts of the periphery are left behind entirely. These are the countries where more than one billion people somehow survive on US$1 a day, or nearly three billion on US$2 a day; where nearly half of humanity has never made or received a telephone call; where one fifth of the world's people lack access to safe drinking water. Africa is less integrated into the global economy today than a decade ago, largely as a result of falling commodity prices.[47] At the level of global economic governance, there is a growing imbalance in global rule making. Those rules that favour global market expansion have become more robust and enforceable – intellectual property rights, for example, or dispute resolution in the World Trade Organization. But rules intended to promote social objectives, such as labour standards, human rights, environmental quality or poverty reduction, lag far behind. In short, the processes of globalization promote 'military deglobalization' in the core, where military expenditures (with the marked exception of the United States) are in decline, incentives for war are reduced (particularly among democracies) and supra-territoriality is on the rise. However, the same processes that have helped to create and maintain 'zones of peace' in the core have contributed to chronic insecurity for people within states in the periphery.[48] Glossing over this co-constitutive relationship between zones of peace and zones of disorder and violence has practical implications for policy making. It renders it difficult if not impossible for the 'zone of disorder' to join the 'zone of peace', notwithstanding the Bush Administration's rhetorical commitment to state building, democratic freedom and economic liberalization on a global scale.[49]

Against this background, one might well doubt whether the United States has sufficient power, rather than too much. Clearly, since 11 September 2001 America's interpretations of the threats to its security have changed. Despotic regimes that were once tolerated (or even supported) for their perceived contribution to wider US strategic interests, and failing states once considered unimportant, are now seen as unacceptable breeding grounds for terrorism and other sources of instability. These new threats have produced new coalitions of convenience between states and non-state actors (such as the Taliban and al-Qaeda) and divided old alliances in the international community. While the cold war united the Western Alliance, the threats of terrorism and Islamic fundamentalism have divided it.

Moreover, these new sets of interests and coalitions, and the preponderance of US power, have severely undermined the multilateral system that the United States constructed after 1945. Over the past three years the United States has demonstrated that it will exercise its hard power, pre-emptively and unilaterally if necessary, where it feels threatened. This has exposed a great gulf between the realities of international politics today and the functioning of the multilateral system, and between the exercise of hard US power and soft European power. The United States demonstrated in Iraq that it needs no significant military support to exercise its hard power. In contrast, it almost certainly will need the economic and political support of the UN system and of other states for post-conflict nation building in Iraq if it is to achieve its ultimate goals of a 'democratic peace' in that shattered country.

There is also a risk of imperial over-stretch through the considerable costs of peacekeeping and nation building which invariably follow regime change. In the case of Iraq, these costs have been high. Ultimately, the ability of the United States to continue to underwrite the economic cost of nation building in Iraq without UN support will depend on tenuous domestic political and economic considerations. One of the greatest uncertainties is the future performance of the US economy, and its capacity to underwrite the implementation of US grand strategy. Again, at issue is not whether the United States is too powerful, but whether it is powerful enough. The United States is running twin budget and current account deficits while granting tax cuts to the rich and maintaining a low dollar, thus failing to integrate its strategic and economic policies on a sustainable basis. The United States is still spending under four per cent of GDP on defence – considerably less than during the cold war – but this does not account for the cost of nation building, both in Afghanistan and Iraq. The current management of the US economy suggests that the United States will not be able to finance the reconstruction of Iraq or Afghanistan alone, and this undermines the goals of peaceful regime change and the pursuit of democratization.

Conclusion

The American empire of today differs from empires of the past through its foundation on mutual interests and benefits within core states rather than intimidation and coercion. The United States is therefore likely to remain the pre-eminent global power for decades to come. There is little prospect of power balancing over the next few decades because of the economic and strategic benefits the United States provides, combined with the absence of any viable rivals for power. Most states will continue to accept US power as legitimate and benign because of its lack of territorial ambition and the global public goods it delivers through international stability and prosperity. However, while US power can be expected to prevail over the next few decades, it will face severe challenges. First, there is a risk of imperial over-extension. Either the continuing ability of the economy to underwrite or the ongoing willingness of the electorate to support the cost of the projection of power may falter. Second, without the support of the international community, questions over the legitimacy of US hard power may undermine the ability of soft power to achieve the outcomes it wants. Ultimately, judgements about the legitimacy of US power will be based on outcomes rather than on process, and on economic, political and humanitarian achievements in the periphery. As Henry Kissinger has argued, the test of history for the United States will be whether it can turn its predominant power into international consensus and its principles into widely accepted international norms.[50] The rise of anti-Americanism is important if only as a barometer of America's failure to pass this test in the 'war on terror'.

Notes

1 J. Nye, *The Paradox of American Power: Why the World's Only Superpower Can't go it Alone*, Oxford: Oxford University Press, 2000.
2 S. Brooks and W. Wohlforth, 'American primacy in perspective', *Foreign Affairs*, 2002, vol. 81, no 4, pp. 20–33.

3 A number of critics have demonstrated a degree of historical shortsightedness in this context. From a long-term perspective, the period of American multilateralism in the post-1945 era needs to be explained, not the United States' reversion to type after 9/11. See J. Gaddis, *Surprise, Security and the American Experience*, Boston, MA: Harvard University Press, 2004.

4 See, for example, G. Breslauer, H. Kreisler and B. Ward (eds.), *Beyond the Cold War: Conflict and Cooperation in the Third World*, Berkeley, CA: University of California Press, 1990; T. Weiss and M. Kessler (eds.), *Third World Security in the Post-Cold War Era*, Boulder, CO: Lynne Rienner, 1991; M. Webber, 'The third world and the dissolution of the USSR', *Third World Quarterly*, 1993, vol. 13, no. 4, pp. 691–713.

5 N. Harris, *The End of the Third World*, Harmondsworth: Penguin, 1995, p. 7.

6 M. Singer and A. Wildavsky, *The Real World Order: Zones of Peace, Zones of Turmoil*, London: Chatham House, 1996; J. Goldgeier and M. McFaul, 'A tale of two worlds: core and periphery in the post-cold war era', *International Organization*, 1992, vol. 46, no. 1, pp. 467–92; K. Holsti, *The State, War, and the State of War*, Cambridge: Cambridge University Press, 1996; R. Harvey, *Global Disorder*, London: Constable, 2003; R. Kaplan, *The Coming Anarchy: Shattering the Dreams of the Post Cold War Order*, New York: Vintage, 2001. For a useful overview of contending metaphors for the post-cold war era, see G. Fry and J. O'Hagan (eds.), *Contending Images of World Politics*, Basingstoke: Palgrave Macmillan, 2000. For a rigorous quantitative study of changing patterns of peace and war, see M. Sarkees, F. Whelan and J. Singer, 'Inter-State, intra-State, and extra-state wars: a comprehensive look at their distribution over time, 1816–1997', *International Studies Quarterly*, 2003, vol. 47, no. 1, pp. 49–70.

7 J. Mueller, *Retreat From Doomsday: The Obsolescence of Major War*, New York: Basic Books, 1989; M. Van Creveld, *The Transformation of War*, New York: The Free Press, 1991.

8 See E. Luard, *The Blunted Sword: The Erosion of Military Power in Modern World Politics*, New York: New Amsterdam Press, 1988.

9 H. Nau, 'Why the Rise and Fall of the Great Powers was Wrong', *Review of International Studies*, 2001, vol. 27, no. 3, p. 582.

10 B. Buzan, 'New patterns of global security in the twenty-first century', *International Affairs*, 1991, vol. 67, no. 3, p. 436.

11 In the 1990s, this became known as the 'democratic peace' thesis. See M. Brown, S. Lynne-Jones and S. Miller (eds.), *Debating the Democratic Peace*, Cambridge, MA: MIT Press, 1996; M. Doyle, 'Liberalism and world politics', *American Political Science Review*, 1986, vol. 80, no. 2, pp. 1151–69; J. Gowa, 'Democratic states and international disputes', *International Organization*, 1995, vol. 49, no. 3, pp. 519–22; J. Ray, *Democracy and International Conflict*, Columbia, SC: University of South Carolina Press, 1995; B. Russett, *Grasping the Democratic Peace*, Princeton, NJ: Princeton University Press, 1993; S. Weart, *Never at War: Why Democracies Will Not Fight Each Other*, New Haven, CT: Yale University Press, 1998.

12 Of course, this was not a new phenomenon, particularly in the North Atlantic. See K. Deutsch, *Political Community in the North Atlantic Area*, New York: Greenwood Press, 1969.

13 M. Ayoob, 'The security problematic of the third world', *World Politics*, 1991, vol. 43, no. 2, p. 258. See also L. Freedman, 'Order and disorder in the new world', *Foreign Affairs*, 1991, vol. 71, no. 1, pp. 20–37; J. Chipman, 'Third world politics and security in the 1990s: the world forgetting by the world forgot', *Washington Quarterly*, 1991, vol. 14, no. 1, pp. 151–68.

14 For a good discussion of the contrasting conditions of core and periphery, see S. David, 'Why the third world still matters', *International Security*, 1992/93, vol. 17, no. 3, pp. 127–59. See also M. Kaldor, *New and Old Wars*, Cambridge: Polity Press, 1999.

15 See, in particular, J. Black, *War and the New Disorder in the 21st Century*, New York: Continuum, 2004, pp. 26–68.

16 K. Holsti, 'Political causes of humanitarian emergencies', in W. Nafziger, F. Stewart and R. Väyrynen (eds.), *War, Hunger and Displacement: The Origins of Humanitarian Emergencies*, Oxford: Oxford University Press, 2000.

17 C. Thomas, 'Third world security', in R. Carey and C. Salmon (eds.), *International Security in the Modern World*, Basingstoke: Macmillan, 1992, p. 109; A. Norton, 'The security legacy of the 1980s in the third world', in T. Weiss and M. Kessler (eds.), *Third World Security in the Post-Cold War Era*, Boulder, CO: Lynne Rienner, 1991, p. 23.

18 H. Seton-Watson, *Nations and States: An Inquiry into the Origins of Nations and the Politics of Nationalism*, London: Methuen, 1977, p. 1. Similarly, Deutsch defined an effective nation-state as independent, cohesive, politically organized, autonomous and internally legitimate. See K. Deutsch, 'Some problems in the study of nation-building', in K. Deutsch and N. Foltz (eds.), *Nation-Building*, New York: Atherton Press, 1963, pp. 11–12.

19 M. Howard, *War in European History*, London: Oxford University Press, 1976; J. Keegan, *A History of Warfare*, New York: Vintage, 1994.

20 C. Tilly (ed.), *The Formation of National States in Western Europe*, Princeton, NJ: Princeton University Press, 1975. See also C. Tilly, 'War-making and state-making as organized crime', in P. Evans, D. Rueschemeyer and T. Skocpol (eds.), *Bringing the State Back In*, Cambridge: Cambridge University Press, 1985, pp. 167–91.

21 R. Jackson, *Quasi-States: Sovereignty, International Relations and the Third World*, Cambridge: Cambridge University Press, 1990.

22 Seton-Watson, *Nations and States*, p. 353. See also, W. Tordoff, *Government and Politics in Africa*, Basingstoke: Palgrave Macmillan, 2002, p. 53.

23 Ayoob, 'The security problematic of the third world', p. 271.

24 J. Herbst, *States and Power in Africa*, Princeton, NJ: Princeton University Press, 2000.

25 The coincidence of colonial boundaries with indigenous boundaries varied around the periphery. In Southeast Asia, for example, it tended to be high, whereas in sub-Saharan Africa it was low.

26 E. Brett, *The World Economy Since the War: The Politics of Uneven Development*, Basingstoke: Macmillan, 1985, p. 183.

27 C. Thomas, *In Search of Security: The Third World in International Relations*, Boulder, CO: Lynne Rienner, 1987, p. 2.

28 Norton, 'The security legacy of the 1980s in the third world', p. 21.

29 See R. Grant and J. Nijman, 'Globalization and the hyperdifferentiation of space in the less developed world', in J. O'Loughlin, L. Staeheli and E. Greenberg (eds.), *Globalization and its Outcomes*, New York: The Guilford Press, pp. 45–66.

30 M. Ayoob, 'Regional security and the third world', in M. Ayoob (ed.), *Regional Security in the Third World*, London: Croom Helm, 1986, p. 12.

31 S. Huntington, *The Third Wave: Democratization in the Late Twentieth Century*, Norman: University of Oklahoma Press, 1993, p. 81. See also I. Hurd, 'Legitimacy and authority in international politics', *International Organization*, 1999, vol. 53, no. 2, pp. 379–408.

32 For a superb analysis of this phenomenon, see W. Reno, *Warlord Politics and African States*, Boulder, CO: Lynne Rienner, 1999.

33 C. Clapham, *Third World Politics*, London: Routledge, 1985, p. 40.

34 R. Jackson, 'Quasi-states, dual regimes and neo-classical theory: international jurisprudence and the third world', *International Organization*, 1987, vol. 41, no. 4, p. 527.

35 As Fukuyama bluntly puts it, 'for the post-September 11 period, the chief issue for global politics will not be how to cut back on stateness but how to build it up. For individual societies and for the global community, the withering away of the state is not a prelude to utopia but to disaster'. F. Fukuyama, *State Building*, Ithaca, NY: Cornell University Press, 2004, p. 162.

36 Prior to 9/11, the debate took place over the costs and benefits of humanitarian intervention. Since 9/11, it has been framed in terms of the costs and benefits of the United States as an empire.

37 For instances of wildly misplaced optimism, see A. Roberts, 'A new age in international relations', *International Affairs*, 1991, vol. 67, no. 3, pp. 509–25; F. Lister, 'The role of international organizations in the 1990s and beyond', *International Relations*, 1990, vol. 10, no. 2, pp. 101–16. For a depressing analysis of the collapse of such optimism, see L. Polman, *We Did Nothing*, New York: Viking, 2003.

38 See, for example P. Anderson, 'Force and consent', *New Left Review*, 2002, vol. 17, no. 1, pp. 5–30; I. Eland, *The Empire Strikes Out: The New Imperialism and Its Fatal Flaws*, Washington, DC: Cato Institute Occasional Paper 459, 2002; E. Goh, 'Hegemonic constraints', *Australian Journal of International Affairs*, 2003, vol. 57, no. 1, pp. 77–97; Nye, *The Paradox of American Power*.

39 For a penetrating analysis of the distinction between liberal democracy and electoral democracy, see F. Zakaria, *The Future of Freedom: Illiberal Democracy at Home and Abroad*, New York: Norton, 2003.

40 For excellent analyses of how neoliberalism is being imposed on Iraq, see R. Looney, 'Neoliberalism in a conflict state: the viability of economic shock therapy in Iraq', *Strategic Insights*, 2004, vol. 3, no. 6. Available <http://www.ccc.nps.navy.mil/si/2004/jun/looneyJun04.asp> (accessed 30 May 2005); N. Klein, 'Baghdad Year Zero: Pillaging Iraq in Pursuit of a Neocon Utopia', *Harper's Magazine*, September 2004, pp. 43–53.

41 J. Williamson, 'What Washington means by policy reform', in J. Williamson (ed.), *Latin American Adjustment*, Washington, DC: Institute of International Economics, 1990, pp. 5–20. See also S. Bessis, *Western Supremacy: The Triumph of an Idea*, London: Zed Books, 2003, pp. 99–130.

42 For the impact of the Washington Consensus on these international organizations, see in particular J. Stiglitz, *Globalization and its Discontents*, London: Penguin, 2002; J. Pincus, and J. Winters, *Reinventing the World Bank*, Ithaca, NY: Cornell University Press, 2002.

43 F. Stewart and A. Berry, 'Globalization, liberalization and inequality: expectations and experience', in A. Hurrell and N. Woods (eds.), *Inequality, Globalization, and World Politics*, Oxford: Oxford University Press, 1999, pp. 150–87.

44 See R. Abrahamson, *Disciplining Democracy*, London: Zed Books, 2000.

45 See, for example, C. Thomas, *Global Governance, Development and Human Security*, London: Pluto Press, 2000.

46 M. Mousseau, 'Market civilization and its clash with terror', *International Security*, 2002/03, vol. 27, no. 3, pp. 5–29.

47 See in particular, P. Schwab, *Africa: A Continent Self-Destructs*, Basingstoke: Palgrave Macmillan, 2001, pp. 119–40.

48 See, in particular, T. Barkawi, and M. Laffey 'The imperial peace: democracy, force and globalization', *European Journal of International Relations*, 1999, vol. 5, no. 4, pp. 403–34; R. Latham, *The Liberal Moment: Modernity, Security and the Making of Postwar International Order*, New York: Columbia University Press, 1997.

49 For a devastating historical overview of the success with which the United States has engaged in these activities, see M. Pei and S. Kaspar, 'Lessons from the past: the American record on nation building', *Policy Brief* 24, New York: Carnegie Endowment for International Peace, 2003; T. Farrell, 'America's misguided mission', *International Affairs*, 2002, vol. 76, no. 3, pp. 583–92.

50 H. Kissinger, 'Our nearsighted world vision', *The Washington Post*, 10 January 2000, p. 19.

7 Anti-Americanism and the clash of civilizations

Richard Crockatt

America is a nation with a mission and that mission comes from our most basic beliefs.

George W. Bush, State of the Union address, 20 January 2004

Among the most striking features of post-cold war debate about international politics has been the revival of talk about 'civilization' and 'civilizations'. Much of it has been stimulated by the publication of Samuel Huntington's argument, first as an article in the influential periodical *Foreign Affairs* (1993) and three years later as a book.[1] His argument was both simple and provocative. 'It is my hypothesis', he wrote, 'that the fundamental source of conflict in this new world will not be primarily ideological or primarily economic. The great divisions among mankind and the dominating source of conflict will be cultural'. Nation states would continue to be important but 'the principal conflicts of global politics will occur between nations and groups of different civilizations'.[2] Commentary on Huntington's argument has reached almost biblical proportions. There are few studies of post-cold war international politics that do not address Huntington's views, and discussion of his theory has extended well beyond the academy.[3] The authors of the Bush administration's *National Security Strategy*, for example, felt it necessary to point out that 'the war on terrorism is not a clash of civilizations', indicating that Huntington's formulation had become common currency.[4]

Civilization-talk has also appeared in other guises, however, which are not related directly to the Huntington debate. Since 9/11 George W. Bush has repeatedly declared that 'this [the war on terror] is the world's fight. This is civilization's fight'. 'The civilized world', he observed in a speech to Congress on September 20, 2001, 'is rallying to America's side'. In his 2002 State of the Union address he declared that 'the civilized world faces unprecedented dangers' and, speaking of Iraq's weapons of mass destruction (WMD), that 'this is a regime that has something to hide from the civilized world'. In his introductory statement to the *National Security Strategy*, issued in September 2002, Bush noted that 'the allies of terror are the enemies of civilization'. 'America's purpose', the President declared in his 2003 State of the Union address, 'is more than to follow a process – it is to achieve a result: the end of terrible threats to the civilized world'. A year later he reminded his audience that 'families and schools and religious congregations' were 'unseen pillars of civilization' which must remain strong in America and be defended.[5] Such rhetoric is to be found in many of President Bush's major speeches since 9/11.

Moral and religious rhetoric in itself is nothing new in American history. The sense of mission expressed in the epigraph to this chapter can be matched by reference to any number of presidential speeches over the last two centuries. However, the moral dimension of the Bush administration's approach to policy is particularly explicit and salient, exceeding even that of the Reagan administration in intensity and consistency. Furthermore, the invocation of 'civilization' and 'civilizations' appears to strike a novel note, suggesting a heightened sense of crisis and of a shift in the very categories of thinking about global politics. Significantly, such rhetoric was also current in the first years of the cold war at the beginning of a historical phase that ended in the early 1990s. Arnold Toynbee's *Civilization on Trial* (1948) captured a widespread sense of being at a momentous historical turning point and also of being challenged by new forces which were at once ideological, moral, and political. Among these the spectre of communism loomed large. Toynbee's *Study of History*, an abridgement of which had appeared to great acclaim the previous year, was widely regarded as a warning of the likely fate of Western Civilization, should it fail to rise to the challenge of communism. The vogue for Toynbee occurred at a time of maximum tension and anxiety. *A Study of History* appeared during the year that the term 'cold war' entered the vocabulary and Truman's doctrine of 'containment' was announced.[6] While Huntington's essay predated the year of greatest crisis in post-cold war global politics – 2001 – his formulation was widely held to define the unfamiliar outlines of the post-cold war world, and for many, the terrorist attacks of 2001 fully confirmed his thesis of the primacy of cultural conflict. For the moment the issue is not the correctness or otherwise of his thesis but rather the unusually wide currency it gained. In this respect, the reception of his writings was comparable with that of Toynbee. A further point of comparison is Huntington's adoption of 'civilizations' as the basic unit of analysis. In this, both Toynbee and Huntington were working in a well-established grand tradition of historical theorizing going back at least to the eighteenth century. 'Civilization' is one of those words bequeathed to us by the Enlightenment, though the idea goes back much further, having roots in any situation in which one society claimed superiority over 'savages' or 'barbarians'.[7] Huntington's scheme of analysis draws heavily on Toynbee and one can assume that the popularity of both was due to the sense they were able to convey, in part through the language they employed, of a depth of historical perspective and weightiness of theme.[8]

It will be clear from the above examples that there is an important distinction to be made between different usages of the terms 'civilization' and 'civilized'. At one end of the spectrum of meaning civilization is a neutral, scientific term indicating a certain kind of society or stage of growth that a society has reached; historians and historical sociologists employ it in the main as a means of categorizing various forms of social organization. In such instances the reference is to a particular civilization or civilizations.[9] At the other end of the spectrum civilization is a politically and ideologically charged abstract noun conveying a partial and self-interested notion of what constitutes 'civilization'. As Huntington himself observed, 'every civilization sees itself as the centre of the world and writes its history as the central drama of human history'.[10] To the extent that the West is dominant in today's world, there is always the suspicion among non-Westerners that the West equates 'civilization' with 'Western civilization'. Such terminology in the mouth of an American president can hardly therefore be regarded as being value neutral. In between these two extremes of usage are a number of intermediate positions, but it is easy for apparently value-neutral uses of the term to spill over into loaded or normative usages. The opening words of Charles and Mary Beard's seminal *The Rise of American Civilization* (1929) neatly encapsulate both meanings: 'The history of a civilization may, if intelligently applied, be an instrument of civilization'.[11] Civilization is evidently, as the social scientists like to say, an 'essentially contested concept' whose meaning will always be a subject of debate and controversy, depending on who is using it and how it is being used.[12]

There are several reasons for being interested in this phenomenon. My concern here is with the degree to which it indicates shifts in attitudes in America since the end of the cold war and in the way America is viewed from abroad. I am less interested in Huntington himself and the fate of his thesis than in the wider phenomenon of 'civilization-consciousness' in the United States.[13] To anticipate my conclusion, I propose the following: that the international conditions of the post-cold war world in general and the post-11 September world in particular have inclined many Americans to accentuate their 'Americanness', to enhance and even exaggerate their sense of the nation as unique and exceptional. The times have reinforced a reassertion of America's core values and a heightened sense of the nation's distinctive destiny and global role. More particularly, the American right has promoted civilization-consciousness as part of its armoury in the effort to reshape American foreign policy. The anti-Americanism that we see around the world is in part a response to this heightened 'civilization-consciousness' and the political and military actions that are prompted by it.

Furthermore, I argue that specific events have served to reinforce the argument Huntington put forward: that cultural conflict is a major and increasing source of global conflict. It is not necessary, however, to follow Huntington the whole way. There are, as we shall see later, certain serious criticisms to be made of his thesis but they are not sufficient to reject out of hand the notion that culture was a major source of conflict in the post-cold war world even if the conclusions he draws from the prevalence of cultural conflict are not the only conclusions which can flow from his premise. The task here is to rescue a cultural interpretation of global conflict both from those who have attacked it and from those who have most forcefully advocated it.

Before proceeding it is necessary to address the meaning and usage of the terms 'culture' and 'cultural conflict'. Is it useful or even possible to distinguish cultural from other sources of conflict? How precisely does cultural conflict differ from political, ideological or economic conflict? In most definitions culture is associated with language, ethnicity, 'way of life' and above all religion and shared meanings and values.[14] Cultures may, but often do not, coincide with national boundaries. A defined culture may be as small as a village or locality or as large as a 'civilization', which Toynbee defined as 'the largest intelligible field of historical study' and which Huntington called 'the highest cultural grouping of people and the broadest level of cultural identity people have short of that which distinguishes human life from other species'. A civilization is, then, 'a culture writ large'.[15] Another way of distinguishing between cultural and other forms of conflict is according to the ways in which conflict is expressed. Characteristically cultural conflicts revolve around issues of identity rather than interests, values rather than material needs, and arise from non-rational levels of experience and behaviour. Furthermore, cultures generally change and develop at a slower rate than do ideologies or political systems. Needless to say, such distinctions cannot be hard and fast; they help to identify family resemblances between different fields of human experience rather than rigid boundaries. It is important, for example, to avoid the trap of assuming that cultures are unchanging essences or that the differences between cultures are always or necessarily more important than common features which they share. Cultures, like political systems, change and evolve; some apparently primordial cultural institutions were created or invented at particular moments in time for particular purposes. Furthermore, fruitful cultural interaction is at least as important as cultural conflict, no more so than in the global age.[16] The necessity of making such qualifications, however, is not a reason for abandoning the attempt to distinguish between cultural and other forms of conflict or interaction. Often in any particular situation the ascription of one term or another will be a matter of emphasis rather than of absolute difference. Nevertheless, it is important to maintain such distinctions. To collapse all facets of human experience into each other is no less distorting than to separate them from each other.

What is meant by 'civilization-consciousness'? I believe that three claims are being made by those who invoke civilization, not all of them obviously compatible. The examples given here are illustrative only and are in keeping with the exploratory nature of this inquiry. The first claim rests on the identification of civilization with America and is therefore an act of appropriation by America. It expresses a sense of America's distinctive identity as a nation and a culture. This is as old as America and is often called 'American exceptionalism' or 'Americanism' or in its more strident forms 'one hundred per cent Americanism'. But more than this is implied. These ideas rest on the notion that America has the capacity to be a world unto itself, that America itself constitutes a 'civilization'. Historically such notions have been as common on the left as on the right. Charles and Mary Beard's history of the United States, as we have seen, was called *The Rise of American Civilization*. Max Lerner's magisterial study of the United States, published in 1957, was entitled *America as a Civilization*. 'Like a person', he wrote, 'a civilization is more than the sum of its parts ... When you have described its people, armies, technology, economics, politics, arts, regions and cities, class and caste, mores and morals, there is something elusive left – an inner civilizational style'. In answer to the question 'is America a civilization?' he answered resoundingly yes: 'to be American is no longer to be only a nationality. It has become, along with communism and in rivalry with it, a key pattern of action and values'. Furthermore, he concluded, 'America represents ... the naked embodiment of the most dynamic elements of modern Western history'.[17]

The argument for an American civilization as distinct from Western civilization has received a great fillip recently in the hands of the New Right in America and in particular in the context of strained relations between America and 'old' Europe. In Robert Kagan's eyes 'it is time to stop pretending that Europeans and Americans share a common view of the world, or even that they occupy the same world'. On major strategic and international questions 'Americans are from Mars and Europeans from Venus: They agree on little and understand each other less and less'. Nor was this a superficial or transitory phenomenon: 'when it comes to setting national priorities, determining threats, defining challenges, and fashioning and implementing foreign and defence policies, the United States and Europe have parted ways'.[18] Kagan presents an array of arguments that explain the outcome he identifies but it is worth pointing out that the notion that Europe and America were different worlds is an old one, as old as the United States itself. Indeed the perception that the old world and the new were incompatible, most forcefully presented by Tom Paine in *Common Sense* (1776), was what tipped the scales in favour of the argument for a declaration of independence. 'It is evident', Paine wrote, 'that [England and America] belong to different systems. England to Europe: America to itself'.[19] What is clear is that since the end of the cold war such perceptions have become prevalent on both sides of the Atlantic. Will Hutton's *The World We're In* (2003) makes another powerful argument, in this case from the point of view of the liberal left, for regarding America and Europe's 'inner civilizational styles' as distinct.[20]

What these arguments come down to is the view, shared by many outsiders as well as Americans, that America is a special kind of nation, a 'nation of nations' as Whitman termed it, granted a special destiny stemming from its uniquely fortunate situation, with claims to be a civilization on its own terms, whether or not the word itself is used. As George W. Bush put it in his 2004 State of the Union address, 'America is a nation with a mission, and that mission comes from our most basic beliefs'.[21] Civilization-consciousness at one level is thus America's peculiar version of nationalism. It expresses claims both to uniqueness and universalism of values, and promotes the argument that America contains within itself all the world's possibilities because it contains elements of all the world's populations and because of the nature of its founding revolution, which was at once unique and exemplary. America is, as one scholar has put it, the 'universal nation'.[22] With such claims to 'specialness' came assumptions of special responsibility. That American exceptionalism is a central feature of the Bush administration is evident in the writings of neoconservatives whose ideas have been such an important influence on his policies. In calling during the mid 1990s for a 'neo-Reaganite foreign policy', leading neoconservatives William Kristol and Robert Kagan observed that 'it is worth recalling that the most successful Republican presidents of this century, Theodore Roosevelt and Ronald Reagan, both inspired Americans to assume cheerfully the new international responsibilities that went with increased influence and power'. Moreover, 'both celebrated American exceptionalism'.[23]

This posture is at once inclusive and exclusive, outward-looking and deeply chauvinist, internationalist and nationalist. Furthermore, this stance expresses something of the effort involved in asserting an American consensus. To make a single entity of all that diversity inevitably involves doing some violence to diversity, setting some limits to difference. One would think that the United States would be well placed to deal with ethnic and cultural diversity but in fact the opposite has often proved to be the case. 'Nativism' has a long history in the United States, particularly at times when American society is perceived to be under pressure from external threats or large-scale immigration.[24] Precisely because it is so diverse, a premium has been placed on unifying institutions, values, and symbols, no more so than at times of national crisis such as the early years of the cold war and the terrorist attacks of 11 September 2001. The expression of those unifying elements has characterized much governmental rhetoric and policies from the passage of the Patriot Act to the key political and military moves in the war on terror. Significantly, Samuel Huntington followed up *The Clash of Civilizations* with a study of the challenges to American national identity resulting from new waves of immigration from Latin America and Asia.[25]

The second claim implicit in 'civilization-consciousness' has to do with leadership and in particular the sense that, in all meanings of the term, America is 'bound to lead':[26] bound in the sense that it is the natural role for a nation of America's size and power and bound in the sense that the role is forced on America whether it wants it or not. America is, from this point of view, inevitably the leader of the civilized world.

This is a much more complicated issue for Americans than most non-Americans acknowledge. Outside observers of America in the last half century have often assumed that America has been determined to spread its influence and to intervene overseas wherever and whenever it had the opportunity to do so. In fact, American policy has been more cautious than such views would suggest, and American public opinion was and still is ambivalent about most overseas ventures.[27] Indeed, for some, America is not decisive enough in the international arena. For all the discussion of 'American empire' at the turn of the millennium, there are those such as British historian Niall Ferguson who note, and bemoan the fact, that 'America has acquired an empire but Americans themselves lack the imperial cast of mind. They would rather consume than conquer'.[28] As leader of the 'civilized' world the United States is generally expected and expects to assume certain responsibilities and the range of economic and strategic interests has increasingly extended the net of commitments. Intervention, however, is rarely automatic, not least because of the well-documented reluctance in the post-Vietnam years of the American taxpayer to accept costly open-ended commitments of substantial numbers of American troops, to say nothing of possible casualties. Indeed this constraint was present during the Vietnam War itself, witness the stealth with which Johnson increased the number of troops and his reluctance to admit the true cost of the war to the American people which would have meant raising taxes and/or taking funds from his cherished Great Society programme, neither of which he was prepared to contemplate. However, the biggest constraint on large-scale overseas actions prior to 1989 was the possibility of direct confrontation with the Soviet Union or China. The deployment of several hundred thousand troops to the Gulf in 1991 and of lesser but still substantial numbers in Afghanistan and Iraq in the ongoing conflict there would have been all but inconceivable during the cold war.

Some traditional constraints still exist on American interventions but the context has changed radically since 1989 and especially after the United States was the target of a direct attack on 11 September 2001. With it the issue of leadership has changed. In one sense the situation has become clearer. The United States has no rival globally, whether one is talking about overall size of the economy, defence budgets, sophistication of weapons systems, global military reach, global economic influence and so on.[29] Not that America is flawless. There are weaknesses as well as strengths in American society and the economy. There is too much domestic debt and too great a gap between rich and poor; growth areas in employment are generally in low-paid casual or temporary service jobs and deregulated capitalism has spawned corporate fraud on a massive scale. There appear also to be signs of social decay in extreme forms of crime and social violence and what one commentator has called 'the collapse of the public realm'.[30] In the short to medium term, however, these weaknesses do not seem likely to affect America's global position. Some of them have long been features of American life; not least levels of social violence, corruption in business, trade imbalances and so on. The basic ingredients of American power remain intact, and with the cold war enemy removed, America is apparently freer to act on the global stage than at any time since World War Two. Hence the continuing relevance of the suggestion that America is 'bound to lead'.

On the other hand, the end of the cold war complicated matters as far as American global leadership is concerned. It is not only the often-remarked absence of a clearly defined enemy so much as the absence of a ready set of rules and justifications for overseas interventions. Rather than the blanket justification of containment of communism, each intervention has to be justified on its own terms or in relation to some as yet not clearly formulated programme – Bush Sr's 'New World Order' or Clinton's 'democratic enlargement'.[31] If cold war 'realism' had supplied the necessary basis for policy choices in the period of East-West confrontation, in the more fluid world that followed the collapse of communism various elements of idealism came more to the fore. To put it another way, the promotion of cultural values featured more prominently than before. The growth of international terrorism in the 1990s, which reached a climax on 11 September 2001, put the 'war on terror' at the top of the political agenda and served to enhance cultural and idealist dimensions of policy. Since the enemy was now not a nation state but shadowy sub- or trans-national organizations, conceptions of realism apparently had limited relevance. If realism assumes a rational actor model, operating on the basis of sovereign nation states, then clearly it could not easily encompass the new threat of terrorism. This is not to say that realism goes entirely out the window. There is not and never has been a simple either/or – realism or idealism – in the making of American foreign policy but rather various complex mixtures of the two. Crucially, a world in which terrorism was the chief threat simply did not accord with the familiar patterns of conflict and policy choices, to the extent that it was necessary to reinterpret that threat to accord more clearly with realist precepts. Hence the 'war' on terrorism and the war on Saddam Hussein's Iraq.

Furthermore, the increasing use of cultural justifications for policy choices lies in the nature of the enemy's agenda, which contains a large cultural and religious element. 'Bin Laden's grievance with the United States', the authors of the *9/11 Commission Report* observed, 'may have started in reaction to specific US policies but it quickly became far deeper. To the ... question, what America could do, al-Qaeda's answer was that America should abandon the Middle East, convert to Islam, and end the immorality and godlessness of its society and culture'. The Report then quotes bin Laden's 2002 'Letter to America' to the effect that 'it is saddening to tell you that you are the worst civilization witnessed by the history of mankind'.[32] Even more pointed is bin Laden's response to the question of whether he agreed with the 'clash of civilizations' thesis. 'Absolutely', he replied. 'The [Holy] Book states it clearly. Jews and Americans invented peace on earth. That's a fairy tale. All they do is chloroform Muslims while leading them to the slaughterhouse'.[33] For his part George W. Bush noted in his 2002 State of the Union address that the challenge posed by al-Qaeda terrorism to the United States was in large part moral. 'Our enemies', he said, 'believed America was weak and materialistic, that we would splinter in fear and selfishness. They were wrong as they were evil ... [and] evil is real and it must be opposed'.[34]

The chances of al-Qaeda actually destroying America are slim. 11 September 2001 had numerous and complex effects but its effects on the American economy were modest, comparable, it has been suggested, with a very severe natural disaster but much less damaging than the stock market collapse of the previous year.[35] The trauma of 11 September arose from the brutally unexpected nature of the attack; its effects were psychological as much as material. The challenge of terrorism is to America's conception of itself rather than to the actual fabric of its institutions, though the effects of the attacks on those directly affected can never be underestimated. It is the nature of terrorism that it seeks to and often achieves an impact far out of proportion to its physical effects and its does so by breaking all the rules of 'civilized' behaviour. One rational response to such a challenge is to reaffirm one's commitment to civilization and civilized values. More specifically, in relation to the issue in question here, the response is to assert American leadership in the fight against barbarism and on behalf of civilization.

The third claim implicit in 'civilization consciousness' in some ways runs counter to the first two. Though treated last here, it is perhaps the most obvious application of the term. It relates to the identification of the United States with the 'civilized world' which is larger than the United States physically and more extensive culturally. Traditionally the identification has been with Western Civilization. Rarely in the contemporary world is it restricted to the 'West' since the United States takes pains to include under the rubric of 'civilized' all those nations and cultures which are willing to join the United States in the war against terror, wherever they are geographically and whatever their religion or culture. That includes Muslims who reject the attempt of bin Laden and others to identify their cause as that of Islam as a whole. America's fight, it has been reiterated by members of the American administration from Bush downwards, is not with Islam but with extremists who have hijacked Islam for their own murderous purposes. For its part, the American Muslim community has declared its allegiance to the United States. The American Council For Islamic Affairs, along with other Islamic bodies in the United States, has taken pains to dissociate itself from 'Islamic terrorism' and to stress the 'Americanness' of American Muslims.[36]

The most obvious manifestation of this aspect of civilization-consciousness lies in the effort to build a coalition against terror and more broadly to associate that effort with the defence of civilization. It is presented as a collective effort, admittedly led by the United States but operating on behalf of the larger whole, indeed the largest possible whole, which includes all those who lay claim to the term 'civilization'. Inclusivity is the goal here with the aim of drawing the clearest possible line between friends and enemies, a line which invokes social and ethical as well as political values.

It would seem that the first and third claims of civilization-consciousness are at odds with each other. In the first aspect the invocation of civilization is an act of national appropriation that lays down a challenge to potential friends and enemies of the United States alike. Can you measure up to our values? Will you support our fight? In the third claim the emphasis lies on collective, cooperative values and is more a matter of the United States reaching out to like-minded nations, drawing the net wide, accentuating supposedly commonly held values. This might be regarded as a contradiction. How can a nation or a culture be both unique and representative of universal values? The answer could be that however contradictory these claims might appear in theory, they are resolved by means of the second claim: in the *practice* of American leadership. There is in practice no fundamental contradiction between the assertion of American nationalism in the name of civilization and the invocation of a world community in the name of civilization. In short, claim number one represents the American argument for the uniqueness of its culture – its 'civilization'; claim three expresses the American argument for the universalism of its values, while claim two is the bridge between them. It is the means by which claim one can give reality to claim three. They are both strategies that rest on the overwhelming 'given' of American dominance and American leadership. Which strategy is employed at any particular time depends on the needs of the moment.

We can link all three aspects by reference to a document which also illustrates some of the political and other difficulties raised by such emphatic and naked assertion of cultural values: the September 2002 *National Security Strategy*. This remarkable document does for the war on terror what *National Security Document 68 (NSC-68,* 1950) did for the cold war: it sets out the political, military and ideological basis for a grand strategy.[37] *NSC-68* was an in-house document, not made public until a quarter of a century later, while the 2002 *National Security Strategy* was a very public document, designed to enlist public support for the war on terror. *NSC-68,* however, was no dry-as-dust position paper but a powerfully rhetorical and ideological effort designed no less than the 2002 strategy to persuade, except that in the case of *NSC-68* the audience was government rather than the people. Significantly, there are close parallels in rhetoric and content between the two documents, not least the conclusion reached in both cases that a transformation of military doctrine was necessary to fight a worsening global threat.

The 2002 *National Security Strategy* notoriously spells out the doctrine of preemption. The concern here is not with that doctrine, important though it is, but with the rhetoric of freedom with which the document is peppered. In itself this is nothing new in American history and foreign policy; it is perhaps America's core value and is regarded as the basis on which all other values are founded. What is particularly significant is firstly, the context of war followed by nation building in Afghanistan followed by the same in Iraq and secondly, the association of this value with what is called the 'non-negotiable demand of human dignity'. Claims are made here on behalf of America's own history and values, on behalf of American leadership in the current crisis and on behalf of the civilized world whose values are taken to be at one with those of the United States. Crucially it is being claimed that these things are all essentially coterminous. American universalism has rarely been more plainly or more comprehensively expressed; to find comparable claims one has perhaps to go back to Woodrow Wilson, though his are in a somewhat different key. Crucially, America's core demand is 'non-negotiable'. This is doubtless intended in a benign sense to convey the deep, self-evident nature of the value of human dignity – self-evidence being a central theme of American discussion of values from the Declaration of Independence onwards – but it conveys also a questionable assumption about the applicability of America's interpretation of 'freedom' and 'human dignity' to other nations and situations. It betrays indeed a potentially coercive and illiberal insistence that America's values are or should be those of all nations. The issue is not whether one believes in freedom – freedom is like food in that you can't be against food – but what freedom means in different cultures. (We don't all need to eat the same food.) The formulation in this document scarcely leaves open the possibility of debate about what freedom means to different peoples. Much of what we call anti-Americanism is a reaction to the sorts of assertions contained in this document. To this we now turn.

Anti-Americanism is one consequence of the growth of America's civilization-consciousness. Having said that, it is necessary to point out that 'anti-Americanism', like all the terms involved in this discussion, refers to a complex set of attitudes and admits of many definitions and explanations. Indeed the term itself is highly political, employed as it often is as a label for attitudes that the user dislikes rather than as a neutral analytical term. Like 'civilization', it is an essentially contested concept. Not least of the difficulties involved is where to draw the line between anti-Americanism and legitimate or rational criticism of American policies. Such decisions are inevitably based on political presuppositions rather than widely agreed canons of evidence. Anti-Americanism is a complex set of attitudes towards the United States whose sources are varied according to the nature of the relationship of particular nations, cultures and individuals with the United States.[38]

What cannot be denied, however, is that public consciousness of negative attitudes towards the United States has been powerfully stimulated by the events of 9/11 and after. Americans and others want to know 'why do people hate America?'[39] It is the disposition to label as much as the meaning of the label which demands explanation. Thus for the purposes of discussion we shall employ an element of short-hand, defining anti-Americanism firstly as a predisposition to doubt whether the United States power can ever be used for good and secondly, a distaste for the way in which America goes about expressing its will and asserting its power. Anti-Americanism thus represents a reaction to the exertion of American power and also to the expression of American culture. Here the focus is on the latter but clearly it is because American power is so great that the nature of its culture matters to so many others.

Anti-Americanism has often attached itself to such apparently trivial matters as the way in which President Bush expresses himself; in particular the (to many non-American eyes) incongruously folksy terms in which he discusses the search for bin Laden and other terrorists. 'We'll smoke 'em out', 'keep those folks on the run' and so on. Behind the reaction to such language in many of the older nations of Europe lie two centuries or more of denigration of American democratic culture combined with growing resentment of American power.[40] The result is that curious amalgam of superiority and inferiority complexes that often characterizes the old world's perception of the new. The American reaction to 11 September 2001 in all its political, military, and cultural ramifications has reminded us how different America is from other cultures. The political complexion of the Bush administration has undoubtedly served to intensify this perception. The American right – and this is arguably the most consistently right-wing administration in post-World War Two history – is generally more nakedly patriotic, more nationalist in complexion, more emphatic in its assertion of traditional American values (especially those associated with the founding period) than Democratic administrations. Policy seems to be forged in the American heartland where 'real' Americans live rather than among the more sophisticated 'European' east coast elites. The current 'culture war' between these two Americas recalls the face-offs during the early cold war between Alger Hiss and his accuser Whittaker Chambers and between Secretary of State Dean Acheson and Senator Joseph McCarthy. There has justifiably been extensive

media and academic commentary on the agenda of the new Right and its influence on the Bush administration.[41]

We shall look at reactions to the three aspects of civilization-consciousness in
turn, though inevitably there will be some overlap in the treatment. It is easy to
see why those who are already firmly opposed to America will react strongly
against America's post-9/11 assertiveness. More significant perhaps are the reactions of those who have no automatic opposition to America but who find
themselves embattled in the new climate of the war on terror. The problem here
is not simple hatred of the United States but the difficulty of living with a United
States that makes such grandiose claims on behalf of its own 'civilization'. This
applies, for example, to many in the Muslim world, including American
Muslims, who fear that the cost of total identification with the war against terror
will be the dilution or even suppression of their own national, religious or
cultural identity. Muslims may regard even gestures of friendship by members of
the American administration towards them with suspicion. Such anxieties
predate the attacks of 9/11. One Muslim observer noted that the Clinton
administration tended to divide Islam into two polarized camps: at one end were
the extremists who advocated a militantly 'political Islam' and were regarded as
terrorists or supporters of terrorism; at the other end of the spectrum was 'Islam'
itself 'represented by the faith that is confined to personal belief and ritual practices'. But while apparently affirming respect for Islam, this latter version of the
religion was 'a disembowelled Islam that has no input into the human, social,
economic and political values, which some Islamists have dubbed "American
Islam"'.[42] As many Muslims see it, the price of friendship with America, or for
citizenship of the United States, is denial of the full expression of Islam. To put
it another way, American civilization does not appear to have a place for Islam.

Under Bush, and especially since 9/11, the dilemma for American Muslims,
indeed Muslims everywhere, has deepened. Despite efforts to insist that the
war against terror is not a war against Islam (some speedy corrections of
earlier faux pas such as terming it a 'crusade' have been required), and despite
efforts by members of the Bush administration – among them Condoleeza
Rice – to reach out directly to the Muslim community, scepticism about the
administration's attitude to Muslims remains. The passage of the Patriot Act,
with its threat to Constitutional rights, is one source of concern, as is the
general climate of suspicion of individuals with Middle Eastern connections or
even appearance.

In this connection America's deep military and political entanglements in the
Middle East complicate matters for Muslims in America and elsewhere. Failure
to make progress on a settlement of the Palestinian-Israeli conflict is doubly
damaging: damaging to the parties directly involved and damaging to Muslims
everywhere who suspect that the American administration's failure to push more
strongly for a settlement reflects its true estimation of the significance of the
Palestinian issue for them and also tends to reinforce the association of Islam
with terrorism. As long as the news about Islam is mainly about terrorist inci-
dents, the deeper the general suspicion of Islam will be and the vulnerability of

individual Muslims will increase. If such scepticism and anxiety is present among Muslims who are basically sympathetic to America and who deplore al-Qaeda *et al*. as perverters of the Muslim faith, how much more alienated will be those Muslims who have no natural sympathy with the United States and regard it simply as an agent of imperialism?

Similar issues apply *pari passu* to Europe, which in the post-cold war world has gained new perception of the differences between European and American 'civilizations'. The same applies, of course, in reverse. Anti-Americanism has its counterpart in anti-Europeanism in America. Cultural differences, needless to say, have been part of the long history of European-American relations, and anti-Americanism is part of that history. The collapse of the cold war, however, has allowed for fuller expression of such sentiments because the tight geopolitical tie promoted by the cold war no longer underpins the relationship. Writing in 1996, a German scholar and convinced Atlanticist, Werner Weidenfeld, noted with alarm that:

> ... the relationship between Germany, Europe and America is no longer based on certainties of the kind that have existed for fifty years ... In terms of communications theory, what is happening is a disintegration of the stabilizers and filters required for information-processing. The dominance of world politics by large blocs and their confrontational relations has gone and with it the antagonisms, stereotypes and political rhetoric that used to provide collective orientation for the "West".[43]

In short, in the post-cold war world, there is more fluidity, less obvious need for coordinated policies especially on defence, more scope for conflict in the relationship, and more opportunities for cultural differences to find expression. American unilateralism has provided a target for these concerns just as it expresses America's own cultural and political imperatives.[44] Following 9/11 such expressions have heightened European sensitivities to American culture as well as American policies. One significant finding of a Pew public opinion survey conducted in 2004 was that, although Europeans continued to make a clear distinction between the Bush administration and the American people, favourable opinion of the American people declined in line with opinion about the Bush administration, in the case of France from 71 per cent to 53 per cent. (In Muslim countries there was little difference between attitudes towards Americans and towards the US government, and they were predominantly negative.)[45]

Of particular significance has been the emphasis in discussions of European attitudes towards America on differences in values. A Marshall Fund study conducted in 2003 reported that, when asked whether Europeans and Americans have different social and cultural values, majorities on both sides of the Atlantic overwhelmingly agreed (83 per cent of American and 79 per cent of European respondents). A detailed analysis of American-German relations has concluded that 'the recent tension demonstrates that US-German relations are characterized by a mutual incomprehension of each other's political culture and deeply held political values'. At the root of the difference, which was sharply brought to the fore in the aftermath of 9/11, were 'vastly differing views of nationalism and flag-waving patriotism ... because the exaggerated nationalism of the Nazi years led to such disastrous results, post-1945 Germany has been characterized by strongly antinationalist and antipatriotic sentiments'. By contrast, such displays are common in the United States and indeed were integral to the morale-building efforts that followed 9/11. Not least among the causes of the difficulties were issues of language, especially the use of the term 'war' in 'war on terror' terminology, which is forbidden in German politics and society.[46]

If anti-American feeling attaches itself to heightened expressions of 'Americanness', it attaches also to America's leadership role; indeed the two areas are obviously closely linked. The awareness that the war on terror is to be fought on America's terms, that America defines these terms, that America supplies the bulk of troops and means to fight the war, and dictates the strategy promotes resentment even among those who share the goals of the United States. The Marshall Fund Survey of 2003 showed sharp declines between 2002 and 2003 in most European countries in the approval ratings of American global leadership, the only increases coming in countries (the UK and the Netherlands) where opinion was already predominantly negative. The Pew survey of 2004 showed an erosion of belief in the trustworthiness of the United States and in its commitment to promoting democracy.[47] The best apparently that could be hoped for among those who wished to influence the way the war on terror was fought – and this was seemingly the basis of Tony Blair's strategy – was to adopt America's goals as their own in the hope that they might be able to influence the direction and pace of American policy. This is not to say that Tony Blair was insincere in his support of President Bush, nor even that he may not have succeeded to some degree in his aim, but it is to say that he has had to go further in 'Americanizing' his approach than normal alliance politics would seem to dictate. To an unusual degree, which was scarcely matched in the cold war years, with the possible exception of the Thatcher/Reagan axis, Blair adopted the American reading of global events and more to the point has adopted an American style of international politicking, including an unusual level of rhetorical inflation.[48]

It seems clear that the dissociation of countries such as France, Germany, and Russia from the American way of fighting the war on terror had partly to do with style. One cost of support for the United States' political goals was a degree of subordination to the style in which they were couched. Evidently resistance on the part of many Europeans had to do with a lot more than style, but the tenor of the debates in the UN Security Council on the proposed second resolution on Iraq indicated that Colin Powell and Dominic de Villepin were not only speaking different languages but were expressing different cultures, voicing different assumptions. Such exchanges were eloquent testimony to the fact that American leadership of the war against terror was both inevitable – in the sense that it could not be resisted – and problematic. From the American point of view (shared by Tony Blair) the idea that a strong Europe should act as a counterbalance to US power was tantamount to obstructionism. Indeed there was no place in the American scheme of things for that old realist nostrum of the balance of power.

Finally, anti-Americanism attaches also to the third aspect of civilization-consciousness: the effort to enlist all nations in an enterprise that transcends the scope and interests of any one nation, that enterprise being civilization itself. At one level there is resistance to the idea that the United States truly represents the ideals of civilization that it claims to uphold. The legal black hole into which the prisoners at Guantanamo Bay were placed and the treatment of them is commonly cited in this connection but the revelations about the treatment of detainees by American soldiers at Abu Ghraib prison in Iraq exposed the moral gap most starkly. Under the heading 'Clash of Civilizations' liberal *New York Times* columnist Maureen Dowd observed that 'after 9/11, America had the support and sympathy of the world. Now awash in digital evidence of uncivilized behaviour, America has careered into a war of civilizations. The pictures [of sexual humiliation of Iraqi prisoners] were clearly meant to use the codebook of Muslim anxieties about nudity and sexual and gender humiliation to break down prisoners'. 'If somebody wanted to plan a clash of civilizations', Senator Diane Feinstein declared, 'this is how they'd do it. These pictures play into every stereotype of America that Arabs have: America as debauched, America as hypocrites'.[49] In short, it was easy to doubt whether the United States could really claim to speak on behalf of global 'civilization'.

Secondly, there was the belief on the part of critics that the fight for 'civilization' was loaded towards America's interests and that it was no more nor less than a fight for America's national interest dressed up to look like a cooperative venture. The 'coalition of the willing' from this point of view was really a coalition of power based on America's ability to exert pressure on other nations. The coalition was in fact, one observer noted, 'an exercise in unilateralism, with a few friends'. It was, wrote another critic, 'inch deep, in large measure a figment of American imagination, energy and money'.[50] American tactics at the UN during the build-up to the war in Iraq were, from this standpoint, the perfect illustration of special pleading, arousing the suspicion among sceptics that America had already made up its mind about Iraq and was merely going through the motions. Once this conviction was established in the minds of unsympathetic observers, it could only become further entrenched as the rhetoric became further inflated. The more insistent was the President on the necessity for war to defend civilization the greater the scepticism with which these claims were regarded. Anti-Americanism, to the extent that attitudes went beyond criticism of policy, fed on a sense of the gap between the nature of the claims being made on behalf of war and the actual motives that were conceived to be the advancement of American interests, whether for oil, a dominant role in the Middle East, or the defence of Israel. The slogan adopted by opponents of the war in Iraq on both sides of the Atlantic, 'Not in our Name', indicated more than a disagreement with the policy but also a dissociation from the larger collectivity being invoked by the United States. Once again, it was easy to doubt whether the United States could claim to speak on behalf of global 'civilization'.

Huntington's clash of civilizations thesis has been the target of some justified criticisms. What he called civilizations are not the discrete entities he imagined. True, he allows for various forms of conflict within civilizations and countries but the larger thesis would fall if he were to allow intra-civilizational cleavages to predominate over those between civilizations. But the fact is that in the age of globalization the boundaries between nations and cultures are increasingly porous and, as many of Huntington's critics have pointed out, there are as many clashes inside civilizations as between them. There is thus a real problem with his use of civilization as his main unit of historical study.

Huntington was not wrong, however, to see cultural, especially religious and ethnic conflict as having increased saliency in the post-cold war world. In many parts of the world where cold war pressures had reduced these to a state of suspended animation, the end of the cold war gave them new life. The task, then, is to adapt Huntington's ideas and make them work for us. If he has done a service, it is to expose the degree to which ethnocentrism can be a source of conflict. He has reminded us that, as Robert Cooper has put it recently, 'foreign policy is not only about interests'. 'At moments of crisis', Cooper continues, 'it is likely that a nation will return to its roots and its myths and respond as the heart urges rather than as the head advises'.[51] The danger is of failing to perceive that this applies to us and not just our adversaries. In Huntington's analysis it is generally other cultures' assertiveness which is the problem, not least Islam, which is said to have 'bloody borders'. Huntington takes less account of how other nations and cultures might regard America's way of acting in the world and in this he reflects the larger problem of ethnocentrism in the American policy making process. The greatest challenge in this more fluid, globalizing world is for nations to develop awareness of how their actions and belief systems impinge on others. For America, because it is so powerful, this means being conscious of the power of culture as well as the culture of power.

There is a second limitation in Huntington's thesis that also gives rise to a challenge. His analysis assumes that cultural difference tends always to produce conflict. In response it can be said that it may do but need not. If you assume that cultural difference will always give rise to conflict, then it is very likely that it will. The challenge is to develop ways of cooperation between cultures and nations which mean different things by words which appear to have self-evident meanings: freedom, democracy, human rights, justice. Rather than assume that we know exactly what these things mean and dismiss those who interpret them differently, it will pay to develop dialogues. At least this may open the possibility of isolating those for whom difference will always and only imply conflict.

Notes

1 S. P. Huntington, 'The Clash of Civilizations?', *Foreign Affairs*, 1993, vol. 72, no. 3, pp. 22–49; and *The Clash of Civilizations and the Remaking of World Order*, New York: Simon and Schuster, 1996.

2 Huntington, 'Clash of Civilizations?', p. 22.

3 See the two subsequent issues of *Foreign Affairs* for the first bout of critiques and Huntington's response (vol. 72, nos. 4 and 5). *Foreign Affairs* has collected these and other commentaries in *Clash of Civilizations: The Debate*, New York: Norton, 1996. Inevitably much of the debate has focused on the West's relations with Islam. See, J. L. Esposito, *The Islamic Threat: Myth or Reality?*, New York: Oxford University Press, 1995, especially Ch. 6; M. Ruthven, *A Fury for God: The Islamist Attack on America*, London: Granta, 2002; F. A. Gerges, *America and Political Islam: Clash of Cultures or Clash of Interests?*, Cambridge: Cambridge University Press, 1999.

4 *National Security Strategy of the United States of America*, 19 September 2002, available at <http://www.whitehouse.gov/nsc/> (accessed 31 May 2005).

5 Bush, State of the Union Address, 29 January 2002, available at <http://www.whitehouse.gov/news/releases/2002/01/> (accessed 31 May 2005); Bush, State of the Union Address, 28 January 2003, available at <http://www.whitehouse.gov/news/releases/2003/01> (accessed 31 May 2005); Bush, State of the Union Address, 20 January 2004, available at <http://www.whitehouse.gov/news/releases/2004/01/> (accessed 31 May 2005); *National Security Strategy of the United States*, p. 1.

6 For a discussion of Toynbee and the cold war see R. Crockatt, 'Challenge and response: Arnold Toynbee and the United States during the cold war', in D. Carter and R. Clifton (eds.), *War and Cold War in American Foreign Policy, 1942–1962*, Basingstoke: Palgrave Macmillan, 2002, pp. 108–30.

7 See R. Williams, *Keywords*, London: Fontana, 1976, pp. 48–50.

8 For all his debt to Toynbee, however, Huntington does not allow for the complexity and variety of interconnections between civilizations which is present in Toynbee's scheme.

9 For a recent example see M. Mozaffari (ed.), *Globalization and Civilizations*, London: Routledge, 2002.

10 Huntington, *Clash of Civilizations*, pp. 54–5.

11 C. A. Beard and M. R. Beard, *The Rise of American Civilization*, New York: Macmillan, 1930, p. vii.

12 For debate over Western civilization courses in the United States see G. Allerdyce, 'The rise and fall of the Western civilization course', *American Historical Review*, June 1982, vol. 87, pp. 695–725, followed by comments and author's rejoinder.

13 The term is used by Huntington. See *The Clash of Civilizations*, pp. 266–72, but the term was employed much earlier by J. Dewey in his *Individualism Old and New*, New York: Capricorn Books, 1962 [1930], Ch. 2.

14 Huntington discusses the definitional problems associated with culture and civilization in *The Clash of Civilizations*, pp. 40–4.

15 A. Toynbee, *A Study of History*, London: Oxford University Press, 1934, vol. 1, pp. 44–5; Huntington, 'The Clash of Civilizations', p. 24.

16 Raymond Williams explores the many meanings and usages of the term culture in *Keywords*, pp. 80–1. Useful discussions of culture in international relations which contain many important cautionary principles are F. Halliday, *The World at 2000: Perils and Promises*, Basingstoke: Palgrave Macmillan, 2001, Ch. 8; and M. Mazarr, 'Culture in international relations', *Washington Quarterly*, Spring 1996, vol. 19, no. 2, pp. 177–97.

17 M. Lerner, *America as a Civilization: Life and Thought in the United States Today*, New York: Simon & Schuster, 1957, pp. 3, 58, 61–2, 65. For a discussion of the rise of 'Americanism' in the context of a discussion of anti-Americanism see R. Crockatt,

America Embattled: September 11, Anti-Americanism and the Global Order, London: Routledge, 2003, pp. 46–51.

18 R. Kagan, *Of Paradise and Power: America and Europe in the New World Order*, London: Atlantic Books, 2003, pp. 1, 2.

19 T. Paine, *Political Writings*, Cambridge: Cambridge University Press, 1989, p. 23.

20 W. Hutton, *The World We're In*, London: Abacus, 2003.

21 Bush, State of the Union address, 20 January 2004.

22 J. Purdy, 'Universal nation', in A. Bacevich (ed.), *The Imperial Tense: Problems and Perspectives of American Empire*, Chicago, IL: Ivan Dee, 2003, pp. 102–10.

23 W. Kristol and R. Kagan, 'Toward a neo-Reaganite foreign policy', *Foreign Affairs*, July/August 1996, vol. 75, p. 32. The major recent study of American exceptionalism is S. M. Lipset, *American Exceptionalism: A Double-edged Sword*, New York: Norton, 1996.

24 See J. Higham, *Strangers in the Land: Patterns of American Nativism*, New York: Atheneum, 1963.

25 S. P. Huntington, *Who Are We? America's Great Debate*, New York: Free Press, 2004.

26 This is the title of a book by J. S. Nye, *Bound to Lead: The Changing Nature of American Power*, New York: Basic Books, 1990.

27 See, for example, Geir Lundestad's suggestion that the growth of American empire was 'by invitation' rather American design (*The American 'Empire' and Other Studies of US Foreign Policy in a Comparative Perspective*, Oxford: Oxford University Press, 1990).

28 N. Ferguson, *Colossus: The Rise and Fall of the American Empire*, London: Allen Lane, 2004, p. 29. Among the other recent works on American empire are A. Bacevich, *American Empire: The Realities and Consequences of US Diplomacy*, Cambridge, MA: Harvard University Press, 2002; and Bacevich (ed.), *The Imperial Tense*.

29 See P. Kennedy, 'Maintaining American power: from injury to recovery', in S. Talbott and N. Chanda (eds.), *The Age of Terror: America and the World After September 11*, Oxford: Perseus Press, 2001, pp. 58–60.

30 See Hutton, *The World We're In*, Chs. 5 and 6.

31 R. Haass, *Intervention: The Uses of American Military Force in the Post-Cold War World*, 2nd edn, Washington, DC: Carnegie Endowment, 1999 usefully outlines the debates as well as providing a good deal of detail on particular interventions.

32 *The 9/11 Commission Report: Final Report of the National Commission on Terrorist Attacks upon the United States*, New York: Norton, 2004, p. 51.

33 Quoted in G. Kepel, *The War for Muslim Minds: Islam and the West*, Cambridge, MA: Harvard University Press, 2004, pp. 123–4.

34 Bush, State of the Union address, 2002.

35 Ferguson, *Collossus*, pp. 126–7.

36 For an early example of the Bush administration's insistence that the war against terror was not a war against Islam see Bush's speech on 20 September 2001. For a perspective on the experience of American Muslims since 11 September see M. Khan, 'Putting the American in "American Muslim"', *New York Times*, 7 September 2003. For a discussion of Islamic-American relations since 11 September see R. Crockatt, 'No common ground? Islam, the United States and anti-Americanism', *European Journal of American Culture*, 2004, vol. 23, pp. 125–42.

37 Note the significance accorded to *NSC-68* by neoconservatives William Kristol and Robert Kagan in 'Toward a Neo-Reaganite Foreign Policy', pp. 28–30.

38 There is now a large and fast growing literature on anti-Americanism especially with regard to Europe. See P. Hollander, *Anti-Americanism: Critiques at Home and Abroad, 1965–1990*, New York: Oxford University Press, 1992; Crockatt, *America Embattled*, Ch. 2; D. Ellwood, *Anti-Americanism in Western Europe: A Comparative Perspective*, Bologna: The Johns Hopkins University, 1999; D. Lacorne, *et al* (eds.), *The Rise and Fall of Anti-Americanism: A Century of French Perception*, New York: St Martin's Press, 1990; P. Roger, *L'Ennemi américain: Généalogie de l'antiaméricanisme français*, Paris: Editions du Seuil, 2002; S. Halper and J. Clarke, *America Alone: The Neoconservatives and the Global Order*,

Cambridge: Cambridge University Press, 2004, Ch. 8; N. Bilge Criss, 'A short history of anti-Americanism and terrorism: the Turkish case', in J. Meyerowitz (ed.), *History and September 11*, Philadelphia, PA: Temple University Press, 2003, pp. 56–72. For a view of anti-Americanism in the Arab world which plays down the 'civilizational' element see U. Makdisi, 'Anti-Americanism in the Arab world: an interpretation of a brief history', in J. Meyerowitz (ed.), *History and September 11*, pp. 131–56.

39 One popular answer to this question is contained in Z. Sardar and M. Wyn Davies, *Why Do People Hate America?*, Cambridge: Icon Books, 2002.

40 See Crockatt, *America Embattled*, Ch. 2, 'How the world sees America: the roots of anti-americanism'.

41 Among the most substantial contributions is Halper and Clarke, *America Alone*. Of particular value in charting the impact of neoconservatism on Bush's policies towards the Islamic world is Kepel, *The War for Muslim Minds: Islam and the West*, Ch. 2.

42 Y. Yazbeck Haddad, 'Islamist perceptions of US policy in the Middle East', in D. W. Lesch (ed.), *The Middle East and the United States: A Historical and Political Reassessment*, 3rd edn, Cambridge, MA: Westview Press, 2003, p. 481.

43 W. Weidenfeld, *America and Europe: Is the Break Inevitable?*, Gütersloh: Bertelsmann Foundation Publishers, 1996, pp. 9–10.

44 See S. Fabbrini, 'Layers of anti-Americanism: Americanization, American unilateralism and anti-Americanism in a European perspective', *European Journal of American Culture*, 2004, vol. 23, no. 2, pp. 79–94.

45 The Pew Research Center, *A Year After the Iraq War: Mistrust of America in Europe Ever Higher, Muslim Anger Persists*, available at <http://people-press.org/reports/display.php3?PageID=796> (accessed 31 May 2005).

46 K. Larres, 'Mutual incomprehension: US-German value gaps beyond Iraq', *The Washington Quarterly*, Spring 2003, vol. 26, no. 2, pp. 23, 30, 31.

47 Marshall Fund, *Transatlantic Trends*, p. 5; Pew Research Center, *A Year after the Iraq War*, p. 7.

48 See Crockatt, *America Embattled*, p. 149.

49 *New York Times*, 13 May 2004.

50 Quentin Peel, in 'Analysis: the sheriff and the posse', BBC Radio 4, 1 November 2001, broadcast transcript, p. 5; T. Judt, 'The War on Terror', *New York Review of Books*, 20 December 2001, p. 102.

51 R. Cooper, *The Breaking of Nations: Order and Chaos in the Twenty-First Century*, London: Atlantic Books, 2003, pp. 127, 136.

8 American grand strategy

The quest for permanent primacy

Andrew O'Neil

The 1990s were largely a decade of frustration for American strategic policy makers. In the decade following the end of the cold war, the United States struggled to formulate a coherent grand strategy[1] for global engagement. Modestly restoring the *status quo ante* in the Persian Gulf in 1991, after having committed over half a million troops to eject Iraq from Kuwait, the United States engaged in several 'brush fire' humanitarian conflicts in Africa and the Balkans; successfully froze North Korea's declared nuclear weapons programme; initiated a vigorous campaign of covert operations against al-Qaeda; reinvigorated efforts to forge a new global trading regime; and fashioned the contours of a containment policy aimed at trimming the sails of China's geo-strategic ambitions. With some notable exceptions, Washington's pursuit of each of these objectives met with success. This success occurred against an unusual historical backdrop: significant geopolitical realignment in the international system in the absence of major power confrontation or major armed conflict.

The United States actually cemented its dominance of the international system during the 1990s. In particular, it reinforced its relative power over all other countries, making a mockery of earlier claims that America's relative power was on the wane.[2] The striking indices of American global power are familiar to all students of contemporary international relations: America accounts for almost one quarter of total world economic output; it outlays more on military spending than the next eight countries combined; and it enjoys widespread international influence flowing from the ubiquity of American culture and its leading role in the global information technology revolution. In short, in terms of its quantifiable 'hard' power and its 'soft' power – the capacity to persuade and influence – America's position in the international system remains unrivalled and unparalleled.

And yet by the end of the 1990s, many Americans continued to portray the previous decade as one of failure for US foreign policy because of what they identified as the absence of a consistent, overarching global strategy. From this perspective, the first Bush (1989–1993) and the Clinton (1993–2001) administrations lacked a comprehensive vision for defining America's proper role and location in the international system. More importantly, both administrations, particularly the Clinton administration, lacked a cogent vision of how American power should be exercised at the global level 'to shape a new century favourable to American principles and interests'.[3] This view was not confined to the neo-conservative wing of the Republican Party. Many others were critical of what they regarded as an excessive degree of 'ad hocery' underpinning US foreign and defence policy throughout the 1990s.

Whatever the shortcomings of the current Bush administration's foreign policy, it cannot be faulted for lacking a grand strategy. Contrary to the views of some critics who maintain that the administration has failed in its attempts to devise a coherent strategic blueprint for the conduct of foreign and defence policy, the Bush administration has been quite successful in elucidating a transparent global strategy for the United States. And it has certainly been much more effective in this respect than its post-cold war predecessors were.

As enunciated in a series of landmark speeches and documents since the terrorist attacks of September 2001, contemporary US grand strategy embraces nothing less than the maintenance of perpetual American primacy in world affairs. But it would be a mistake to assume that the Bush administration's grand strategy necessarily represents a sharp break with the past. Indeed, the very idea of equating America's preponderance of relative power with the pursuit of global primacy can be traced to influential thinking inside the Truman administration shortly after World War Two.[4] Moreover, many of the underlying themes of *Pax Americana* that permeate America's post-9/11 strategy were evident in early post-cold war US pronouncements about the emergence of a 'new world order' and the Clinton administration's ambitious plans for global 'democratic enlargement'.[5]

This chapter explores the links between the 9/11 terrorist attacks, the subsequent 'war on terror' declared by President Bush, and the changes to US grand strategy in the 2001–2004 period. My central argument is that the Bush administration has embraced the 'war on terror' in an attempt to both clarify *and* legitimise a more coherent American global strategic agenda. I also argue that rather than representing a revolutionary shift, the administration's grand strategy of actively seeking US primacy in perpetuity should be seen as a more robust expression of existing themes in American strategic policy articulated under previous administrations. To elucidate this point, in the third section of the chapter I examine briefly pre-emption and capabilities-based military planning, two of the most prominent tenets underpinning the Bush administration's grand strategy. In the concluding section, I discuss the international political and strategic backlash provoked by American grand strategy since 9/11. While US officials appear unperturbed by the international political backlash, American policy makers *are* concerned increasingly about the strategic dimension of the backlash where US adversaries are seeking to accelerate their acquisition of dedicated asymmetrical war-fighting capabilities, particularly nuclear weapons, to counter America's more assertive global military posture.

The dual-edged impact of 9/11

On the morning of 11 September 2001, al-Qaeda operatives hijacked four US domestic flights, two of which were flown into the World Trade Center in New York, the third into the Pentagon, while the fourth crashed in a deserted field en route to Washington DC. In addition to the colossal financial cost of the attacks, the human cost was immense with the final death toll reaching in excess of 3000 fatalities. The events of 9/11 set entirely new precedents for international terrorism. Never before had thousands been killed in a single coordinated terrorist act. And never before had civilian airliners been used as guided missiles against civilian targets. That the most powerful country in the international system was the target of the attacks merely added potency to their psychological impact. While the attacks on the continental United States (CONUS) did not 'change everything' as some have claimed, the repercussions of 9/11 continue to be felt in different ways at numerous levels of the international system.[6]

For the United States, the attacks essentially had a twofold impact. First, they underscored America's continuing vulnerability to asymmetric warfare attacks against core national assets. As Richard Betts notes, the human cost caused by the attacks, as well as the financial and psychological damage, was massively disproportionate to the cost and effort of mounting the attacks.[7] The attacks appeared designed deliberately to highlight the point that while the United States remains largely invulnerable to conventional military defeat, American citizens remain acutely vulnerable to terrorist attacks in large urban centres. In this sense, 9/11 demonstrated graphically that American global pre-eminence offers no protection against catastrophic attacks on the American homeland and may, in fact, serve to heighten the level of risk. As outlined in the next section, these negative implications combined to have a major catalysing effect on the direction of American global strategy.

The second impact of the attacks was to expose the enormous gaps in America's strategic early warning capabilities.[8] A distinction needs to be drawn here between US intelligence *collection* capabilities on the one hand, and intelligence *assessment* capabilities on the other. Clearly, America's capacity to collect intelligence from a diverse range of sources remains second to no other country. Yet the ability of US government agencies to cooperate with each other and coordinate their efforts in formulating adequate and timely early warning of threats to national security remains far from satisfactory.[9] While the Bush administration has emphasised that there was no 'single piece of information' that it could have acted on to prevent the 9/11 attacks, the analogy with Pearl Harbor is more compelling than many Americans would like to admit. Then, as in the months leading up to September 2001, US intelligence agencies and middle ranking and more senior level officials failed to appreciate the significance of the various warning signs that pointed to the likelihood of an attack from the source and on the scale that materialised.

Oceans of ink have been spilt in an endeavour to explain the impact of the 9/11 terrorist attacks on the United States. Many of these interpretations vary, but there is a striking level of convergence on one point: 9/11 is seen as having ended decisively the post-cold war interregnum. In this sense, if somewhat para-

White House. When a leaked version of the Pentagon's revamped
Policy Guidance emerged in the last year of the Bush adminis
that recommended explicitly the pursuit of US global pri
concept of 'benevolent domination' – it provoked a stor
versy that ensured the draft never saw the light of da
fashion and articulate a definitive grand strategy
1990s, the United States pursued a hybrid grand
'uneasy amalgam' of selective engagement, coo

In the aftermath of 9/11, the Bush admin
Congress and backed by public opinio
terrorism' as synonymous with US gr
national affiliates were neutralis
America's defining mission in int
session of Congress nine da
prepare 'not for one battl
seen'.[14] The US-led ov
the first step in a m
nothing less than t

As a purely d
devoid of a
warfare p
politica
warf

incredulity among US strategic policy makers. In a very real sense,
'futures' oriented tone of current American strategic planning, endorsing as it
does the pursuit of perpetual primacy, appears to be an effort to compensate
partly for this earlier inability to plan for life after the Soviet Union.

The nature of US strategic thinking has altered dramatically over the last
decade. Caught largely unaware when the Soviet Union disintegrated, American
policy makers, together with many strategic analysts in the academic community,
struggled to deal with the radically different global environment well into the
1990s. It was never entirely clear what the precise role of the United States
would or should be in a fluid post-bipolar world. Both the Bush and Clinton
administrations failed to sanction coherent strategic guidance that defined in
clear and specific terms the task and longer term mission of the United States in
world affairs.

This is not to say that policy makers, especially those in Pentagon, did not try.
Yet, efforts to conceptualise an ambitious American grand strategy typically
encountered strong bureaucratic resistance from the State Department and the

draft Defense
ration – a draft
acy based on the
n of political contro-
[12] This unwillingness to
eant that for much of the
strategy that incorporated an
perative security, and primacy.[13]
istration, with the strong support of
n, determined to treat the 'war on
nd strategy. Until al-Qaeda and its inter-
d, defeating global terrorism would be
rnational affairs. In his speech to a special joint
s after the attacks, Bush warned US citizens to
, but a lengthy campaign, unlike any other we have
rthrow of the Taliban regime in Afghanistan would be
ch larger and drawn out campaign whose goal would be
e defeat of global terrorism.

escriptive term, however, the 'war on terrorism' has always been
y real meaning. Terrorism is an age-old strategy of asymmetric
actised by the relatively weak against the relatively strong; it is not a
ideology. Above all, terrorism is an archetypal manifestation of irregular
are where entities with relatively weaker conventional war-fighting capabili-
s target stronger actors where they are most vulnerable and avoid deliberately
engaging the strong where they are strongest.[15] Moreover, groups and individuals do not subscribe to 'terrorism' *per se* as a political, social, or economic creed.
Thus the idea that terrorism can, like fascism and communism, be effectively
nullified by any state or coalition of states runs sharply counter to historical
experience.

However, as a political cloak to rationalise action, the 'war on terrorism' is
manifestly rich with potential. A number of analysts predicted in the immediate
wake of 9/11 that the Bush administration would use the terrorist attacks as a
pretext to pursue a more assertive foreign policy. At the time, these observers
were themselves roundly condemned for 'exploiting the dead' to score cheap
political points against the administration. Some were even dismissed as being
motivated exclusively by anti-Americanism. But with the advantage of critical
hindsight some five years later, it is now evident that these analysts were fairly
accurate in their predictions.

In essence, the 'war on terrorism' has become Washington's moral fig leaf for
cementing American global primacy. The evident righteousness of the cause
(who can oppose defeating terrorism?) has itself become a thinly veiled instrument for deflecting criticism of the litany of foreign policy failures committed by
the Bush administration since 9/11. These include the administration's unwillingness to devote sufficient funds to reconstructing Afghanistan; its mishandling
of the post-war situation in Iraq; its unwillingness to consult in any serious way

with US allies; and its willingness to deal with a host of unsavoury totalitarian regimes while loudly condemning 'anti-democratic' forces worldwide. In short, from the perspective of the Bush administration and its supporters, the 'war on terror' has become an all-purpose moral justification for just about all US international activity since 9/11. This was a central theme in the campaign strategy adopted by the Republican Party during the 2004 presidential race.[16]

The trend towards embracing a range of seemingly disparate aims under the single banner of the 'war on terrorism' evolved quickly after September 2001 hand in glove with the administration's increasingly expansive pronouncements about American grand strategy. In his second State of the Union address in January 2002, President Bush sought to draw a strong link between terrorists of the al-Qaeda variety, state sponsors of terrorism, and 'terrorist' rogue states that possess weapons of mass destruction – Iran, Iraq, and North Korea.[17] Without even endeavouring to justify, much less explain, why any possible link could be drawn between an extremist Islamic group like al-Qaeda and a secular *status quo* oriented Stalinist state like North Korea, Bush elevated the threat from Iran, Iraq, and North Korea to the same level as that emanating from al-Qaeda. By effectively linking (however spuriously) this 'rogue' state *troika* with Osama bin Laden, Bush signalled that the United States would be justified in taking equally decisive action against these states at some future point.

The 'axis of evil' theme was developed further in a landmark presidential address at the West Point Military Academy in June 2002. This time, Bush spelt out an additional layer of US doctrine: Washington would consider itself justified in carrying out pre-emptive military action against those states 'engaged in terror and aggression'.[18] The threat was of a sufficiently generic and abstract nature to allow the United States considerable room for manoeuvre in deciding when and where to employ force pre-emptively. According to Bush, the international security environment had altered radically since 9/11 to the extent that traditional forms of deterrence were essentially outmoded. In a theme that would be repeated relentlessly by the administration during the prelude to war with Iraq in early 2003, Bush invoked what he saw as the key lesson of 9/11: 'If we wait for threats to fully materialise, we will have waited too long'.[19]

Bush's West Point address was also significant for another reason. It was the first time the administration signalled that perpetual primacy would be an explicit objective of US grand strategy. As Bush noted, 'America has, and intends to keep, military strengths beyond challenge – thereby, making the destabilizing arms races of other eras pointless, and limiting rivalries [with other states] to trade and other pursuits of peace'.[20] This theme was followed up in the National Security Strategy released exactly one year after the 9/11 attacks. The document provided the clearest snapshot yet of America's increasingly ambitious grand strategy, with its emphasis on American exceptionalism and global pre-eminence. By stressing that the United States would continue to 'extend the benefits of freedom across the globe', the National Security Strategy declared boldly that America would 'use its strength to promote a balance of power that favours freedom'.[21]

Less than meets the eye: assessing the shift

Superficially at least, American grand strategy has experienced a radical shift since the events of 9/11. The conventional wisdom in much of the academic literature is that the Bush administration has forged a 'new' grand strategy of primacy that signifies a radical break with established tradition in America's approach to the international system.[22] The linking of primacy with notions of American 'imperial' expansion has reinforced this perspective.[23]

As noted in the introduction to this chapter, however, it is important not to exaggerate the shift in American grand strategy under the Bush administration. While the administration's rhetoric has been more assertive and muscular than that of the previous two administrations, the tenor of its pronouncements remains eerily familiar to those of the first Reagan administration (1981–1985). More significantly, though, two of the key doctrinal developments often identified by observers as confirming the shift to a decidedly new grand strategy – the formal embrace of pre-emption and the move to capabilities based military planning – can be traced directly to the thinking evident in previous administrations. The concept of pre-emption has a long lineage in American strategic culture, while capabilities based planning had already emerged as the template for US force structure and acquisition policy during the last year of the Clinton administration.

Embracing the doctrine of pre-emption

Speaking shortly after the formal cessation of combat hostilities in Iraq in May 2003, the neo-conservative commentator Charles Krauthammer observed that the Bush Doctrine of pre-emptive war was akin to the Truman Doctrine in its 'revolutionary' implications.[24] Interestingly, many analysts on the left have also characterised the doctrine of pre-emption as signifying a 'radical' shift in US strategy.[25] Leaving aside the vast gulf separating those on the right and left over the merits of pre-emption – one side welcomes it, the other side censures it – there is generally strong agreement that it represents a new addition to US strategy.[26]

Pre-emption constitutes the anticipatory use of force by one state against another from whom an attack is judged to be imminent. By its very nature, the concept assumes that the benefits of resorting to military force to forestall an armed attack outweigh the costs of defending against an attack that is regarded as inevitable. In this sense, pre-emptive use of force enshrines the 'superiority of the offensive' in international relations. It assumes explicitly that the momentum for victory in any armed conflict lies with the state that retains the initiative in conducting offensive operations against an enemy. The operative words contained in the above definition of pre-emption – anticipatory and imminent – presuppose that the state doing the pre-empting possesses two distinct capabilities. First, the capacity to verify through early warning intelligence sources that there is an attack pending; and second, the military wherewithal and political will to use force decisively to neutralise an attack before it materialises.

A number of analysts have pointed to the Bush administration's deliberate blurring of the traditional distinction between the pre-emptive use of force and preventive military strikes – i.e. strikes that aim to prevent a specific capability from emerging rather than destroying an existing capability poised for use. The absence of any explicit distinction between pre-emption and preventive war was first evident in the 2002 National Security Strategy[27] and was reinforced by the administration's stated justification for invading Iraq in March 2003. Although invoking the term 'pre-emption' to justify military action, the administration's pronouncements about Iraq's alleged WMD programme focussed more on preventing a situation from evolving whereby Iraq could eventually strike American soil rather than destroying a capability poised for use. If the Bush administration had believed genuinely that Iraq's WMD was poised for use against US targets or Israel, it would not have endeavoured to gain UN Security Council backing in the latter stages of 2002. And it certainly would not have waited until March 2003 to give the green light for an invasion of Iraqi territory.[28]

The concepts of pre-emptive use of force and preventive war have both been mainstays in American strategic doctrine since World War Two. Indeed, pre-emptive strikes formed an integral component of US nuclear war-fighting strategy for the best part of the cold war. Despite the stated aversion of successive administrations to the idea of undertaking a 'sneak attack' – largely the result of Pearl Harbor experience – both pre-emptive and preventive strikes have formed part of the American military's suite of options since 1945. In the early post-war world, the Truman administration considered closely various options for striking the Soviet Union's nuclear weapons programme prior to, and shortly after, Moscow's successful test of an atomic device in 1949, while the Kennedy and Johnson administrations displayed a similar interest in exploring preventive war options against China's nuclear programme during the 1960s.[29] More recently, in the midst of the 1993–1994 nuclear crisis, the Clinton administration examined carefully a series of 'surgical' military operations designed to destroy North Korea's nuclear capability.[30]

Capabilities-based planning

Given that the US military is by far the dominant material component in America's panoply of global power projection capabilities, military planning is critical to achieving the core objectives of national strategy. A common theme in sections of the academic literature examining American strategy is that US military doctrine has been reconfigured dramatically since President Bush's declaration of the 'war on terrorism' in September 2001. The American military has certainly been more active in terms of the scope of its overseas combat deployments since 9/11 than at any stage since the end of World War Two. And, largely as a corollary of this, the demands on the thinly stretched US armed forces have never been greater. Such demands have been amplified by the demanding requirement laid down by the Bush administration for US forces. Under the previous Clinton administration, the American military was required to be capable of waging (and winning) two major theatre wars simultaneously while deterring an attack on the United States. The Bush administration has signalled that, in addition to deterring attacks against US territory, it expects US forces to achieve the '4–2–1' benchmark: 'deter in four places, counter-attack in two, and if necessary, go to the enemy's capital in one of the two'.[31]

However, a more significant development at the doctrinal level has been the decision to replace a 'threat-based' approach to strategic planning with a 'capabilities-based' approach. Put simply, this entails planners in the Pentagon improving American force capabilities exponentially *irrespective* of the nature of prevailing threats to American security. Thus, although there is no current missile threat from North Korea or Iran against the United States, the fact that these states may attain an operational inter-continental ballistic missile capability at some point in the future serves to justify acquiring a national missile defence network. Missile defence has more to do with enhancing US force capabilities relative to those of all other countries in the international system than it does with protecting the American homeland from 'rogue' state attacks. From this administration's perspective, the focus must be on widening further the already massive gulf between American military capabilities and those of all other countries, including friends as well as foes, in the international system.[32] This is a key avenue for attaining the broader national strategy of preventing the emergence of peer competitors now and into the future.

Many have identified the adoption of a capabilities based approach to planning force structure and acquisition policy as a radical departure from established US practice, with one leading scholar classifying it as one of a number of 'wholesale changes to America's military-strategic doctrine and posture' under the Bush administration.[33] However, like pre-emption, a capabilities-based approach to US military planning owes more to the strategic rationale outlined prior to the arrival of George Bush in the White House than it does to any innovative change countenanced by the Bush administration in the wake of 9/11.

The shift to capabilities-based planning was already well in train under the Clinton administration. For instance, in 1996 the Clinton White House endorsed a National Space Policy that outlined explicitly the need for the US to maintain and bolster its supremacy in the use of outer space for military purposes. Significantly, it also underscored the importance of actively denying other countries capabilities that could challenge this supremacy in the longer term.[34] Similarly, although at a broader level, the Pentagon's *Joint Vision 2020* document released in the last year of the Clinton administration accorded strong emphasis to the importance of the United States maintaining 'full spectrum dominance' in its war-fighting capabilities with a view to 'defeating any adversary and controlling any situation across the full range of military operations … unilaterally or in combination with multinational partners'.[35]

A political and strategic backlash

In the run-up to the 2004 presidential election, two unmistakable trends dominated surveys of international public opinion regarding the United States. The first was that most respondents, in virtually every country surveyed, were hoping for the defeat of the incumbent, George Bush. The second trend was that the majority of respondents, again among US allies and adversaries alike, identified what they saw as America's increasingly unbridled arrogance in world affairs.[36] Clearly, the first desire was related closely to the second perspective. George Bush, rightly or wrongly, is perceived by those who hold adverse impressions of America's contemporary role in international relations as personifying US imperiousness. It would be mistaken to assume that this anti-Bush sentiment was (or still is) confined to the Middle East or 'old' Europe. In Australia, for instance, one of Washington's staunchest allies in the 'war on terrorism', the majority of public opinion has reflected starkly negative images of President Bush.[37]

Of course, it would be an exaggeration to ascribe all of this sentiment to the policies of the Bush administration. There can be little doubt that a reasonable portion of it is attributable to the ever-present residual anti-Americanism evident in almost every country around the globe. Still, there can be little doubt that a good portion of the growing anti-US sentiment worldwide derives from a genuine aversion to the accentuated unilateralism of America's global strategy under George Bush. A key factor driving this sentiment is widespread disenchantment internationally over US policy in Iraq, and the specific belief in some quarters that the Bush administration was disingenuous with the rest of the international community about its reasons for invading in the first place. As one American critic observes:

> The failure to honour promises to secure Iraq immediately, to feed and fight simultaneously, tarnished the lustre of US omnipotence. The subsequent failure to find weapons of mass destruction in Iraq, and ultimately the revelation that there had almost certainly been none to find – after the Pentagon had said it knew where those weapons were – is seen as a sign of falseness on the part of the United States and has deeply undermined American credibility.[38]

Some, to be sure, are repelled by the very idea that a single country possesses such unrivalled power internationally. As Robert Jervis points out, 'the United States is probably as benign a hegemon as the world has ever seen … [b]ut a hegemon it remains, and by that very fact it must make others uneasy'.[39] Yet, it is striking the degree to which the widespread international sympathy for the United States triggered by the 9/11 attacks has been supplanted by an equally striking that degree of underlying mistrust that at times borders on blatant hostility towards America's policy on specific issues and its broader motives globally.

The Bush administration has essentially squandered the reservoir of international goodwill towards the United States that emerged following the terrorist attacks in September 2001. But the administration remains unconcerned with this development for what it sees as two good reasons. The first is that it believes the international community has little choice but to acquiesce to US global dominance in the foreseeable future because of America's hegemonic status. The second reason is that the core objective of US grand strategy post-9/11 is profoundly adversarial in nature – preventing actively the emergence of any peer competitors, friendly or otherwise, in perpetuity. In this sense, the Bush administration sees international criticism of its policies and global strategy as a relatively small price to pay if this core objective is to be achieved. Indeed, many of those in Bush's political heartland in the South and Midwest of the United States wear disparagement from the likes of France and Germany as a badge of honour.

Ironically, the political backlash against American unilateralism has been provoked at least in part by the Bush administration's *success* in articulating a more transparent US grand strategy. America's intentions are more clear-cut than ever and its approach to international relations increasingly absolutist (good versus evil, 'you're either with us or you're with the terrorists'). Inevitably, this has flow on effects for American foreign policy. One of the more salient features of the Bush administration's diplomatic offensive in the lead up to the US invasion of Iraq in March 2003 was its failure to convince a significant number, let alone a majority, of countries of the merits of deposing the Baathist regime in Baghdad. This exposed a key disjuncture between American hard power on the one hand, and its capacity to influence on the other, raising serious questions about the perceived legitimacy of US global leadership.[40]

Although expending considerable diplomatic capital in building a case in favour of overthrowing Saddam Hussein's regime – which included linking regime change with degrading al-Qaeda's capabilities in the Middle East – the Bush administration provoked a groundswell of international opposition to the invasion of Iraq in 2003. Much of this opposition sprang not from unease over the prospect of the US military forcibly ejecting Saddam Hussein from office *per se*, but from genuine apprehension about American primacy and unilateralism evident in earlier criticism of the Bush administration's rejection of the Kyoto Protocol, its withdrawal from the Anti-Ballistic Missile Treaty, and its strong opposition to the creation of the International Criminal Court. More tellingly, however, despite America's overwhelming relative power internationally, there was no discernible 'bandwagoning' of allies in favour of invading Iraq. Not only did Washington fail to persuade some of its closest allies to support military action, it actually had to contend with spirited opposition from key NATO allies such as Canada, France, and Germany. In the end, a mere handful of states proved willing to support the invasion, and even fewer committed military forces. Perhaps surprisingly, though, US officials did not appear to be particularly concerned with the dearth of international support for the Bush administration's Iraq expedition.

As we now know, at no point did Saddam Hussein's Iraq pose an imminent threat to the core national security interests of the United States. It is increasingly evident, however, that the same may not be said for much longer about North Korea and Iran, two countries whose respective nuclear weapons programmes are provoking serious consternation among Bush administration officials. Most independent estimates place North Korea at or over the threshold of possessing nuclear weapons, while British and French intelligence sources estimate that Iran's accelerated programme will put it in a position to acquire an operational nuclear force by 2007.[41]

In their occasional moments of public candour, both countries have signalled that their quest to acquire nuclear weapons is motivated largely by the belief that they are necessary to deter a US-led invasion. There is, undoubtedly, a degree of exaggeration in these statements designed to appeal to caricatures of US unilateralism internationally. After all, both countries continued to devote scarce national resources to attaining a nuclear capability in the past when relations with Washington were not as tense. Nevertheless, from the strategic perspective of Pyongyang and Tehran, the argument that nuclear weapons provide the best means of deterring US conventional military action is both logical and compelling, particularly in light of Bush's decision to classify these two states as belonging to 'an axis of evil'. The North Korean regime has indicated publicly that it believes the critical lesson to be drawn from American-led military action against Iraq is that the latter was invaded because it did not have nuclear weapons.[42] The logic of nuclear acquisition for Pyongyang and Tehran has probably been reinforced by leaked details of the 2001 US Nuclear Posture Review, which specified North Korea and Iran as two of the key targets in the Bush administration's nuclear contingency planning.[43]

In a very important sense, North Korea and Iran represent the strategic dimension of the international backlash against contemporary US power and global strategy. The shift to a more transparently assertive American grand strategy predicated on perpetual primacy has had the effect of intensifying defensive measures from those countries with which the US has an adversarial strategic relationship. Weaker adversaries have responded not by competing with the US at the conventional level – the cost is prohibitive –- but by seeking asymmetric warfare capabilities that provide a modicum of 'strategic equalization' in an endeavour to offset American conventional and nuclear superiority. As the events of 9/11 and the ongoing campaign by insurgents in Iraq demonstrate, the US remains acutely vulnerable to asymmetric warfare strategies. Even if North Korea or Iran prove incapable of delivering nuclear weapons against US targets via conventional means (missile or aircraft), both countries could probably pass on elements of their fissile material stocks, or possibly a complete warhead, to a terrorist group better placed to carry out an attack against targets on the American mainland.[44]

For this reason alone, US strategic planners have very good reason to be concerned about the respective nuclear programs of North Korea and Iran. Two points should be made here. The first is that a nuclear North Korea and a nuclear Iran potentially threaten not just US security, but also the security of other countries, including American allies, in Asia, the Middle East, and Europe.

The second, perhaps less obvious, point is that if the United States is to address these threats without resorting to military force – which in both cases is fraught with tremendous risks and potentially enormous costs for Washington – it needs the close cooperation of other states which do have some leverage over Pyongyang and Tehran. This is something that Bush administration officials would do well to ponder when they are next inclined to dismiss the relevance of international criticism of American unilateral action in world affairs.

Notes

1 Definitions of grand strategy in the academic literature vary widely in scope. Consider the following metaphorically based definition by one of America's leading strategists, Edward Luttwak: '[G]rand strategy may be seen as a confluence of the military interactions that flow up and down level by level – forming strategy's vertical dimension – with the varied external relations that form strategy's horizontal dimension at its highest level. In this image, the rivers and rivulets of international transactions would radiate from a central vertical flow, violating the laws of hydrodynamics in their reciprocal movement as military preparations and actions have their effects on the non-military dealings of states, and as the latter in turn affect the military realm'. In contrast, Barry Posen defines grand strategy simply, as 'a political-military, means-ends chain, a state's theory about how it can best "cause" security for itself'. For the purpose of this chapter, grand strategy can be defined as the broad strategic goals that drive a state's conduct of foreign and defence policy. See E. Luttwak, *Strategy: The Logic of War and Peace*, Cambridge, MA: The Belknap Press, 1987, pp. 179–80; B. Posen, *The Sources of Military Doctrine: France, Britain, and Germany Between the World Wars*, Ithaca, NY: Cornell University Press, 1984, p. 13.

2 See, for example, P. Kennedy, *The Rise and Fall of the Great Powers: Economic Change and Military Conflict from 1500 to 2000*, New York: Random House, 1987.

3 T. Donnelly, *Rebuilding America's Defences: Strategy, Forces and Resources for a New Century*, Washington, DC: Project for the New American Century, 2000, p. i.

4 For an excellent discussion of the Truman administration's grand strategy, see M. Leffler, *A Preponderance of Power: National Security, The Truman Administration and the Cold War*, Stanford, CA: Stanford University Press, 1992.

5 C. Dueck, 'New perspectives on American grand strategy: a review essay', *International Security*, Spring 2004, vol. 28, no. 4, p. 212.

6 One of the most significant, yet frequently underestimated, costs has resulted from the response by governments to what they regard as the increased likelihood of terrorist strikes on their own soil following 9/11. For most states, certainly those in the developed world, the financial cost of implementing new security measures at airports and seaports has been enormous.

7 R. Betts, 'The soft underbelly of American primacy: tactical advantages of terror', *Political Science Quarterly*, Spring 2002, vol. 117, no. 1, p. 27.

8 For a surprisingly critical analysis of the performance of US intelligence agencies in the lead up to 9/11, see National Commission on Terrorist Attacks on the United States, *The 9/11 Commission Report: The Authorized Edition*, New York: Norton, 2004, pp. 339–60.

9 For discussion on this point against the background of America's covert war against al-Qaeda during the 1990s, see D. Ball, 'Desperately seeking Bin Laden: the intelligence dimension of the war against terrorism', in K. Booth and T. Dunne (eds.), *Worlds in Collision: Terror and the Future of Global Order*, Basingstoke: Palgrave Macmillan, 2002, pp. 60–73.

10 N. Lemann, 'The next world order', *The New Yorker*, 1 April 2002, p. 44.

11 For an interesting, if somewhat sympathetic, account of the administration's approach in the months after 9/11, see B. Woodward, *Bush at War*, New York: Simon & Schuster, 2002.

12 P. Tyler, 'US strategy plan calls for insuring no rivals develop', *The New York Times*, 8 March 1992.

13 B. Posen and A. Ross, 'Competing visions for US grand strategy', *International Security*, Winter 1996–1997, vol. 21, no. 3, p. 5.

14 The White House, 'President Bush's Address to a Joint Session of Congress and the American People, Washington, 20 September 2001', available at <http://www.whitehouse.gov/news/releases/2001/09/20010920-8.html> (accessed 31 May 2005).

15 On this point, see J. Kiras, 'Terrorism and irregular warfare', in J. Baylis, J. Wirtz, E. Cohen and C. Gray (eds.), *Strategy in the Contemporary World: An Introduction to Strategic Studies*, Oxford: Oxford University Press, 2002, pp. 208–32.

16 It should therefore have come as no surprise that the rhetoric of George Bush following his re-election in November 2004 implied that his victory over Democrat candidate John Kerry vindicated not only his administration's conduct of the 'war on terrorism', but also its broader foreign policy including the invasion and occupation of Iraq.

17 The White House, 'The President's State of the Union Address, Washington DC, 29 January 2002', available at <http://www.whitehouse.gov/news/releases/2002/01/20020129-11.html> (accessed 31 May 2005).

18 The White House, 'Remarks by the President at the 2002 Graduation Exercise of the United States Military Academy, West Point, 1 June 2002', available at <http://www.whitehouse.gov/news/releases/2002/06/20020601-3.html> (accessed 31 May 2005).

19 Ibid.

20 Ibid.

21 The White House, *The National Security Strategy of the United States of America*, September 2002, available at <http://www.whitehouse.gov/nsc/nss.html> (accessed 31 May 2005).

22 See, for example, E. Sloan, 'Beyond primacy: American grand strategy in the post-September 11 era', *International Journal*, Spring 2003, vol. 58, no 2, pp. 303–19; S. Schwenninger, 'Revamping American grand strategy', *World Policy Journal*, Fall 2003, vol. 20, no. 3, pp. 25–44; and C. Dueck, 'Ideas and alternatives in American grand strategy, 2000–2004', *Review of International Studies*, October 2004, vol. 30, no. 4, pp. 511–35.

23 One of the more lively discussions on this theme can be found in M. Cox, 'The Empire's back in town: or America's imperial temptation – again', *Millennium: Journal of International Studies*, 2003, vol. 32, no. 1, pp. 1–27.

24 Quoted in T. Judt, 'Dreams of Empire', *The New York Review of Books*, 4 November 2004, p. 39.

25 See, for instance, P. Dombrowski and R. Payne, 'Global debate and the limits of the Bush doctrine', *International Studies Perspectives*, November 2003, vol. 4, no. 4, pp. 395–408.

26 Although Litwak concedes that '[t]he origins of the current Bush administration's pre-emption policy date to the early 1990s', he nevertheless characterizes the rise of pre-emption as a 'new' development. See R. Litwak, 'The new calculus of pre-emption', *Survival*, Winter 2002–2003, vol. 44, no 4, p. 54 and *passim*.

27 The White House, *The National Security Strategy of the United States of America*.

28 For further discussion on this point, see A. O'Neil, 'The Bush administration, pre-emption, and the absence of consistency', *AQ: Journal of Contemporary Analysis*, May/June. 2004, vol. 76, no. 3, pp. 9–14.

29 Litwak, 'The new calculus of pre-emption', pp. 61–2.

30 Senior Clinton administration officials have since confirmed that during the 1993–1994 crisis, the Pentagon examined in detail the feasibility of selective military strikes against North Korea's nuclear infrastructure and concluded that such strikes were 'technically possible'. The study concluded that US and allied air power would be able to destroy key nuclear facilities, including the lynchpin reactor at Yongbyon, without causing the release of radioactive materials into the atmosphere. While never presented formally to President Clinton for consideration, it is highly likely that the Pentagon study forms the backbone of current American planning for preventive/pre-emptive strikes on the Korean peninsula. See J. Wit, D. Poneman, and R. Galluci, *Going Critical: The First North Korean Nuclear Crisis*, Washington, DC: The Brookings Institution, 2004, pp. 210–11. On current US military planning for a North Korean contingency, see R. Ayson and B. Taylor, 'Attacking North Korea: why war might be preferred', *Comparative Strategy*, 2004, vol. 23, no. 3, pp. 263–79.

31 B. Posen, 'Command of the commons: the military foundation of US hegemony', *International Security*, Summer 2003, vol. 28, no. 1, p. 7.

32 US Joint Chiefs of Staff, *National Military Strategy of the United States of America 2004: A Strategy for Today, A Vision for Tomorrow*, Washington, DC: US Government Printing Office, 2004, pp. 18–20.

33 C. Reus-Smit, *American Power and World Order*, Cambridge: Polity Press, 2004, pp. 74–5.

34 The White House, *National Space Policy Fact Sheet*, 19 September 1996. In October 2004, the US Air Force announced that the Counter Communications System (CCS) had become operational. The CCS is an anti-satellite system designed to jam 'enemy' spaced based communications with a view to denying such countries early warning of US military operations in specific regional theatres and/or worldwide. See J. Wolf, 'US deploys satellite jamming system', *Reuters*, 29 October 2004.

35 US Joint Chiefs of Staff, *Joint Vision 2020: America's Military Preparing for Tomorrow*, Washington, DC: US Government Printing Office, 2000, p. 6.

36 A. Travis, 'Poll reveals world anger at Bush', *The Guardian*, 15 October 2004.

37 P. Hartcher, 'Attitudes harden as Bush seeks fresh mandate', *The Sydney Morning Herald*, 15 October 2004.

38 N. Crawford, 'Principia Leviathan: the moral duties of American hegemony', *Naval War College Review*, 2004, vol. 57, no. 3, p. 86.

39 R. Jervis, 'Understanding the Bush Doctrine', *Political Science Quarterly*, Fall 2003, vol. 118, no 3, p. 385.

40 For discussion, see J. Nye, 'US power and strategy after Iraq', *Foreign Affairs*, July–August 2003, vol. 82, no. 4, pp. 60–73. It should be borne in mind, however, that the US failed to convince a large number of its key cold war allies of the merits of involvement in Vietnam during the 1960s. This, along with subsequent defeat in 1975, did have an impact on America's global standing, though it was not as serious and enduring as many at the time predicted.

41 On the history and scope of both respective programmes, see International Institute for Strategic Studies, *North Korea's Weapons Programmes: A Net Assessment*, Basingstoke: Palgrave Macmillan, 2004, pp. 27–48; W. Bowen and J. Kidd, 'The Iranian nuclear challenge', *International Affairs*, March 2004, vol. 80, no. 2, pp. 257–76.

42 A. Ward, 'Iraq shows deterrent needed, says N. Korea', *The Financial Times*, 6 April 2003.

43 A. Newman, 'Arms control, proliferation and terrorism: the Bush administration's post-September 11 security strategy', *The Journal of Strategic Studies*, March 2004, vol. 27, no. 1, p. 69.

44 For a pessimistic, though refreshingly non-alarmist, discussion of this possibility, see G. Allison, *Nuclear Terrorism: The Ultimate Preventable Catastrophe*, New York: Times Books, 2004, pp. 61–8

9 The Bush elite

Aberration or harbinger?

John Higley

Ruling elites in Western countries during the twentieth century's second half were seldom clearly distinct from their predecessors and successors. Typically, they were enmeshed in extended circles and networks of political influence and personal acquaintance that tied together several thousand of the uppermost figures in politics, government administration, business, trade unions, the media, and assorted interest groups. These interlocked formations were tighter than the 'pluralist elite' depicted, but more far-flung than the 'power elite' model portrayed.[1] Through such circles and networks, individuals and factions rose to executive power, osmosis-like, *via* lengthy careers in elective, party, administrative, and other politically relevant arenas. Once in power, elites found their actions checked in many ways. Radical policy innovations were stymied by the complexity of established institutions and by programs inherited from the previous holders of executive office. Truculent congressional or parliamentary supporters had to be placated; political debts incurred during the rise to power had to be paid; preparations for the next election tempered actions; the power of elites in other societal sectors had to be respected; the personal behaviors and political decisions of the ruling group were subject to intense media scrutiny and criticism. All in all, a single-minded pursuit of political aims that broke sharply with what had gone before was exceedingly difficult. As S. E. Finer put it, elites in most Western countries routinely took in each other's washing.[2] The complexity and extent of this elite laundry gave rise to the view among political analysts that 'ruling elite' was a gross simplification, if not a wild exaggeration.

The elite clustered around President George W. Bush requires reconsidering this view. In composition and structure, the Bush elite is exceptionally well articulated and tightly woven. Its principal members have long been political intimates who possess a marked *élan* and share a distinctive set of moral and political beliefs. The elite possesses an internally agreed and remarkably ambitious program as regards America's role in the world and domestic changes that it believes are imperative. Most of this program was formulated years before the elite gained power at the start of 2001, and the 9/11 attacks that year provided a public justification for implementing it. Although some amount of improvisation has since been unavoidable, the Bush elite has been tenacious – many would say ruthless – in pursuing its program and the beliefs that underpin it. These aspects of the Bush elite have no clear precedent in American history. In this chapter, I ask if the Bush elite is an aberration in American politics or the harbinger of a new kind of elite rule in the United States. Are concatenating domestic trends and international pressures, the latter manifested so grievously by the 9/11 attacks and by many attacks on Americans and American installations abroad, altering the character of American ruling elites in some long-lasting way? If so, how, and what are the implications for America's liberal democracy?

The Bush elite

The Bush elite's gestation can be traced to the emergence of a pronouncedly conservative and nationalist elite faction in the Republican Party that fueled Barry Goldwater's campaign for the presidency in 1964.[3] This faction expanded and consolidated ideologically when neo-conservatives in the Democratic Party decamped to the Republicans in the wake of the Vietnam War, the Munich Olympics terrorist attack in 1972, and the Yom Kippur War in 1973. The oil price shocks and stagflation of the mid and late 1970s, combined with the Carter administration's perceived weakness at the time of the Iranian revolution and Soviet invasion of Afghanistan, put wind in the nascent elite's sails. It acquired robust form during the 'evil empire' rhetoric and counter-insurgency actions of the Reagan administration in the 1980s, the demise of the Soviet Empire that was said to flow from Reagan's tough stance, and the string of Likud-dominated governments in Israel that Menachem Begin initiated.

Except that the elite lacked a sturdy presidential horse to ride, it became fully formed when in opposition to the Clinton administration after 1992 – courtesy of Ross Perot's third-party candidacy in that year's presidential election. An esti-mated US$300 million was spent to smear and defeat Clinton's proposed health care program during 1993, and it was in large measure because of this that Republicans won and proclaimed 'revolutionary' control of the House of Representatives in 1994. The elite and its congressional allies then launched a ferocious assault on Clinton's administration and person. This climaxed in late 1998 and early 1999 when Republicans in Congress used the pretext of Clinton's sexual misconduct to impeach and nearly convict him for 'high crimes and misdemeanors'. Possessing the detailed foreign and domestic program alluded to above, members of the elite settled quickly on George W. Bush, the unworldly Governor of Texas with a household name, as its horse for the 2000 presidential election. When, at the last minute, a maverick Republican Senator, John McCain, threatened to de-rail the elite's drive for power, McCain's campaign was overpowered by a combination of demagogy and huge Bush campaign expenditures. Essentially the same tactics were then employed to convert the pivotal Florida election into a legal standoff that a majority of Supreme Court Justices, all of them Republican appointees, resolved in the elite's favor.

The Bush elite is a study in network density and integration – of circles within circles and hubs within hubs. Although no formal analysis of this network has been conducted, there are numerous well-documented books and articles by journalists and persons who held important positions in the first Bush administration that portray the elite's exceptional integration and uniformity of belief.[4]

The elite's core consists of the Bush family dynasty and a handful of close and trusted Texas advisers and allies: political tactician Karl Rove; media advisor Karen Hughes; White House chief of staff Andrew Card; White House press secretary Scott McClelland; and, until late 2004, Secretary of Commerce Donald Evans.[5] Several dense circles overlap and intersect at the elite's core and have various labels: 'Vulcans' (a self-selected label inspired by the god of fire and steel), neo-conservatives, assertive nationalists, democratic imperialists, old-school conservatives, etc. The most conspicuous and powerful of these circles are the 'Vulcans', whose members are foreign and defense policy veterans of the Reagan and Bush Senior administrations and even of the Ford and Nixon administrations.[6] They are led by Vice President Dick Cheney and his assistant Lewis Libby, Defense Secretary Donald Rumsfeld and his deputy Paul Wolfowitz, and, until the 2004 election, National Security Adviser Condoleezza Rice and her assistant Stephen Hadley, together with former Secretary of State Colin Powell and his former deputy, Richard Armitage. Although often squabbling about the extent of military deployments in Iraq and how hard a line to take toward Iran, North Korea, and other trouble spots, the Vulcans are as one in believing that US military power, which they perceive to have few limits, is the central means for unseating dictatorial regimes and promoting democracy and freedom worldwide. The Vulcans insist that the use of US military power must not be fettered by agreements and accommodations with other countries and that the United States must block any rival hyper-power from emerging. Vulcan leaders are key nodes in an extended network of like-minded associates and former aides who are strategically located in cabinet departments and the intelligence agencies. An important circle within the Vulcan circle consists of persons with close ties to Israel and the powerful Israeli lobby in Washington: former Chairman of the Defense Advisory Board Richard Pearle; Defense Undersecretary for Policy Douglas Feith and his deputy Stephen Cambone; Undersecretary of State for Arms Control John Bolton now America's representative at the UN and his adviser David Wurmser; plus a handful of others who belonged to a committee that advised Benjamin Netanyahu when he became Israeli Prime Minister in 1996.

Following the Bush elite's victory in the 2004 election, the Vulcan circle was made still more powerful by leaving Rumsfeld and his team in control of the Pentagon and putting the president's closest Vulcan advisors in two key positions: Rice as Secretary of State and Hadley as National Security Adviser. Altogether, nine of Bush's fifteen cabinet secretaries were replaced, in most cases by persons closer to Bush and the White House than the previous secretaries had been. Among these White House legal counsel Alberto Gonzales was named attorney-general; White House domestic policy adviser Margaret Spellings was made Secretary of Education; a staunch congressional supporter, J. Porter Goss, took over as Director of Central Intelligence, and another prominent ally, Tom Ridge, continued as Secretary of Homeland Security (having been appointed to this post in January 2003). A number of important officials below cabinet level who had sometimes been out of step with the White House were purged and replaced by loyalists. From late 2004, in short, a small knot of Bush confidants had thorough control of the executive branch, eradicating or at least reducing the jurisdictional rivalries and policy disagreements that sometimes occurred during the elite's first four years in power.

The Bush elite's beliefs have a strong religious coloration and its élan is Spartan.[7] Bush is a 'born again Christian' rescued by God, he believes, from a dissolute life and destined to serve a Divine purpose. Cabinet and other meetings begin with prayer; Bible study sessions are held among White House personnel; the president's speeches are laced with references to God. 'Evil' is a meaningful concept, and shifting responsibility for the provision of welfare services to 'faith-based' organizations is a prime domestic aim. There is a quasi-military code of behavior and dress to which elite members adhere. A flag button is on every member's lapel. Loyalty to the president and secrecy in elite decision-making are watchwords.

A blueprint for the Bush elite's defense program, titled *Rebuilding America's Defenses: Strategy, Forces and Resources for a New Century* (2000), was drawn up during the three years before the elite took power in 2001. Among its co-authors were Paul Wolfowitz and several close associates who now hold high Pentagon and State Department positions – Cambone and Dov Zakheim in the Pentagon, Bolton at State, Elliot Cohen and Devon Cross at the Defense Policy Board, together with Lewis Libby, Cheney's chief assistant. Work on the blueprint was co-chaired by William Kristol, editor of *The Weekly Standard*, which is the print media organ for political class supporters of the Bush elite, and Robert Kagan. Kagan's book, *Of Paradise and Power* (2003), has been regarded by many in and around the elite as a seminal essay on post-9/11 trans-Atlantic relations and the 'Hobbesian' world in which the United States finds itself.[8] The defense blueprint refined a plan conceived and recommended by Wolfowitz as early as 1992, when he was deputy to Cheney, who was then Defense Secretary in the Bush Senior administration. Much of the blueprint was implemented during and after 2001. The 1972 anti-ballistic missile treaty with the Soviet Union/Russia was repudiated; construction of a missile defense system got underway and was to be declared 'operational' late in 2004, until another of its tests failed. The defense budget was increased from three per cent of GDP to the recommended four per cent; weapons systems that had been identified as outmoded were cancelled and the development of small nuclear warheads for use against hardened bunkers was authorized. The Saddam Hussein regime was decapitated and efforts to de-stabilize 'rogue' regimes in Iran and North Korea were given a green light.

In step with this defense blueprint, the elite's *National Security Strategy*, announced in September 2002, asserts a number of initiatives. It endorses pre-emptive attacks against countries posing an imminent threat to the United States, rejects strategies of containment and deterrence as cold war relics, charts a global structure of US military bases and long-distance troop deployments, and asserts that no country will be allowed to equal or surpass American military power during the next several decades. The Bush elite's policy toward the Israel-Palestine conflict also reflects documents written well before the elite gained power. One was an advisory paper prepared for Netanyahu by members of the Vulcans' Israel-oriented circle in 1996. Entitled *A Clean Break: A New Strategy for Securing the Realm*, this recommended de-emphasizing the Oslo peace process in favor of a balance of power strategy for Israel that would involve, *inter alia*, eliminating Saddam Hussein's regime. Another anticipatory document that has had more than a few echoes in the Bush elite's strategy toward the Middle East was a 1999 book by David Wurmser (since 2001 the senior adviser to John Bolton in the State Department). Wurmser predicted that liquidating the Iraqi regime would de-stabilize the regimes in Syria and Iran, neutralize Lebanon and its support for Hezbollah, and thus deprive the Palestine Liberation Authority of external support.[9]

The Bush elite's domestic program rests on a vision of 'markets released' and an 'ownership society' in which citizens take greater responsibility for their financial well-being through tax-favored 'lifetime savings accounts' that they use to pay for their education, health care, and retirement. Much of what government agencies have customarily done is outsourced to private companies, not least companies that provide paramilitary security specialists on a contract basis to the Pentagon. This has the political benefits of weakening public sector trade unions and avoiding the conscription of civilians to sustain military engagements like those in Afghanistan and Iraq. Environmental protections are loosened or removed in the name of de-regulation. Much of the federal government's Medicaid spending for indigent citizens is shifted to the states, which are typically unable to bear the costs, so that the Medicaid program is whittled down. Above all, federal taxes on income are slashed on the theory that supply-side economic growth will generate new tax revenues with which to eliminate the large budget deficit created by the tax cuts, the defense buildup and military engagements, and the large amount of pork-barrel spending by Republicans in Congress. *A National Strategy for Homeland Security*, announced in July 2002, results in a vast Department of Homeland Security that absorbs and controls agencies responsible for preventing, pre-empting, and, if necessary, recovering from attacks by terrorists who employ nuclear, chemical, or biological weapons. The previous strict domestic/foreign boundary between the FBI and CIA is substantially dismantled, the Immigration & Naturalization Service and Border Patrol are fused and a color-coded scale of 'terrorist alerts' is in use. Thousands of foreign aliens are registered, photographed, fingerprinted, and deported when found to be residing illegally in the United States whilst educational institutions are compelled to certify the enrolled status of international students. In addition to these the so-called Patriot Act 2002 and a sweeping National Intelligence Act in late 2004 ease restrictions on the surveillance and detention of persons suspected of terrorist ties.

The elite's mobilization of public support is impressively choreographed. Bush and his most senior associates, especially the Vice President, regularly invoke the horrors of 9/11 and the necessity for a 'global war on terror'. The elite's program is couched in strong value terms: 'spreading democracy and freedom', 'an era of responsibility', 'leave no child behind', 'compassionate conservatism' etc. It is also dressed in nationalist garb, to wit, 'America's duty as the greatest and strongest country the world has ever seen'. Speeches by Bush, Cheney and principal cabinet members are carefully sequenced by the White House Communications Office to escalate public awareness of threats facing the country. Key elite members are made available for background briefings of local television news anchors to promote a nationally uniform and sympathetic media presentation of the case for forceful actions. Cable television channels, especially Rupert Murdoch's *Fox News Channel*, are given large dollops of Defense Department film footage for programs that demonize America's enemies and glorify America's military might, depict heroic sacrifices in places like Falujah, and rehearse victories in previous wars fought to 'defend freedom'. Television and radio talk-show hosts sympathetic to the Bush elite are regularly fed leaks and materials by the public relations offices of government departments, Republican Party national headquarters, and the array of conservative think tanks allied with the elite, so that talk-show hosts are better able to deride domestic critics and unreliable allies such as 'the French'.

Despite its tight integration and programmatic coherence, the Bush elite has not been without internal divisions, which the placement of trusted White House advisors in key departments and agencies after the 2004 election is intended to eliminate. A policy fault line between top-level actors located in the Pentagon and White House, who helped fashion the elite's program during the 1990s, and those who did not, such as Colin Powell, the State Department's professional diplomats, and key figures in the CIA, was apparent during the elite's first four years in power. Powell and his camp clashed with the 'unilater-alist' proclivities of the Pentagon leaders clustered around Rumsfeld and Wolfowitz, the National Security Council run by Rice, and Cheney and his advisers. After the election, however, Powell was replaced by Rice, a number of State Department diplomats resigned, the CIA's upper echelons were swept clean of skeptics by J. Porter Goss and his lieutenants, and the unilateralists appeared to obtain seamless control. Moreover, the plebiscitary 2004 election campaign, the interpretation of its outcome as a mandate for the 'war against terror', and a perception that the stakes in Iraq had become too large to permit 'throwing in the towel' muffled many of the elite's external critics and boosted Bush's public popularity.

Finally, although the Bush elite has gained sweeping control of the executive branch, Congress has been less reliably under its sway. Before the November 2002 mid-term elections the Democrats had knife-edge control of the Senate, while the Republicans, who controlled the House of Representatives, had to contend with diverse factions and constituencies that diluted their leaders' support of the White House. The victory won by Bush for his Senate supporters in the 2002 elections was so narrow that the elite's ability to get important parts of its domestic program through Congress remained limited. However, the plebiscitary campaign waged by Bush in the 2004 presidential election, coupled with an unscrupulous Republican re-districting of congressional House seats in Texas during 2003, produced substantial Republican majorities in both the House and Senate. From November 2004, in short, the Bush elite and its congressional and judicial allies have held full control of the federal government, as well as 34 of the 50 state governments.

An aberration?

Is the Bush elite an aberration in American politics that will prove to be of short duration? It was certainly possible to regard its initial ascendancy as the accidental result of the political train wreck that the 2000 presidential and congressional elections constituted. Not only did Al Gore fumble his presidential campaign, but the third-party candidacy of Ralph Nader and Florida's deeply flawed voting machinery combined to deprive Gore of an Electoral College majority that would have reflected his nationwide vote total. The Bush elite's accession to power in early 2001 thus appeared to result from a unique conjunction of electoral circumstances and the elite's fairly ruthless exploitation of it, especially in Florida. Even then, the elite had to rely on a friendly majority of Supreme Court Justices to gain power through a decision, in Bush v. Gore, that most constitutional scholars agreed was without sound basis. In short, the elite's initial hold on power could be seen as an accident and as wafer thin, with its program, which was largely concealed from the public during the 2000 campaign, lacking an electoral mandate. It was plausible to expect that in the normal cycles and practices of American politics the elite would be stymied and soon driven from office. It was simply an aberration.

Since the 9/11 attacks and the elite's political exploitation of them in the 2002 and 2004 elections, this assessment has become less plausible. The elite's long gestation and exceptional coherence, its concerted assault on the competing Democratic elite, and its use of power to entrench itself – breathtakingly manifest in the White House's tightened command of government departments and purge of dissenting officials after the 2004 election – could not be ignored. From virtually its first day in power, and despite its lack of an electoral mandate, the Bush elite began implementing its domestic and foreign programs, as I have summarized. It did so, however, in the face of Democratic opposition so intense that by the first week of September 2001 the elite's programs were judged by the bulk of political observers to be 'dead in the water'. But the 9/11 attacks on the following Tuesday gave Bush and his compatriots an unparalleled opportunity to claim 'wartime' leadership of a suddenly vulnerable United States. The trauma of 9/11, which was perhaps nowhere greater than inside the elite itself,[10] opened the way to stifling Democratic opposition. The attack on the Taliban regime in Afghanistan was launched a month later, and the decision to attack and destroy the Saddam Hussein regime in Iraq is believed to have been taken as early as May-June 2002, nearly a year before the Iraq invasion was launched and many months before a UN resolution sanctioning it was sought.[11] Invoking still fresh memories of the 9/11 attacks, Bush and his allies overpowered the Democrats in the 2002 mid-term elections, enlarging the Republican majority in the House of Representatives and winning enough seats in the Senate to gain Republican control. This was accomplished by 'nationalizing' election contests in a number of key states through a questioning of the patriotism and 'anti-terror' bone fides of Democratic candidates. A variant of this strategy produced a resounding victory in the 2004 presidential and congressional elections. With US forces confronting a violent insurgency in Iraq, the fortitude and toughness of John Kerry and other Democratic candidates were systematically portrayed as insufficient for the task of wartime leadership. Only Bush understood the true magnitude of the threats to America and only he had the will to counter them. The outcome, as recounted above, was a major strengthening of the Bush elite and its control of all branches of government.

Ominous world trends constitute a second reason for doubting that the Bush elite is simply an aberration. Strong centripetal pressures on the United States (and other Western countries) are here to stay. The flight of millions of people to the United States and to the West more generally from stagnating or deteriorating economic and political conditions in much of the non-Western world has been accelerating for at least two decades. The spread of easily deliverable and highly destructive weapons among states and fanatical political movements hostile to the United States – 'lethal globalization' – can probably not be contained, let alone reversed. These and other ominous trends – mounting environmental problems such as global warming and the HIV-Aids pandemic come most quickly to mind – imply that leonine elites not greatly dissimilar to the Bush elite may become the norm as the United States and other Western countries seek to counter these world trends.

Symptomatic of this prospect is the shift that has occurred among Democratic Party elite factions. Although Democratic leaders have not simply mimicked the Bush elite, neither have most of them desisted or dissented in any fundamental way from using force to counter external pressures on the United States. During the eight years of the Clinton administration, as Dana Priest has observed, 'the military slowly, without public scrutiny or debate, came to surpass its civilian leaders in resources and influence around the world'.[12] Spending on diplomacy continued the decline that began in the 1970s, while military spending increased, as it had done massively during the preceding Reagan and Bush Senior administrations. Tasks that were once civilian responsibilities were assigned to the military: clearing landmines; disrupting drug trafficking; countering terrorism; disaster relief; even allowing the military's powerful four-star regional commanders-in-chief to conduct diplomacy. In 1998, Clinton initiated sustained bombing in Iraq's 'no-fly zones' and under heavy pressure from the elite that was gathering around George W. Bush he made 'regime change' in Iraq official US policy. Madeline Albright, while serving as Clinton's Ambassador to the UN and arguing for military intervention to stop the bloodletting in Bosnia, had famously exclaimed to a reluctant General Colin Powell, then Chairman of the Joint Chiefs of Staff: 'What's the point of having this superb military that you're always talking about if we can't use it?'.[13] In 1999, as

Clinton's Secretary of State, Albright championed 'coercive diplomacy' against Slobodan Milosevic's campaign of ethnic cleansing in Kosovo. Without approval by the UN Security Council, Clinton initiated the 78-day bombing of Yugoslavia that brought about Milosevic's downfall.

Following the 9/11 attacks, every Democratic senator and all but one Democrat in the House voted for the joint congressional resolution authorizing Bush to use military force against 'individuals and nations that planned, authorized, committed or aided the terrorist attacks'. A majority of Democratic senators voted for the October 2002 congressional resolution that authorized Bush to use force in Iraq, although a majority of House Democrats voted against it. During their 2004 presidential campaign, John Kerry and John Edwards criticized the Bush administration for rushing into war in Iraq, for badly mishandling Iraq's subsequent occupation, and for failures in reconstructing Afghanistan and hunting for Osama bin Laden. But they did not disavow their Senate votes for the Bush policies, they pledged to 'stay the course' in Iraq and the wider 'war on terror', and the central thrust of their campaign was playing up Kerry's military experience and toughness.

Several long-term developments in American society are a third reason, or set of reasons, for regarding the Bush elite as more than an aberration. There is space to highlight just two of these developments. The first is the spread of employment insecurities. The strict need for many jobs is nebulous and uncertain; the proportion of orderly and predictable careers shrinks and that of chaotic job patterns grows. It is widely sensed that the sudden obsolescence of a particular skill may occur at any point in a career, as evidenced by the many careers that are cut short ten, fifteen, or even twenty years before normal retirement age. The political ramification is that employment insecurities contribute to a crisis of morale among citizens and voters. Demoralization – the loss of individual morale and loss of respect for the economic, political and social order that generates insecurities – becomes widespread. Demoralized people are prone to seek essentially magical 'salvations' for their plights, salvations of the kind that religious fundamentalists promise. As has been evident in recent electoral contests, religious fundamentalists are now a force that American political elites must reckon with and try to harness. Competing for voters of one or another fundamentalist persuasion require, however, that elites traffic in the language of absolutes, portraying themselves as protectors of 'right values' and their opponents as bearers of moral darkness. Contests of a plebiscitary and polarized character are a consequence, and in such campaigns an elite tightly organized around a leader who invokes a sense of overwhelming crisis, the need for a closer integration of a purer community, and the superiority of his or her instincts is advantaged.[14]

The second development is the swollen size of the American political class. Prosperity and the expansion of higher education have increased the proportion of citizens who are knowledgeable about political developments and whose circumstances – for some quite leisured, for others quite insecure – incline or impel them to engage in politics on a regular basis. Prime examples are professional social movement organizers who make careers out of crystallizing and representing mass discontents and interests. Other examples are self-appointed fundamentalist religious leaders who achieve political prominence and influence by demanding a return to 'basic values'. Still others are professional campaign consultants steeped in manipulating electorates for handsome incomes. The number of persons with major career stakes in electoral and lobbying outcomes becomes very large. Consider that the winning side in a presidential election disposes of 7,000 reasonably plum political appointments and it can affect the career fortunes of approximately 10,000 political consultants, more than 20,000 full-time legislative staff, and close to 100,000 policy advocates and registered lobbyists. It is not surprising, therefore, that electoral contests are struggles between armadas of political class members for whom the outcomes have pivotal personal implications. As the deeply divisive struggle that followed the 2000 presidential election and the viciousness of the 2004 presidential campaign illustrate, top political leaders have great difficulty resisting the pressures from these armadas to win at any cost – to 'go down and dirty'.[15]

When asking if the Bush elite is more than an aberration it is also important to remember that the personalities, choices and mentalities of elites do much to shape the contours of politics. They alter political agendas and institutions in ways that make the *status quo ante* irretrievable. They create foreign and domestic enemies who outlive them and economic problems that encumber their successors. Such lasting changes are likely to be the Bush elite's legacy. Even if its *National Security Strategy* proves in time to be more bark than bite, the *Strategy* has altered the assessments and actions of the elite's opponents at home and abroad. Likewise, even if the Bush elite's zealous tax cuts are reversed, they have created a mammoth budget deficit that will constrain domestic policies for many years to come. In sum, is there anyone who does not think that the current and foreseeable contours of American politics would be significantly different, even without 9/11, had the Bush elite failed to gain power in 2000? As a corollary, is it likely that the Bush elite's successors in power will depart in major ways from its tight integration, programmatic coherence, secrecy, and bare-knuckled political actions? It is worth considering, in conclusion, what answers to these questions may portend for America's liberal democracy.

A more elitist democracy

It is plausible to think that the Bush elite alters the balance between American democracy's vertical and horizontal dimensions. As Giovanni Sartori explains:

> Politics has to do, in the main and most of the time, with subordination, superordination, and coordination ... I shall call this the vertical dimension of politics. Politics also has a horizontal dimension, but this dimension becomes salient only in democracies ... Public opinion, electoral democracy, participatory democracy, referendum democracy – all represent a horizontal implementation and diffusion of democracy.[16]

American democracy's horizontal dimension has always been pronounced. Tocqueville thought nineteenth-century America virtually unique in this respect. Strong populist movements and reforms during the decades before World War One and in the 1920s were further evidence for his thesis. The civil rights, women's, and student movements of the 1960s–1970s, which levied strong demands for greater democratic access and participation, blazed a trail that movements throughout the Western world followed. But American democracy's historically robust horizontal dimension sits uneasily with the Bush elite's tight integration, programmatic zeal, penchant for secrecy, and reliance on force – all of which are manifestations of Sartori's 'subordination, superordination, and coordination'. First, an increasingly centralized and secretive military-security apparatus bulks large, with many of its actions receiving little scrutiny and its needs and recommendations receiving much deference. Second, the ease with which the Bush elite is able to mould public support for its 'war on terror' and its invasion of Iraq indicates greater verticality in American politics. This molding of public support has many aspects, but one of the most important is the elite's careful orchestration of commercial broadcast media in a strongly nationalist, even jingoist, direction. Third, the Bush elite is adept in sanitizing its use of force in Afghanistan and Iraq. The Pentagon succeeds in minimizing media coverage of combat casualties and 'collateral' civilian casualties and property damage. For example, of 772 stories about the Iraq invasion aired by the prime time news shows of the four main TV networks from the first missile strike on Baghdad on 19 March 2003 through the fall of Tikrit on 14 April, just 81 of them showed US military casualties, only 61 contained images of civilian casualties, and only 190 depicted property damage.[17] The Pentagon allows no media coverage of soldiers' coffins returning to the United States or of the steady streams of military ambulances bearing grievously wounded soldiers to US hospitals in Germany, Washington and other locations. A further Pentagon media control measure is the 'embedding' of journalists in combat units, which results in dramatic ground level reporting but contains few assessments of how the overall military effort is going. Fourth, and perhaps as a consequence of all this, popular protests against the elite's actions and policies – the most important of which has been the attack on Iraq – have little size or political punch.

Some theorists and analysts of contemporary democracies – of whom Sartori is probably the most influential – worry that the balance between their vertical and horizontal dimensions has tilted too strongly toward the horizontal dimension. There is an excess of popular inputs and pressures, so that democracies are becoming rudderless. Those who hold power devote themselves to placating popular demands while losing the independence that is a prerequisite for tackling multifaceted issues, the complexities of which lie beyond the grasp of mass publics. 'The deregulation of democracy has gone too far', writes Fareed Zakaria, so that we now have 'an unwieldy system, unable to govern or command the respect of people; although none would dare to speak ill of present-day democracy, most people instinctively sense a problem'.[18] Zakaria's prescription, which is in line with Sartori's, is 'that those with immense power in our societies embrace their responsibilities, lead, and set standards that are not only legal, but moral. Without this inner stuffing, democracy will become an empty shell, not simply inadequate but potentially dangerous, bringing with it the erosion of liberty, the manipulation of freedom, and the decay of a common life'.[19] Put somewhat differently, as G. Lowell Field and I did 25 years ago, 'elites in the developed societies desperately need to reconstitute a self-consciously elitist frame of reference'.[20]

Is the Bush elite the prescription that Sartori, Zakaria and others who worry about democracy from this standpoint have called for? Bush and his tightly knit associates constitute a ruling, self-conscious elite. There is, of course, widespread questioning of whether they are an 'elite' in the term's qualitative sense of 'the best' or 'the select'. Doubts about that are evident in the enormous attention paid to the adequacy of Bush's intellectual and other qualifications for the presidency and in the suspicion that Bush and his associates are but a cabal that has hijacked the government by systematically misleading the public. Nevertheless, an important consequence of the Bush elite's ascendancy, form and actions is a much greater awareness of the centrality of elites in shaping America's fate and, thus, the need to inspect closely the quality of any elite seeking to replace them.

Does the Bush elite presage the character of American ruling elites henceforth? Looking for an answer, it is worth recalling one of Vilfredo Pareto's *dicta*:

> The need of the weak for protection is constant and universal, and seeks fulfillment at the hands of whoever possesses power. In a period when centrifugal forces prevail, this protection will be sought for at the hands of certain outstandingly powerful men: the great lords and magnates. When centripetal forces are dominant, the central government will be called on to provide it. Whenever circumstances turn in favor of this second, centripetal phase, a pre-existing central government, or a central authority new both in form and substance, asserts itself sooner or later. Either by sudden violence or by protracted effort it subdues the dominant oligarchy and sets about the task of concentrating all sovereignty in itself.[21]

In his *Treatise on General Sociology* (1915), Pareto held that 'in international relations, beneath all the surface tinsel of humanitarian and ethnical declamation, what prevails is force alone'.[22] When war or the threat of war impinges, lion-like individuals and groups rise to power. The ruling elite becomes more bellicose and prone to use force. It appeals to patriotic, religious, and xenophobic sentiments to mobilize mass support for the reliance on force. This describes, well enough I believe, current and foreseeable US circumstances and their political ramifications. Centripetal pressures on the United States are unlikely to lessen; on the contrary, there is every reason to expect their increase. It is, consequently, hard to conceive of responses by future American ruling elites that will be less hierarchical and more pacific than the Bush elite's.

What are this scenario's implications for America's liberal democracy? A consensus among elites about fundamental democratic game rules and the worth of established democratic institutions is the *sine qua non* of liberal democracy. Only where there is such elite consensus are restrained political competitions, which are the hallmarks of liberal democracies, possible. This postulate is not in itself controversial, although some of its implications are unsettling to exuberant democrats. One such implication is that it is elite cooperation that keeps explosive and potentially ruinous issues and conflicts from being fully expressed. Bluntly put, liberal democracy requires regular political policing by an internally consensual and mutually accommodative elite stratum. For this to work, elites must be satisfied, individually and collectively, that they can realize their divergent interests through the existing liberal democratic order. As Pareto might say, elites must have ample opportunities for mutual back scratching. In this respect, and like any other kind of political regime, a liberal democracy is at base an arrangement among elites. It differs from other regimes primarily in the representative practices and political protections on which elites have at some earlier time agreed and which they sustain because it is in their collective interest to do so.[23]

The danger is that the Bush elite and succeeding ruling elites will upset this apple cart. The Bush elite acts with a political zeal, even a brutality, which injures wider elite comity. This was evident in its single-minded drive for power in all phases of the 2000 presidential election, in the way it 'nationalized' pivotal Senate and House contests in the 2002 mid-term elections, and in its stoking of voter fears to secure re-election in 2004. Many politicians and political observers sense that these actions test the limits of acceptable and customary behavior in American politics – that they push the envelope of elite probity and restraint too hard. To this extent, the Bush elite threatens the elite foundations of liberal democracy in the United States.

Notes

1 J. Higley, U. Hoffmann-Lange, C. Kadushin and G. Moore, 'Elite integration in stable democracies', *European Sociological Review*, 1991, vol. 7, pp. 35–53. See also W. Bürklin and H. Rebenstorf, *Eliten in Deutschland*, Opladen: Leske und Budrich, 1997; T. Gulbrandsen and F. Engelstad, *Norske makteliter*, Oslo: Gyldendal, 2002.

2 S. E. Finer, 'Introduction', in *V. Pareto: Sociological Writings*, New York: Praeger, 1965, p. 67.

3 See, inter alia, J. Mann, *Rise of the Vulcans: The History of Bush's War Cabinet*, New York: Viking, 2004; S. Halper and J. Clark, *America Alone: The Neo-Conservatives and the Global Order*, New York: Cambridge University Press, 2004; G. Hodgson, *More Equal Than Others: America from Nixon to the New Century*, Princeton, NJ: The Century Foundation, 2004, esp. pp. 29–60.

4 Among portraits of the elite's composition and workings between 2001 and early 2004 are B. Woodward, *Bush at War*, New York: Simon & Schuster, 2002, and *Plan of Attack*, New York: Simon & Schuster, 2004; D. Frum, *The Right Man: The Surprise Presidency of George W. Bush*, New York: Random House, 2003; R. Suskind, *The Price of Loyalty: George W. Bush, the White House, and the Education of Paul O'Neill*, New York: Simon & Schuster, 2004; R. A. Clarke, *Against All Enemies: Inside America's War on Terror*, New York: The Free Press, 2004.

5 K. Phillips, *American Dynasty: Aristocracy, Fortune, and the Politics of Deceit in the House of Bush*, New York: Viking, 2004; M. Lind, *Made in Texas: George W. Bush and the Southern Takeover of American Politics*, New York: Basic Books, 2003.

6 Mann, *Rise of the Vulcans.*

7 Frum, *The Right Man.*

8 W. Kristol and R. Kagan, *Rebuilding America's Defenses: Strategy, Forces and Resources for a New Century*, Washington, DC: Project for the New American Century, 2000; R. Kagan, *Of Paradise and Power: America and Europe in the New World Order*, New York: Knopf, 2003.

9 N. Lemann, 'After Iraq', *The New Yorker*, 17 and 24 February 2003, pp. 70–6; D. Wurmser, *Tyranny's Ally: America's Failure to Defeat Saddam Hussein*, Washington, DC: AEI Press, 1999.

10 See, e.g., Woodward, *Bush At War*; Frum, *The Right Man.*

11 Woodward, *Plan of Attack*, pp. 1–4.

12 D. Priest, *The Mission: Waging War and Keeping Peace with America's Military*, New York: Norton, 2004, p. 42.

13 Ibid., p. 52.

14 R. O. Paxton, *The Anatomy of Fascism*, New York: Knopf, 2004, pp. 219–20.

15 J. Tapper, *Down and Dirty: The Plot to Steal the Presidency*, New York: Little Brown, 2001; G. Palast, *The Best Democracy Money Can Buy*, London: Pluto, 2002; S. E. Schier, *You Call This an Election? America's Peculiar Democracy*, Washington, DC: Georgetown University Press, 2003.

16 G. Sartori, *The Theory of Democracy Revisited, Part I: The Contemporary Debate*, Chatham, NJ: Chatham House Publishers, 1987, p. 131.

17 *Media Monitor*, 2003, vol. 17, pp. 7–8.

18 F. Zakaria, *The Future of Freedom: Liberal Democracy at Home and Abroad*, New York: Norton, 2003, pp. 240–1.

19 Ibid., p. 256.

20 G. Lowell Field and J. Higley, *Elitism*, London: Routledge, 1980, p. 130.

21 V. Pareto, *The Transformation of Democracy*, New Brunswick, NJ: Transaction Publishers, 1984 [1921], p. 47.

22 V. Pareto, *Treatise on General Sociology*, New York: Harcourt, Brace and Co., 1935 [1915], paras 2180, 2274–7.

23 J. Higley and M. Burton, 'Elite settlements and the taming of politics', *Government and Opposition*, 1998, vol. 33, pp. 98–115.

10 Anti-Americanism and the major foundations

Inderjeet Parmar

The major American foundations – especially the 'Big Three' (Ford, Rockefeller, and Carnegie) – have been linked with controversies over Americanism, anti-Americanism and un-Americanism almost from their very beginnings. Right-wing Americans, in particular, accuse the foundations of being anti- or un-American. Others argue that the foundations have effectively promoted Americanism and/or opposed anti-Americanism. This chapter shows that – rather than being un- or anti-American – the major foundations have been vehicles for promoting, at different times, 'liberal-internationalist' and 'neoliberal' Americanism at home and abroad, and for challenging specific political tendencies and elites around the world for being 'anti-American'. Today, the Ford, Carnegie and Rockefeller foundations promote Americanism principally through their support of globalization, and better understanding of Islamic societies and belief systems, while the German Marshall Fund of the United States (GMFUS) specializes in combating anti-Americanism by promoting transatlantic unity.

Virtually all of these actions were and are carried out either in line with dominant thinking among US economic and political elites and/or in direct concert with official foreign policy makers. The Big Three foundations are part of an east coast foreign policy establishment that is globalist, expansionist, and imperial in orientation, in line with the overall objectives of the American state since World War Two.[1] Despite their declarations to the contrary – that they are non-political, non-ideological and independent of the American state[2] – the major American foundations are ideological and political: they mobilize intellectual power to support American foreign policies and they put 'knowledge to work' for the American national security state. Their actions are best understood in Gramscian terms: they are builders of an intellectual consensus that spans America and strategic regions of the globe, elements of an historic bloc of international corporations and banks, official state policy makers, and Ivy League universities, supports that American global domination.[3]

This chapter begins by discussing controversies surrounding the foundations' (and general definitional problems concerning) Americanism, anti-Americanism and un-Americanism. Second, the chapter examines the foundations' origins, aims, worldviews and operating procedures. Third, it considers the elite backgrounds of foundation trustees, showing their connections with the east coast establishment and today's 'globalizers'. Finally, the chapter turns to the promotion by foundations of (historically) liberal and (contemporary) 'soft' neoliberal versions of Americanism and examines three cases of how foundations challenge anti-American elites and tendencies abroad.

Foundations and anti-Americanism or un-Americanism

The Big Three foundations' loyalty to American core values has been questioned. In 1915, the (congressional) Walsh Commission investigated the charge that the foundations were undemocratic concentrations of corporate-political power.[4] During the 1950s, the McCarthyite Reece Commission tried, unsuccessfully, to demonstrate that the Ford-Rockefeller-Carnegie complex aided international communism by backing such groups in America and abroad. Today, right-wingers assert the un- and anti-American character of the foundations. For example, Malcolm Hoenlein, executive vice chairman of the Conference of Presidents of Major American Jewish Organizations, has called for a congressional investigation of Ford Foundation grants to Palestinian NGOs.[5] Others charge Ford for funding Mexican-Americans' anti-Americanism.[6] In fact, a cursory web search under 'Ford Foundation and anti-Americanism' yields several pages of right-wing websites railing against Ford's anti-Semitism, anti-Zionism, pro-terrorist, and generally anti-American grant-making.

The very idea of Americanism, un-Americanism and anti-Americanism is the subject of great controversy. As Hofstadter wrote long ago, America does not have an ideology, it *is* one;[7] its meaning is politically and culturally contested; it changes over time, ebbing and flowing from liberal to illiberal interpretations.

Anti-Americanism, Americanism and un-Americanism

The struggle over the definition of Americanism is concerned with power: the definition that prevails determines the underlying assumptions of state policies, and how 'anti-Americanism' and 'un-Americanism' are acted upon. The favoured definition is used to reward allegiance and punish disloyalty. The Big Three foundations, and other 'pro-Americans', tend to see anti-Americanism in very broad terms, though rarely as caused by US foreign policy, as is shown below.

For some, anti-Americanism is a form of racism, 'the anti-Semitism of the [European] intellectuals'.[8] That is, Americans are viewed with 'racial' prejudice in a manner identical to that utilized by anti-Semites in relation to Jews: Americans rule the world, determine all outcomes, and promote their own interests at the expense of others. They are therefore to be openly criticized, vilified, and expelled. The problem with this particular argument, however, is that critical Americans often advance such arguments about their own country.[9] H. L. Mencken, noted, for example, that his fellow-Americans were 'the most timorous, snivelling, poltroonish, ignominious mob of serfs and goose steppers ever gathered under one flag in Christendom since the end of the Middle

Ages'.[10] Clearly, this is not anti-American prejudice akin to anti-Semitism. Yet such labelling has great coercive power: it may easily be used to silence legitimate criticism.[11]

Another way of explaining anti-Americanism is as a form of cultural snobbery on the part of European and other older civilizations, resulting, in part, from the loss of European power after 1945.[12] Clearly, snobbery and resentment are a part of the cultural prejudice against American power, but it must also be stressed that anti-American feeling may be caused by anti-foreigner xenophobia in the United States, which sees other peoples as inferior and suffering from inexorable decay.[13] Relatedly, some contend that anti-Americanism is an unjust label, applied by American elites and pro-Americans, for justified criticisms of American corporate, governmental or military behaviour abroad.[14] Still others suggest that anti-Americanism is a *psychological* disorder, a rejection of the father/leader by the son, an infantile response by dysfunctional individuals.[15]

A more historical-sociological view suggests that what often manifests itself as anti-Americanism may more accurately be termed 'anti-modernism' – an anxious reaction to rapid cultural and economic change.[16] What is generally agreed upon, however, is that the label is a pejorative one: few wear the badge of anti-Americanism with pride. Anti-Americanism is, therefore, a multifaceted and complex phenomenon and it is important that its varied meanings are explicated. Attitudes that may appear, at face value, to be based on prejudice often mask a deeper set of critiques about the nature of American society and its foreign policies.

Relatedly, of course, anti-Americanism is a variant of *un*-Americanism. Domestically, political forces/movements tend to apply the label 'un-American' to their opponents, 'unpatriotic' violators of American traditional values. Just as the 100 per cent Americans – such as the Ku Klux Klan, American Legion, and the McCarthyites – label liberal-leftist forces un-American so do, in a subtle way, the Foundation-liberals label their enemies on the left and right as 'un-American'. The precise interpretation of Americanism at any one period of time is politically contested; its application in everyday politics and government, involves fierce partisan debate.[17] Liberal east coast philanthropic foundations, therefore, defined the world through the lens of their particular definition of Americanism, and it is to these institutions that attention now turns.

The 'Big Three' foundations: origins, aims and worldviews

Philanthropic foundations are key institutions in American society, bolstering (right-of-centre) liberal values and institutions, and are intimately connected with modernization. They are key agencies for problem-identification and change-management, placing strategically targeted funds behind innovative techniques to solve age-old problems both within and outside the United States such as poverty and economic underdevelopment.[18]

Founded in the main at the turn of the twentieth century, the Big Three foundations owe their origins to massive industrial fortunes, a phenomenon of the Progressive era of mass immigration, urbanization and industrialization.[19] The United States was transformed into an industrial, urban, and ethnically mixed society, rapidly losing its agricultural, rural, and White Anglo-Saxon Protestant (WASP) character. Such change frightened American elites who sought to develop institutions (private and public) that would manage change to preserve the capitalistic and liberal character of American society – especially to avoid social chaos and the threat of left-wing ideologies, as espoused by the Socialist Party and the Industrial Workers of the World.[20] Additionally, America's rapidly-expanding population, status in the world economy, and victory over Spain in the 1898 war, turned east coast elites' attention to world affairs and a growing awareness of the need to develop political and executive institutions capable of exercising power in international relations.[21]

Progressives proliferated a variety of educational, professional, scientific and reform organizations dedicated to 'public service' and the 'national interest'. Such organizations were 'para-states' – private institutions that were simultaneously 'state-oriented'. Consequently, they built alliances with the federal executive branch – the state – and also sought to mobilize public opinion behind their own worldview. Effectively, they bypassed electoral processes, the main political parties, and legislatures at state and national levels, because progressives considered them parochial and corrupt.[22]

In important respects, in promoting globalization, and in claiming to ameliorate its negative effects on the worlds poorest, the foundations follow their domestic experience. In the United States, they had first tried to *nationalize* the country, to strengthen it as a national entity, to transform its parochial consciousness into an American one, to 'Americanize' the immigrant, to strengthen the federal executive branch at the expense of the parochially-based Congress, to concentrate power in elite/expert hands as opposed to mass-oriented populist institutions dominated by party machines, and challenge inward-looking 'isolationism' in favour of internationalism. In doing this at home, the foundations developed and adapted 'modernizing' strategies for the world: international government/institutions, later global governance; economic and political modernization, that mirrored the development trajectories of the West to be promoted in the Third World; Americanizing the world's elites; undermining national sovereignties in favour of international arrangements/globalization/global governance. What we observe is a domestic model, followed by an international model for the cold war era, and then a global model – one that works through non-state actors within and between states in a more consistent and comprehensive way – from the late 1980s. In each era, the foundations have their definition of Americanism as the basis of their activities; that also defines the forces in the United States they consider un-American e.g., isolationists, McCarthyites, left-liberals/communists, and anti-globalizers; those they consider pro-American, i.e., the elite universities, think tanks, research institutes, and publicity organizations, and elements of the US state; those they think are anti-Americans in the world, for example, Indonesia's

President Sukharno, and back policies that foster pro-Americanism or temper anti-Americanism.

The Carnegie Corporation (CC) owes its inspiration to Andrew Carnegie, who made his wealth through the forerunner corporation of United States Steel, the world's first billion-dollar company.[23] The CC was formed in 1911 as a non-political organization that was prohibited from 'propaganda' and empowered only to provide 'information and understanding'.[24] It had an endowment of US$135 million.[25] The Rockefeller Foundation, founded in 1913, promoted nothing less than the welfare of mankind, using scientific methods both to distribute its funds and to assist in solving America's and the world's most intractable problems.[26] The Ford Foundation, though founded in 1936, began its modern career in 1951, with an endowment – at US$3 billion – that dwarfed its older counterparts.[27] Despite its later emergence, Ford continued the tradition of scientific philanthropy pioneered by Rockefeller and Carnegie.

All three foundations advance a philosophy of human capital development to justify their activities,[28] viewing education as the means of constructing human capital: people with 'brains' and potential for leadership in solving social problems and assisting American foreign policy.[29] The foundations' philosophy is pragmatic and utilitarian, funding empirical research to generate knowledge for practical use by policy makers, to 'put knowledge to work'. They champion positivistic social science in order to apply the benefits to society and politics, to solve the problems of poverty, crime and the urban slum.[30] The foundations are elitist, convinced of their superior wisdom and their duty to alleviate society's ills in the manner they see fit – through certified experts – without the necessity of consulting those upon whose behalf they claim to act.[31]

These are the principles that motivate foundations' behaviour within the United States: elitist, technocratic, utilitarian, 'scientific'. These principles were, and are, realized by the investment of large funds in a range of individuals, universities, think tanks, and policy research institutes from the cold war period to the era of globalization.

The foundations aimed at building up a network of key institutions connected to each other through fellowships and scholarships for advanced research and training either at US universities, such as Chicago, Harvard and Yale, or at other key elements of a nascent international network, such as the London School of Economics in Britain. Disciplines such as economics, cultural anthropology, international relations, public administration and sociology were developed in such directions by the foundations with important effects in academia and public policy.[32]

It is clear, therefore, that the overall world outlook of the foundations strongly favours a strategy of scientific, technical, economic, political and administrative modernization at home and abroad, based on a vibrant university sector that champions utilitarian conceptions of the practical role of knowledge in society. They are fiercely independent of the state in their rhetoric, valuing the age-old voluntarist tradition of private, charitable and other action – public service – yet completely state-oriented in their mindset: they see the problems of the state as their own, and seek to assist the modernization of the state itself in order to meet the challenges of a changing social and world order. In foreign affairs, foundation leaders were often referred to as 'liberal internationalists': this actually meant that they were 'nationalist-internationalists', patriots who believed that American national interests could best be pursued in the context of a world-system of international institutions (UN, IMF, World Bank), under the enlightened leadership of the United States.

Today, Americanism is effectively promoted through the foundations' support of globalization: as scholars argue, the dominant structures and processes of the world are global in scope, and the United States is the world's leading globalizer. For Thomas Friedman, globalization is the world's 'super story', the framework for world development, and the United States heads the system.[33] The opponents of globalization, and critics of America's war on Iraq, are designated anti-American: those who, as Friedman notes, live in 'failing states in the Muslim and Third World … [who] do not share our values … [and] … resent America's influence over their lives, politics, children … and they often blame America for the failure of their societies to master modernity'. The left, argues Friedman, hates America for 'its free-market capitalism, death penalty, and globalization'.[34] Criticisms of American society, government or culture, within the mindset of the national security state, have seen as 'anti-American'.

The foundation elite

According to a former Ford Foundation staff director 'foundations are at or near the centre of gravity of the American Establishment'.[35] Arnove argues that the foundations represent a class-divided and elitist society, as their trustees are unaccountable and unrepresentative.[36] The statistics below demonstrate that foundation trustees are recruited from the east coast elite and are intimately interconnected with other influential institutions – large corporations, prestigious universities, the American state, and US-led international institutions. Far from being part of a pluralistic system of interest group competition and independence from the state, the foundations can justifiably be classified as part of the power elite of the United States.

According to Whitaker, more than half the trustees from the thirteen largest foundations were educated at Harvard, Princeton or Yale. Racially and ethnically, they were almost all white, aged between 55 and 65 years, and members of either the Episcopalian or Presbyterian denominations.[37]

Analysis of the boards of trustees of the foundations demonstrates that one third of trustees held upper-class social club memberships (listed in *Who's Who*, which is based entirely on self-reported information and, therefore, understates the actual position). More significantly, one third of the trustees of Carnegie, Russell Sage, and Rockefeller Foundations were members of the same New York City club, the Century Association, a prime location for informally discussing the nation's business.[38]

Between 40 to 47 per cent of Ford, Rockefeller and Carnegie trustees held high positions within the federal government, including cabinet secretaries and assistant secretaries, representing further opportunities for the consensus-construction.[39] Bipartisanship is indeed one of the hallmarks of 'establishment'.[40]

Colwell's examination of the interconnections of foundation boards and grant-recipient organizations shows extensive overlaps. The elitist Council on Foreign Relations (CFR) is the most thoroughly interconnected with the foundations. In 1961, the CFR received one quarter of its annual income from the Big Three foundations. At the same time, on the CFR's membership rolls were 10 of the 14 Carnegie, 10 of 15 Ford, and 12 of 20 Rockefeller, trustees.[41] The CFR was also interlocked with serving government officials:[42] from 1945 to 1972, 45 per cent of top foreign policy officials were Council members.[43] There is indeed a 'revolving door' between key elements of the establishment in the United States.

Since the 1980s, the foundations have diversified their leadership, recruiting more minorities (up from 6 per cent to 24 per cent in the Ford Foundation), women (up from 13 per cent to 18 per cent at Ford) and overseas members (including the president of Nigeria, General Obasanjo). Ford's Susan Berresford is the first woman to head one of the Big Three. Overall, however, women and minorities constitute only 14 per cent of Big Three trustees.[44]

Additionally, the RF's trustees have been joined by Mamphela Ramphele, the World Bank's managing director, and by David de Ferranti, the Bank's vice-president (Latin America and Caribbean Office). At the end of 2001, RF also announced the recruitment of Fernando Henrique Cardoso, the former two-time president of Brazil and neoliberal economic reformer, and of Thomas J. Healey, former managing director of Goldman Sachs, senior fellow at the Kennedy School of Business, Harvard, and President Ronald Reagan's assistant secretary to the US Treasury.[45]

The social composition and worldview of the foundations, as outlined above, suggests something of the flavour of their domestic and foreign activities and programmes. The trustees are/were, and see/saw themselves, as modernizing elites, armed with expert knowledge and understanding of American society and the world and a sense of their destiny, leading a movement for modernization. The promotion of their vision of 'Americanism' is, of course, central to their goals and strategies, as is the marginalization and/or defeat of its antitheses: foreign 'anti-Americanism'. It is to their promotion of liberal and neoliberal versions of Americanism that the following section of the chapter is devoted.

Promoting Americanism through neoliberal globalization

In the era of America's *rise* to globalism, the foundations constructed and promoted, at home and abroad, *liberal-internationalist* versions of Americanism. In the era of *globalization*, they promote a 'transnationalized' Americanism that

backs the neoliberal project but seeks to blunt its harsher edges.[46] The foundations are not (necessarily) neo-conservative supporters of George W. Bush,
however, as even a cursory glance at the website of the Carnegie Endowment for
International Peace (CEIP) shows.[47] Overall, however, the foundations today are
replicating their historical strategies at home and abroad; they seek to protect the
existing system of power by engaging in activities to ameliorate the negative
consequences of that very system – the same system of which they are a central
component and beneficiaries.[48] At the beginning of the twentieth century, the
foundations targeted the alleviation of domestic poverty and the slum – brought
on by American urbanization and capitalist industrialization; today they focus on
the worldwide social fallout of neoliberal globalization strategies.[49] In the cold
war, they backed efforts to stem anti-Americanism; today, in the war on terror,
they continue to do the same.

The IMF and the World Bank are widely considered, along with the US
Treasury, to be the nerve centres of the 'Washington Consensus', the motors of
neoliberal globalization.[50] The former two organizations – formed at Bretton
Woods in 1944–1945 with full support from the Rockefeller/Carnegie foundations – continue to garner sponsorship and sustenance from east coast
philanthropy. As is shown below, the World Bank has received grants from the
Ford Foundation, while David Rockefeller has been a consistent IMF stalwart.[51]

As was historically the case when American foundations often carried out
programmes that the state would not or could not, it is also the case today – with
the dramatic loss of state legitimacy associated with the rise of free market liberalism – that non-state actors are scurrying to perform key functions. The
proliferation of domestic and international non-governmental organizations
(NGOs and INGOs), the rise of the 'third sector', is partly explained by the 'roll-
back' of state social support programmes in the wake of Reaganomics and
Thatcherism. Offsetting the fallout of increasing gaps between rich and poor has
become a key foundation task, especially by backing 'pivotal institutions that can
shape behaviour away from risk factors and *dangerous directions* [i.e., anti-
Americanism and anti-globalization protests]', according to the Carnegie
Corporation.[52] Part of the solution is seen to lie in 'promoting democracy,
market reform and the creation of civil institutions …'[53], that is, in the neoliberal project itself. Carnegie actively promoted, during the 1990s, 'Partnerships
for Global Development', headed by prestigious academics, scientists and politicians, that promoted liberalization of markets as a core concern. Contrary to
Peet *et al.*, neoliberal globalization's foundation-backers do not see a wide gulf
between neoliberalism and its critics: by their social amelioration policies, they
hope to promote the market *and* social justice.[54]

In the same vein, the Rockefeller Foundation declared in 1985 that social
inequality reduction lay at the heart of its economic developmental concerns.
Yet, just prior to this, due to the rise in anti-American sentiment around the
world, the Rockefeller Foundation had reduced its overseas personnel from 136
to just 34.[55] In 1999, the incoming president of RF, former vice-chancellor of
the University of Sussex, Gordon Conway, stressed that the foundation had two

priorities: 'first, to understand the processes of change spurred by globalization and second, to find ways that the poor and excluded will not be left out'. Inherent in both foundations' attitudes is the taken-for-granted neoliberal character of globalization.[56] Therefore, it is unsurprising that the third of what some may call an 'unholy trinity', the Ford Foundation, granted the Hudson Institute, a conservative think tank, US$150,000 to assist 'economists and officials of Estonia, Latvia, and Lithuania [to] develop plans to transform their economies and integrate them into the world economy'.[57] To examine the consequences of market reforms, the Rockefeller Foundation administered a project, at a cost of US$150,000, towards 'an exploration on trade liberalization and its impacts on poor farmers'.[58]

The American foundations are important supporters of the key engines of the globalization process, as their records show. For example, Ford awarded a grant of US$400,000 to the World Bank to fund the latter's 'Consultative Group to Assist the Poorest to develop the capacity of microfinance institutions and improve member donor practices in supporting microfinance'.[59] Microfinance is a strategy for lifting into the marketplace those too poor to get loans from mainstream commercial banks. In 1999, RF granted US$800,000 to the World Bank's Economic Development Institute for economic growth acceleration strategies.[60] Further Ford grants were made in 2003 to institutions that try to build interconnections between large Western corporations and small enterprises in the Third World.[61] During the 1990s, the head of the Rockefeller family – David Rockefeller – offered unconditional support for the International Monetary Fund's global programmes: without the IMF, the world would return to the economic crises of the 1930s and the threat of global economic and military conflicts.[62] A grant of US$250,000 aimed to finance 'strategic workshops and meetings among Asian government officials, academics and civil society groups on the governance of the World Trade Organization', another motor of globalization processes.[63]

The American foundations are globalizing forces in their own right too – historically and today. They consciously create, finance and strengthen global knowledge networks between universities, think tanks, research centres, government agencies, and philanthropies.[64] The International Network for Strategic Philanthropy (INSP) – set up by the German Bertelsmann Foundation – with US foundations' support – encourages the global spread of philanthropy. The (American) Philanthropy Initiative, Inc., aims to ensure the 'strategic and systematic investment of private philanthropic resources to address complex, interconnected manifestations of chronic underdevelopment [including] escalating ethnic conflicts that threaten world peace'. At the forefront of encouraging global giving are the American Big Three. RF has backed several initiatives to train a new generation of global givers, 'promising leaders in the field of philanthropy and civil society'. The Ford, Hewlett, Kellogg and Charles Stewart Mott Foundations run similar programmes. Even philanthropy-strengthening groups have access to a network of support groups such as the Council on Foundations and the European Foundation Centre. The global givers are further networked with regional and national philanthropies, such as the Asia Pacific Philanthropy Consortium, and to international networks and associations, such as the World Economic Forum, which in turn, has its own global social investors programme.[65]

In that context, the grants information that follows proves to be just the tip of a very large iceberg. The Ford Foundation granted US$400,000 to the Academy for the Development of Philanthropy in Poland (ADPP) – which grew out of a USAID project – in order to strengthen foundations locally. A Ford grant of US$220,000 supports efforts to link-up Polish and Belarusian NGOs. Relatedly, Ford awarded US$500,000 to the Brazilian Association of NGOs to help organize the World Social Forum, a body that tries to develop 'social and economic alternatives to current patterns of globalization'.[66]

The Ford Foundation is an enthusiastic supporter of the World Social Forum (WSF), an international network of liberal-reformist globalizers. FF has invested well over US$1,000,000 in WSF to help it organize events and globally to disseminate its message.[67] At its third annual meeting, WSF attracted 100,000 delegates from 156 countries – feminists, trades unionists, political leaders, churchmen and so on. According to Michael Edwards, director of the Ford Foundation's Governance and Civil Society unit, WSF has changed the 'terms of the debate about globalization... . There's [now] an inescapable public debate about the role of corporations and the distribution of globalization's benefits, and I think that's largely due to the WSF crew'.[68] WSF, with the FF's and others' sponsorship, promotes critiques of some of the 'negative side effects of market liberalization: growing economic disparity, the privatization of health care and environmental degradation'. The ultimate aim, according to Ford's Edwards, is a 'global civil society' the influence of which would bear comparison to the impact of the Bretton Woods system formed in World War Two.[69] WSF aims to construct 'an alternative development model and to construct a new form of globalization', as opposed to rejecting globalization per se.[70] A Carnegie Corporation grant of US$25,000 assists 'dialogue on globalization between representatives of the World Economic Forum and the World Social Forum'.[71] A FF grant to the London School of Economics of US$500,000 aims to help scholars explore 'the depth of global governance and its accountability to a polity', another reformist measure promoted by all three major US foundations.[72]

The WSF, however, is the subject of much Third World criticism. For example, MumbaiResistance, a radical Indian organization opposed to capitalist globalization, argues that the WSF is 'No Real Threat to the Imperialist System'. This is, it is claimed, because the sponsors of the WSF have co-opted anti-globalization forces, channelled them away from 'direct and militant confrontation ... into discussions and debates that are often sterile, and mostly unfocused and aimless'. Some participants at WSF meetings complain that they are expected mostly to 'listen' to WSF leaders rather than to participate; the aim was 'putting a human face on globalization'. The World Bank refers to the WSF as 'a maturing social movement' and the Bank's officials have been granted observer status at WSF meetings. WSF's supporters include Brazil's President Lula, head of the Workers' Party and proponent of IMF policies and US free trade agreements, and opponent of peasants' land struggles. WSF is, ultimately, a 'safety valve' trying to blunt the harsher edges of capitalist globalization.[73]

Combating anti-Americanism

To *some* extent, Hutton's views are seen as threatening to American interests by a number of US liberal internationalist foundations, particularly the German Marshall Fund of the United States (GMF).[74] The GMF now has a larger circle of funders, including the Ford and Rockefeller philanthropies, the Council on Foreign Relations (CFR), North Atlantic Treaty Organization (NATO), and US Agency for International Development (USAID).[75] GMF's programmes are essentially focused around two *complementary* goals: promoting transatlantic cooperation and combating anti-Americanism in Europe by building collaborations between US and European elites, including academics, journalists, policy makers, business leaders, think tanks, and philanthropies. GMF builds partnerships across the Atlantic, with Eastern Europe, and the wider world, by pooling 'intellectual ... analytical ... [and] financial resources'. Its projects are designed to develop 'innovative solutions' to transatlantic problems, 'an opportunity for American voices to be heard in Europe and for European voices to be heard in America, and for both Americans and Europeans to be heard throughout other world regions'. GMF locates itself at the centre of numerous global networks that include universities, mass media, US Congress and Senate, the European Union, industrialists' organizations like the Confederation of Indian Industry, and George Soros's Open Society Institute.[76]

In 2003, GMF engaged in a wide range of activities to build transatlantic cooperation. Critically interested in understanding and acting upon public opinion, GMF financed a survey of *Transatlantic Trends* across seven European countries plus the United States. In June, GMF organized a symposium of 28 American and European think tanks, shadowing the official US-EU Summit. The symposium analysed diverging attitudes towards the Middle East and on global trade, as well as examining 'the prospects for resolving the tensions' between the power blocs. Presentations of the findings and recommendations were made at the US Capitol by Doug Bereuter, US Congressman, Pat Cox, president of the European Parliament, Marc Grossman, Under-Secretary of State for Political Affairs and George Papandreou, Greek Foreign Minister. Continuing the examination of European-American divergent opinion-consideration, as the basis for future consensus building, GMF arranged a special 'Strategic Discussion with Henry Kissinger' for emerging German leaders.[77] Finally, GMF launched the Trade and Poverty Forum in February 2003, with the aim of developing US-European and Third World leaders' dialogue on those matters, in order to assist 'the global trading system to better address development challenges'. Its first report, 'Restoring Trust in the WTO: The Challenge for Cancun', is to be followed up by 'attention to how to respond to the

breakdown of trade negotiations in Cancun, and how to advance broad development goals'. The TPF consists of six delegations from the United States (headed
by Robert Rubin, former Secretary to the Treasury), Japan, India, Brazil, South
Africa and Europe.[78] The TPF wants to 'focus on rebuilding the confidence of
developing countries in the importance of world trade for their economic well-
being' and to 'educate the press and public about the importance of US-EU
leadership on trade and development matters'.[79]

An important part of GMF's work since 2000 has been its annual meetings of
'Emerging Foreign Policy Leaders', at Hotel Tremezzo, Lake Como, Italy. This
programme is conducted in partnership with the Bertelsmann Foundation and
the Center for Applied Policy Research. Over 30 US-EU leaders – 'from a range
of professions, from the private sector and media to government and think tanks'
– examined the causes of transatlantic division, the Israeli-Palestinian conflict,
'the future of international organizations such as the UN and NATO, economic
and financial interdependence, and what steps can be taken to renew and
rebuild transatlantic relations'.[80]

The GMF has a significant research fellowships initiative. In 2003, Mark
Leonard was awarded a Fellowship to travel in the United States. Leonard is
Director of Prime Minister Tony Blair's think tank, the Foreign Policy Centre,
and editor of a book, *Re-Ordering the World*, a call for a new 'liberal imperialism'
in the wake of 9/11. Leonard asserted that '[Osama] Bin Laden is an aftershock
of the mistakes made after 1989' by Presidents George HW Bush and Bill
Clinton, and by Prime Minister John Major.[81] This is an echo of the perspectives
shared by the current Bush administration and some of its ideological supporters
in the neo-conservative Project for the New American Century (PNAC).[82] An
essay in the same volume by Robert Cooper, a former Blair foreign policy
adviser, Foreign Office diplomat and adviser to Javier Solana, the EU's High
Representative for Foreign and Security Policy, argued that the world was
divided into three kinds of state: post-modern, modern and pre-modern. In
Cooper's view, the EU and the United States are, more or less, in the post-
modern camp and are obliged, for their own security, to cooperate in dealing
with al-Qaeda and other terror bases in pre-modern states.[83] In so doing, they
would need to use any means necessary, including 'force, pre-emptive attack,
deception', a series of strategies associated with Anglo-American aggression in
Iraq in 2003.

Leonard's principal product during his fellowship was to research and write
an article, 'The US Heads Home: Will Europe Regret It?' His travels took
Leonard to numerous American cities, think tanks, and universities, conducting
interviews with 40 elite national and community leaders. Analysing the unravelling of the three core elements of Bush's pro-Iraq War coalition – traditional
security concerns (alleged Iraqi weapons of mass destruction claims), assertive
nationalism (Iraq's alleged al-Qaeda links and 9/11), and Wilsonian idealism
(promoting democracy) – Leonard claims that the United States is set to draw
back from its crusading foreign policy to *relative* isolationism. He emphasizes
relative isolationism because total withdrawal from world affairs is impossible for a

nation that has troops in 130 countries and a globalized economy. He concludes that such relative isolation may be regretted by European critics of the United States, as world crises mount and Europe's own inability to assert power and influence, highlighted by the Kosovo crisis, is exposed.[84] His conclusions are in line with the attitudes of the German Marshall Fund.

Among its past fellows, the GMF's Transatlantic Fellows Program cites a roster of prominent figures from academic, political and business life, including G. John Ikenberry (Princeton), Christopher Makins (Atlantic Council), Lee Feinstein (CFR), Ellen Bork (Project for the New American Century), Barry Posen (MIT), Cindy Williams (MIT), and John Harris (*Washington Post*).[85]

GMF is actively doing – in its own way – what some Americans claim that the US government is not – a long tradition in American philanthropy. The context of the GMF's programmes may be set by its president's most recent writings. In an important article in *The National Interest*, President Craig Kennedy advanced the argument for more powerful, effective and better-financed attempts by the US administration to combat anti-Americanism and better to promote the country's image and foreign policies abroad, especially in Europe.[86] Also in 2003, Kennedy was one of 29 prominent Americans – including Lynne Cheney, William J. Bennett, James Q. Wilson and Walter Russell Mead[87] – who contributed to a right-wing volume, *Terrorists, Despots and Democracy: What Our Children Need to Know*. In it, the central argument was that the terrorist attacks of 11 September 2001 were sourced in hatred of American values and freedoms, and had *no relation whatever* to American foreign policy. Any arguments to the contrary, the volume stridently argued, were misguided, pacifistic, relativistic, 'long on tolerance', multiculturalistic, and unpatriotic.[88] Kennedy's contribution echoed those themes by criticizing the 'wrong-headed view' that 9/11 *had anything whatsoever* to do with 'the irresponsible use of American economic and military power in the rest of the world'.[89]

In his article in *The National Interest*, Kennedy argued that anti-Americanism was being inadequately tackled by the American administration. Indeed, the United States has a 'public diplomacy crisis' of rising anti-Americanism in Europe, as erstwhile allies turn against the United States 'in droves'. The United States needs a 'serious campaign to open European minds to our positions', drawing on how historically the Central Intelligence Agency (CIA) and the Ford Foundation helped battle anti-Americanism during the cold war. In particular, Kennedy focused on the anti-communist Congress for Cultural Freedom (CCF), which was unfairly portrayed as a 'CIA front', in Kennedy's view – although that is exactly what it was.[90] Its principal achievement, despite its failure completely to stem the tide of European anti-Americanism, was to 'nurture a nucleus of thinkers and activists who were open to American ideas and willing to engage in serious discourse on the major issues of the day'.[91]

Today, in the wake of 9/11 and the Iraq War, it is vital, according to Kennedy, to recognize the correctness of Robert Kagan's views vis-à-vis American military strength and European weakness.[92] While there are differences of opinion and worldview, there are also important areas of cooperation and convergence – especially on terrorism and globalization – upon which the United States should try to make 'more palatable' US-European differential capabilities 'by building a base of support for active engagement with America'. Kennedy advised that the Bush administration must take four steps to 'advance its strategy of stemming the loss of public support among Europe's elites and common citizenry'. Firstly, public diplomacy to mobilize public opinion; secondly, more overseas travel to Europe by administration officials to *debate* policies and issues; thirdly, more financial resources for public diplomacy information officers, restoring spending to cold war levels. And finally, to ensure that the kind of public diplomacy engaged in be active, explanatory, and combative, and not merely an exercise to 're-brand' American diplomacy, as Colin Powell's efforts had tried, in vain, to achieve.[93]

Recommending a strategy that resembles, and complements, the programmes of the GMF, Kennedy urges the administration to 'support those European political leaders and intellectuals who are willing to take the increasingly unpopular stand of backing America'. We need both to ensure that the 'good news' gets out about American policy and also 'to knock down slander of the United States in a comprehensive and timely fashion'. As an example of such 'slander', Kennedy points to 'unfounded' allegations of torture and mistreatment of prisoners at Guantanamo Bay: in fact, they were only 'shackled and blindfolded … [as] reasonable precautions … while the detainees were being transported'.[94] The administration's diplomatic machinery alone, however, is too slow, inflexible, and unskilled to meet current needs.

> These sorts of challenges require serious intellectual combatants. This means a critical mass of writers, thinkers and diplomats who can engage editorial boards, join the television talk show circuits, participate in internet chat rooms, operate websites – not to mention debate Europe's scholars, business leaders and university students alike. Above all, it means developing a broader, non-partisan network of like-minded individuals on both sides of the Atlantic who are dedicated to the cause of keeping the idea of the West and its ever expanding community of liberal democracies alive. Though times have changed … institutions like the Congress for Cultural Freedom once worked. Perhaps it is time to consider what additional lessons history can offer.[95]

It is to two major historical examples of foundations' efforts to eliminate anti-Americanism that we now turn, beginning with CCF.

The Ford Foundation and the Congress for Cultural Freedom

Combating anti-Americanism and fighting communism were very closely related, given the breadth of definition of both concepts, in the eyes of the Ford Foundation and of the US Department of State and other state agencies. In fact, it is clear that communism represented the starkest version of anti-Americanism – a coherent worldview that challenged the free market, private property, limited government, and individualism. It should occasion little surprise, then, that Ford took a favourable view of one of the most notorious CIA programmes – the Congress for Cultural Freedom (CCF),[96] seen by its founders as 'the cultural-intellectual equivalent to the political economy of the European Recovery Program (ERP) and the security framework of NATO ...'[97] CCF received important support from Ford's board of trustees, which was packed with former CIA and OSS members, in addition to Marshall Planners and members of the US High Commission in Germany. The relationship with CIA, CCF, and numerous other opponents of communism and anti-Americanism was close, enduring and smooth.[98]

CCF's anti-communism lost its edge after the death of Stalin in 1953, and it found its new mission in promoting the benefits and advantages of Western freedom, pluralism and social democracy. They championed revolution-free welfare capitalism and the rise of the classless society. As with Ford's economists in Indonesia (more below), CCF stalwarts promoted Keynesian economic management. In Europe, this line of thought led directly to 'end of ideology' thinking from a trio of American social scientists – Daniel Bell, Seymour Martin Lipset and Edward Shils.[99]

The political impact in Britain of the CCF was felt primarily in the politics of the Labour Party, which critics claimed had too powerful a left-wing anti-American element.[100] Opposition to the establishment of US military and air bases on British soil and the Party Conference's decision in 1960 unilaterally to disarm Britain's nuclear weapons indicated Labour's 'anti-Americanism'. Therefore, CCF, funded by the CIA, fostered the *right-wing* of the Labour Party – including Hugh Gaitskell, Denis Healey, RHS Crossman, Tony Crosland and Roy Jenkins. CCF's Milan Conference of 1955 provided these Labour leaders – all MPs, and Gaitskell set to became Labour's leader later the same year – a chance to build alliances with European 'moderate' socialists and with the 'reformist wing of the US Democratic Party as represented by such luminaries as J. K. Galbraith and Arthur Schlesinger Jnr'. The aim was to strengthen the reformist left and maintain their 'Atlantic alignment'. Healey was a leading Bilderberger in the 1950s and 1960s.[101] In 1961, of course, Gaitskell was able to reverse the 'unilateral nuclear disarmament' decision.

A key player in the Ford Foundation, CCF and European labour politics was Shepard Stone.[102] It was Stone with whom Denis Healey conducted the preliminary negotiations, at a Bilderberg meeting in 1954 that led to Ford's funding the new London-based Institute of Strategic Studies. Ford provided US$150,000 over three years to the new think tank that supported the Atlantic Alliance, boosted right-wing labour ideas favouring nuclear weapons and the American-led North Atlantic Treaty Organization (NATO).[103] It therefore provided intellectual and political support for opposing the left-wing, 'anti-American' forces in the labour movement.

Although CCF was exposed as a CIA-front in 1967, the Ford Foundation continued to support the organization. The only issue was over whether it ought to change its name, given that it had become discredited in some circles and because some prominent former supporters – such as Raymond Aron, the French sociologist, and the Labour theoretician, W. Arthur Lewis – were unwilling to have anything more to do with it unless it changed its name, address, and funding sources. According to Aron, the anti-Soviet role of CCF was no longer necessary. CCF supporters agreed that 'its functions in the Western world need new definition'. Francis X. Sutton, Ford official and author of an internal appraisal of the CCF, noted that 'anti-Americanism is now an important intellectual phenomenon in Western Europe. An American-financed organization cannot readily cope with this phenomenon; either it is actively pro-American or it bends unnaturally and awkwardly to be "fair"'. The Sutton memorandum noted that CCF publications – especially *Encounter*, a significant magazine of current affairs, arts and literature – had not been 'sufficiently critical of the United States', excluding intellectual critics from its pages. In particular, American policy in Vietnam had escaped censure in *Encounter* as had any thing 'anti-American'. Sutton concluded that CCF or something similar was an absolute necessity in 'the modern world', especially in dealing with 'problems of irresponsibility [among intellectuals] and decay of purpose'. And if there is 'a certain tension' in Ford's supporting a CCF-style semi-secret activity, it 'ought to be tolerated'.[104] Sutton recommended that Ford award US$4.65 million over five years to a revamped CCF, to deal with the 'disorientation and irresponsibility now common among Western intellectuals'. In order to alleviate the suspicion that this is a pro-American organization, Sutton recommended that Ford should urge on CCF 'substantial internationalization of financial support'.[105]

That the German Marshall Fund of the United States seeks to resurrect a CCF-style organization indicates that there are sufficient positive and negative reasons for US-EU cooperation. First, both blocs have a vested interest in globalization processes from which they derive huge economic benefits; cooperation over global trade, finance and economics lubricates the globalization process and ensures the smoother functioning of the system as a whole. Secondly, both have a vested interest in co-opting and defeating, as the case may be, those global, regional and national forces that oppose globalization. Finally, both the US and EU share attitudes towards international terrorism and the global 'war on terror', although they differ over means. They are agreed that it is the 'premodern' states – failed, collapsed or rogue states – that constitute the greatest threat to the West. It is this threat that – negatively – is being used to bring the two blocs together, especially through attempts at public diplomacy by the United States. As there is a new ideological/theological division in the world, organizations similar to the old CCF may develop to fight a new 'cold war' against the enemies of the West. It is certainly the hope of the GMF. Yet, a secretly funded CIA front-organization is deeply undemocratic and incompatible with the principles of an open society. It clandestinely intervenes in the internal affairs of democracies, sponsoring right-wing forces at every level of society and marginalizing dissenting voices. It advances its sponsored publications, leaders and organizations as evidence of the healthy functioning of democracy, of the free market of ideas and the inevitable triumph of capitalist democracy. In today's context, a CCF-style organization is likely to combat anti-neoliberal globalization forces by co-opting less radical organizations and promoting them as the 'true' voice of the people. It thereby subverts the very democratic system it professes to protect and promote.

The next section of this chapter considers the role of the Ford Foundation in Indonesia's globalization, its transformation from a country inimical to US interests – anti-American – to one that became a 'model pupil of globalization' and, therefore, 'acceptable'.

Indonesia: model pupil of globalization

The Ford Foundation played an active role in Indonesia from the early 1950s, particularly in building a 'modernizing elite' that would examine national economic and political problems from a Western perspective. Ford initiatives across the Indonesian university system dovetailed with more aggressive policies of covert arms drops by the Central Intelligence Agency (CIA) to rebels opposed to the leftist-nationalist government of Sukharno. Both Ford and the CIA defined the Sukharno regime and its nationalist supporters as 'anti-American' and unstable. When attempts to overthrow Sukharno failed in the 1950s, the more subtle methods of the Ford Foundation came to the fore.[106] Interestingly, Ford records show that during the early years of his rule, Sukharno was seen as Indonesia's own George Washington, a national liberation struggle leader. The shift in Ford's thinking occurred in line with official US foreign policy's increasing anti-communist attitude to developments in Korea, Vietnam, and in India, particularly due to the rise of the 'non-aligned movement' that tried to provide a neutral path between the two superpowers. In line with this, Ford converted Sukharno from identification with an authentic American hero to an enemy of order, stability, and rationality.[107]

Ford initiated, with enthusiastic regime approval the teaching of English as the language of 'development', in order to improve Indonesian access to valuable Western development strategies. Additionally, the University of Indonesia (UI) received funding to reform its economics faculty, development programmes, graduate training, and for research. Ford constructed an elite cadre of pro-American upper-class economists wedded (quite willingly) to a worldview and to economic theories that favoured open economies, foreign investment, low taxation, foreign loans, and World Bank/IMF development strategies. This group was also, in effect, preparing economic reforms for the day when Sukharno would no longer be in power.[108]

The principal vehicle for the penetration of Indonesian academia was the small cadre of scholars around Sumitro, a 'socialist' opponent of the Sukharno regime. In the late 1950s, Sumitro, who headed the Faculty of Economics at UI, went into exile after an armed insurrection that he led ended in failure. Dozens of leading Indonesian economists were identified by Sumitro's group and sent to the University of California, Berkeley, on doctoral programmes, returning thereafter to take up full-time positions at home. In contrast to the 'anti-Americanism' of the Sukharno administration, the Ford Foundation viewed Sumitro's group as patriotic, rational, technocratic and progressive modernizers. Ford invested US$2.5 million in the tie-up between the two universities, transforming the Economics faculty into an American-style school of business administration, economics and statistics.

Ford invested large funds in developing Southeast Asian studies in elite US universities – especially at Harvard, UC Berkeley, Massachusetts Institute of Technology (MIT), and Cornell. For example, Ford financed the Modern Indonesia Project at Cornell in 1954 in order to examine its social and political structures. Some of Ford's American Indonesia scholars were in contact with the Indonesian military – parts of which were actively opposed to the government, causing two American academics to resign in protest. Professors Len Doyle (UC Berkeley) and Ralph Anspach refused to participate in Ford programmes they claimed were either a 'rebellion against the government' or an 'American policy of empire'.[109]

Ultimately, the Sukharno regime gave way – after the bloody massacre of hundreds of thousands of 'communists' – to the pro-American administration of General Suharto in 1966. It came as little surprise that the five man Team of Experts for Economic and Financial Affairs was furnished by the Faculty of Economics at UI, and that it suggested reforms favouring the United States, the IMF and the World Bank. The New Order in Indonesia promised political stability, modernization and economic development, and was decidedly not 'anti-American', in contrast to its irrational predecessor.[110] Thirty-five years later, the World Bank declared Suharto's Indonesia a 'model pupil of globalization'.[111]

Promoting globalization, fighting anti-Americanism

The foundations have combated anti-Americanism in a number of ways, especially through network-construction for consensus building, through financing clandestine organizations such as the CCF, as well as through direct overseas interventions such as that in Indonesia. These initiatives have also been related to the cold war construction of 'area studies' as a distinct academic discipline. As shown above, American foundations have promoted Americanism primarily through promoting neoliberal globalization and through incorporating 'moderate' dissenting voices. It is also clear, however, that understanding Islamic societies and ideas today – important hotbeds of contemporary anti-Americanism – are central to foundations' concerns. The section below examines some evidence of this recent development in foundations' efforts to smooth the path to complete globalization.

'There is rarely a direct link between terrorism and poverty and exclusion. But it is evident that terrorists draw much of their support and justification from those who are, or *perceive themselves* as, unjustly impoverished'. So wrote the president of the Rockefeller Foundation in 2002.[112] In addition to those programmes, RF also launched a number of 'area studies-type' initiatives to illuminate the nature of modern Islam as a precursor, or in addition, to further interventions in the 'war on terror' and anti-Americanism.

In May 2004, RF allocated US$700,000 to a series of conferences on 'Muslim Worlds and Global Futures'. No further information is available on this conference series, yet its title suggests an interesting initiative in examining the Muslim 'mind' and its impact on the globalization process.[113] Further initiatives being funded by RF on aspects of the 'Islamic question' include a series of meetings, the preparation of new studies, and research fellowship programmes. RF has also awarded US$50,000 to the American Sufi Muslim Association towards the cost of the 'Cordoba Dialogues, an interfaith effort to heal the relationship between Islam and America'.[114] The Asian Resource Foundation in Thailand has been granted US$252,000 for its research fellowships programme for 'young Muslim scholars in the region' entitled, *Islam in Transition in Southeast Asia: A View from Within*.[115] Other initiatives explore how Middle Eastern Islam looks from African and Asian perspectives, the nature of 'Radical Islamic Organizations in Central Asia', or are pointedly combative – the Sisters in Islam group, Malaysia, was funded for its meeting in 2003, 'Muslim Women Challenge Fundamentalism: Building Bridges between Southeast Asia and West Asia [Middle East]'.[116]

Inherent in these initiatives is the idea that the *principal* cause of terrorism and anti-Americanism is *insufficient knowledge and understanding* between communities or a failure to communicate. The initiatives suggest that the foundations, echoing the current Bush administration, believe that the problem lies in people's hearts and minds rather than in any desire to retain national cultures or autonomy from American domination. As Conway told delegates to the International Symposium of the World Conference on Religion and Peace, we must act now to 'bridge the potential fissures that terrorism can create. Civilized societies should not fall victim to a manipulation of human understanding'. Here, terrorism itself is given an *independent* causal role in spreading misunderstanding between peoples, rather than being seen, in any way as *symptomatic* of significant globalization processes.[117]

The Carnegie Corporation, in some respects, has focused on the 'problem' of Islam and globalization for some time, even prior to 9/11. For example, in June 2000, CC awarded US$237,000 to the University of California, Santa Cruz, for 'research on globalization and Islam'.[118] This grant should be seen in the context of other CC funding of studies of the impact of globalization on national self-determination and 'ethnopolitics': to UCLA (US$312,000 in early 2001) and Yale (US$445,000 in early 2001); UC, San Diego (US$260,000 in 2002); and University of Pennsylvania (US$248,000 in 2000).[119] In effect, this helps strengthen an existing network of American Islamicists, a contemporary version of cold war students of Communism.

Post-9/11, however, a more sharply-defined investment strategy has been forged at Carnegie. Its International Peace and Security Programme is more pointedly aiming at 'global engagement' as 'the United States and other states face new global threats and opportunities'. In particular, CC focuses on the problems posed by 'states at risk for instability' that may be attacked by new 'nation-building' measures, a policy now espoused, according to CC, by the Bush administration in Iraq and Afghanistan. According to Carnegie, there are, 'on the horizon ... other candidates for external intervention by both the United States and other members of the international community', presenting CC with an opportunity to support efforts at 'generating policy-relevant scholarship on the challenges posed by states at risk; and promoting new multilateral approaches to confronting these challenges'.[120]

In light of the above, CC has funded a plethora of scholars and institutes to study Islamic ideas, political Islam, and terrorism. For example, the University of Maryland was awarded US$25,000 to finance a workshop on 'non-state actors, terrorism and the proliferation of the weapons of mass destruction'; a Carnegie scholar, Robert A. Pape, was granted US$100,000 to research 'The Strategic Logic of Suicide Terrorism'; and the National Academy of Sciences given US$220,000 to study 'US-Russian challenges in countering urban terrorism'.[121] Domestically, there is a growing interest in Arab and Muslim communities in America: in 2003, CC granted Louise Cainkar US$100,000 for 'A Sociological Study of the Islamicization of Chicago's Arab Community: Implications for Democratic Integration'.[122]

Additionally, like Ford, CC also considers the principal cause of anti-Americanism to be in misunderstanding and, therefore, backs several initiatives to extend understanding. For example, in March 2002, Boston University was awarded US$100,000 for its radio stations to develop 'programming on Islam and foreign policy'; and in 2003, the American University in Beirut received US$94,900 'toward a program to promote understanding between the United States and the Islamic world'. Likewise, the Brookings Institution received US$11,000 in 2004 towards 'creating new dialogues between the United States and the Muslim world'.[123] The ultimate aim of these efforts is indicated in the title of a grant (US$100,000) for scholar Carrie Rosefsky Wickham, in 2003, to research 'The Path to Moderation: Lessons from the Evolution of Islamism in the Middle East'.[124]

Carnegie has also prepared for the worst, however, by financing two grants in 2002–2003 (totalling US$75,000) to the neo-conservative think tank, American Enterprise Institute (AEI), 'Toward a joint project with the Brookings Institution to form a bipartisan commission to consider ways to ensure the continuity of government after a terrorist attack'.[125] To monitor human rights abuses in Afghanistan and in the domestic fight against terrorism, CC awarded US$100,000 to Human Rights Watch in 2002,[126] indicating its continuing commitment to liberal checks on the US administration.

Conclusion

The American foundations are major engines for promoting Americanism and for challenging anti-Americanism. Their messages and strategies are honed to suit historical time and political-ideological conditions. They are highly consistent but adaptive institutions. In their early years up to 1945, they laboured in an environment hostile to American expansion and engagement with the world. Their strategy then was to foster internationalist thought, opinion, study, research and networks inside and beyond America's borders, and to connect their programmes with those (few and uninfluential) elements in the American state that were engaged in America's foreign affairs. During and after World War Two, their strategies switched to developing an intellectual infrastructure of area studies, international relations, and economic development studies programmes, as well as backing globalist think tanks and connecting them with the national security state. In addition, they constructed an array of international knowledge networks. Today, in the post-cold war era of globalization, the foundations promote neoliberal globalization; try to co-opt 'moderate' anti-globalization protesters, and combat anti-Americanism in Europe and the Islamic world. They are at the forefront of efforts to construct global alliances of networks of philanthropies, NGOs and INGOs, universities, think tanks, international financial institutions, and governments. Although this has been going on for some time, it is now far denser, better funded and more organized than it was in the 1990s.

The foundations are immersed in elite networks inside the United States, in international organizations, and global corporations. Their efforts to combat the opponents of globalization and of US foreign policy must be seen in light of their attempts to build an 'Americanized' global civil society in which their American-style politics, their neoliberal economics, and their free world ideology predominate. The world may lack a global executive committee, as the World Bank complained recently, to govern its affairs.[127] It already has the key components of a well funded and globally networked civil society led by American and European foundations and their core concerns. These philanthropic networks are grounded in global corporations, interconnected with civil society, and enmeshed in multi-level relationships with American, other Western, and other allied states' agencies and priorities. Their advantage is that they claim to be non-political and non-ideological and therefore are able to intervene where governments often dare not or cannot.

The above structure of global elite power, within whose context the foundations' struggle to promote Americanism and counter anti-Americanism must be viewed, sits uneasily with the theory of their own roles that foundation insiders and others advance. The foundations, it is suggested, are independent of politics, ideology, the state, big business; they are, it is claimed, part of a 'third sector' beyond politics and the market; they are impartial, objective and 'scientific' – motivated by a desire to 'do good'.

Their myriad connections, examined above, place the foundations at or near the centre of the American system of power and, increasingly, of the global power structure. Neoliberalism, featuring the withdrawal of the state from social support, employment, and other interventionist strategies, has opened the space for massively increased opportunities for private actors at national and global levels. The foundations have taken full advantage and are well positioned to dominate the social and political agenda of global politics and global civil society. As they act within the patterns of corporate power which brought them into being, and are state-oriented in their mind-set – Gramsci would say 'state-spirited'[128] – they act in accord with the principal contemporary underlying power concept: US-led neoliberal capitalist globalization. They are therefore part of the continuing and renewed American hegemonic, imperial project of the late 1990s but particularly after 11 September 2001.

Notes

1 M. Rupert, *Ideologies of Globalization: Contending Visions of a New World Order*, London: Routledge, 2000.
2 B. D. Karl and S. N. Katz, 'Foundations and ruling class elites', *Daedalus*, 1987, vol. 116, no. 1, pp. 1–40.
3 I. Parmar, 'Engineering consent: the Carnegie Endowment for International Peace and the mobilization of opinion in the United States' rise to globalism, 1939–1945', *Review of International Studies*, 2000, vol. 26, no. 1, pp. 35–48; R. F. Arnove (ed.), *Philanthropy and Cultural Imperialism*, Boston: GK Hall, 1980.
4 B. Howe, 'The emergence of scientific philanthropy, 1900–1920', in Arnove, *Philanthropy and Cultural Imperialism*, pp. 25–54.
5 E. Black, 'Funding hate: Ford Foundation draws scrutiny as terrorism rules begin to bite', *New York Sun*, 21 October 2003.
6 D. Montgomery, 'Mexican anti-Americanism in America', *FrontPageMagazine*, 6 December 2002.
7 Hofstadter, cited in S. M. Lipset, *American Exceptionalism*, New York: Norton, 1996, p. 18.
8 Andre Glucksmann cited in M. Cunliffe, 'The anatomy of anti-Americanism', in R. Kroes and M. Van Rossem (eds.), *Anti-Americanism in Europe*, Amsterdam: Free University Press, 1986, p. 20.
9 See for example, Noam Chomsky's, *Necessary Illusions*, London: Pluto Press, 1989; C. Wright Mills, *The Power Elite*, London: Oxford University Press, 1956; G. William Domhoff, *Who Rules America?*, Mountain View, CA: Mayfield Publishing Co., 1998; C. Johnson, *Blowback: The Costs and Consequence of American Empire*, London: Little, Brown, 2000; P. Hollander, *Anti-Americanism: critiques at home and abroad 1965–1990*, Oxford: Oxford University Press, 1992.
10 Cunliffe, 'The anatomy of anti-Americanism', p. 27.
11 H. S. Becker, *Outsiders*, New York: The Free Press, 1963.
12 President George W. Bush, for example, often refers to dissenters against US power as people who 'resent our success and hate our values'. See G. W. Bush, *A Charge to Keep*, New York: William Morrow, 1999, p. 239.
13 Cunliffe, 'The anatomy of anti-Americanism', pp. 28–9.
14 David Strauss; cited in Cunliffe, 'The anatomy of anti-Americanism', p. 20.
15 B. Appleyard, 'Why do they hate America?', *The* (London) *Sunday Times (News Review)*, 23 September 2001.
16 R. Weitkunat, 'The philosophical origins of European anti-Americanism', *Contemporary Review*, July 2002; P. W. Rodman, 'The world's resentment', *The National Interest*, Summer 2000.
17 M. Foley, *American Political Ideas*, Manchester: Manchester University Press, 1991.
18 Arnove, *Philanthropy and Cultural Imperialism*; E. C. Lagemann, *The Politics of Knowledge: The Carnegie Corporation, Philanthropy, and Public Policy*, Middletown, CT: Wesleyan University Press, 1989.
19 RF in 1901; CC in 1911; FF in 1936.

20 S. Slaughter and E. de Silva, 'Looking backwards: how foundations formulated ideology in the Progressive period', in Arnove, *Philanthropy and Cultural Imperialism*, pp. 55–86.

21 W. E. Leuchtenberg, 'Progressivism and imperialism', *Mississippi Valley Historical Review*, 1952, vol. 5339, pp. 483–504.

22 I. Parmar, *Think Tanks and Power in Foreign Policy: A Comparative Study of the Council on Foreign Relations and the Royal Institute of International Affairs, 1939–1945*, London: Palgrave Macmillan, 2004, especially chapter 3.

23 I. Moore, *Andrew Carnegie*, New York: Carnegie Corporation, 1995, p. 5. Carnegie sold his company for US$400 million to J. Pierpont Morgan in 1901.

24 I. Parmar, 'The Carnegie Corporation and the mobilization of opinion in the United States' rise to globalism, 1939–1945', *Minerva*, 1999, vol. 37, p. 356.

25 Carnegie Corporation, *Annual Report*, 1952, pp. 19–20.

26 B. Howe, 'The emergence of scientific philanthropy, 1900–1920', in Arnove, *Philanthropy and Cultural Imperialism*, pp. 25–54.

27 F. S. Saunders, *Who Paid the Piper?*, London: Granta Books, 1999, p. 139.

28 D. Fisher, 'American philanthropy and the social sciences', in Arnove, *Philanthropy and Cultural Imperialism*, pp. 233–68.

29 I. Parmar, 'American foundations and the construction of global knowledge networks', *Global Networks*, 2002, vol. 2, no. 1, p. 16.

30 Arnove, *Philanthropy and Cultural Imperialism*.

31 E. H. Berman, *The Influence of the Carnegie, Ford, and Rockefeller Foundations on American Foreign Policy*, New York: SUNY Press, 1983.

32 E. C. Lagemann, *The Politics of Knowledge*, Middletown, CT: Wesleyan University Press, 1989.

33 B. E. Moon, 'The United States and globalization', in R. Stubbs and G. Underhill (eds.), *Political Economy and the Changing Global Order*, 2nd edn, Ontario: Oxford University Press, 2000, pp. 342–51; see also T. Friedman, *Longitudes and Attitudes*, London: Penguin, 2003, p. 5.

34 Friedman, *Longitudes and Attitudes*, p. 33; p. 25.

35 W. A. Nielsen, *The Big Foundations*, New York: Columbia University Press, 1972, p. ix.

36 Arnove, *Philanthropy and Cultural Imperialism*, p. 1.

37 B. Whitaker, *The Philanthropoids: Foundations and Society*, New York: William Morrow, 1974, p. 90.

38 M. Colwell, 'The foundation connection: links among foundations and recipient organizations', in Arnove, *Philanthropy and Cultural Imperialism*, pp. 413–52.

39 Ibid., pp. 428–9.

40 G. Hodgson, 'The establishment', *Foreign Policy*, 1972, vol. 739, pp. 3–40.

41 Berman, *The influence of the Carnegie, Ford, and Rockefeller Foundations on American foreign policy*, p. 36. In 1964, John J. McCloy was simultaneously chairman of the CFR, of the Ford Foundation, trustee of the Rockefeller Foundation, and chairman of Chase Manhattan Bank.

42 Ibid.

43 L. Shoup and W. Minter, *Imperial Brain Trust*, New York: Monthly Review Press, 1977, p. 59.

44 R.F Arnove and N. Pinede, 'Revisiting the "Big Three" Foundations'. pp. 32–3.

45 *RF News Archive*, 13 December 2001. Healey is also a regent of Georgetown University and of the Hoover Institution.

46 Robert F. Arnove and Nadine Pinede, 'Revisiting the "Big Three" Foundations'.

47 CEIP asserts the liberal internationalist critique of Bush's unilateralism, military pre-emption, and of sidelining the United Nations, fearing the anti-American fallout from such policies. Even so, Robert Kagan, a leading member of the neo-conservative Project for the New American Century, is senior associate at CEIP.

48 Arnove and Pinede, 'Revisiting the "Big Three" Foundations', pp. 2–3. A 'break-out session [on] globalization' at a meeting of the International Network for Strategic Philanthropy (INSP) concluded that 'foundation portfolios have benefited from globalization'. Plenary Meeting, 22 March 2002, facilitated by Paula Johnson (The Philanthropic Initiative, USA), Adele Simmons (World Economic Forum), and David Winder (Synergos Institute).
49 J. D. Wolfensohn, *Development and Poverty Reduction*, Washington, DC: International Bank for Reconstruction and Development/World Bank, 2004.
50 J. Stiglitz, *Globalization and its Discontents*, London: Penguin, 2002.
51 Ibid.; See also S. Gill, *Power and Resistance in the New World Order*, Basingstoke: Palgrave Macmillan, 2003.
52 David Hamburg, CC president (1983–1997), cited by Arnove and Pinede, 'Revisiting the "Big Three" Foundations', p. 10, emphasis added.
53 Arnove and Pinede, 'Revisiting the "Big Three" Foundations', p. 13.
54 R. Peet, *Unholy Trinity: The IMF, World Bank and WTO*, London: Zed Books, 2003, p. 14.
55 Arnove and Pinede, 'Revisiting the "Big Three" Foundations', p. 18.
56 Ibid., p. 19.
57 Ibid., p. 29.
58 Rockefeller *Global Inclusion Programme*, October 2003. Available <www.rockfound.org> (accessed 02 June 2005).
59 Foundation website available at <www.fordfound.org> (accessed 02 June 2005); grant awarded in 2003.
60 Arnove and Pinede, 'Revisiting the "Big Three" Foundations', p. 22.
61 The Prince of Wales International Business Leaders Forum received US$100,000 to 'build, study and promote mutually advantageous business links between large corporations and small or micro-enterprises worldwide'; www.fordfound.org.
62 D. Rockefeller, 'Why we need the IMF', *Wall Street Journal*, 1 May 1998.
63 See <www.fordfound.org>; granted in 2003 to the Third World Network.
64 Ford granted US$350,000 to Yale University in 2003 to fund 'the research practice and outreach activities of the Center for Cities and Globalization and to strengthen an interdisciplinary network on globalization'.
65 The Philanthropic Initiative, Inc., *Global Social Investing: A Preliminary Overview*, Boston: TPI Inc., 2001, pp. 4–5, pp. 37–42.
66 All three grants – to Poland, Poland-Belarus and Brazil – were in 2003; see Ford websites TPI, p. 20.
67 Ford gave US$153,000 to Internews Interactive, Inc., as part of its 'Bridge Initiative on Globalization', to assist the WSF to communicate with members of the World Economic Forum.
68 S. Charle, 'Another way: leaders of a global civil society chart an alternative to globalization', *Ford Foundation Report*, Spring 2003.
69 Ibid.
70 J. Gabriel Lopez, 'Green Globalization', *Ford Foundation Report*, Summer 2003.
71 *CC Grants for Globalization Initiatives*, CC website.
72 Grant to the LSE Foundation, 2003, FF website.
73 W. Hutton, 'Is globalization Americanization?', *BBC News* UK Edition, 16 June.
74 GMF was originally founded by a West German government grant in 1972 in appreciation of US Marshall Plan assistance; headquartered in Washington, DC, it also maintains five offices in Europe – Belgrade, Berlin, Bratislava, Brussels, and Paris; *GMF Annual Report*, 2003. Available <www.gmfus.org> (accessed 02 June 2005).
75 Ibid.
76 Ibid.
77 *GMF Annual Report*, 2003, pp. 1–6.

78 Rubin held that post in President Clinton's second administration, 1995–1999; he was a partner at Goldman Sachs from the early 1970s; he is a former trustee of the Carnegie Corporation.
79 *GMF Annual Report*, 2003, pp. 7–10.
80 Ibid., p. 11.
81 M. Leonard (ed.), *Re-Ordering the World*, London: The Foreign Policy Centre, 2002.
82 I. Parmar, 'Catalysing events, think tanks and American foreign policy shifts: a comparative analysis of the impacts of Pearl Harbor 1941 and 11 September 2001', *Government and Opposition*, Winter 2005, vol. 40, no. 1 pp. 1–25.
83 R. Cooper, 'The post-modern state', in Leonard (ed.), *Re-Ordering the World*, pp. 11–20. Since then, Cooper has published an important book, *The Breaking of Nations*, New York: Atlantic Monthly Press, 2003.
84 M. Leonard, 'The US heads home: will Europe regret it?', available on GMF website, <www.gmfus.org> (Recent Publications section) (accessed 02 June 2005).
85 'Transatlantic Fellows program: past fellows', GMF website. Other past fellows have included the former President of Bulgaria, Peter Stoyanov, Todd Stern, former Clinton White House Staff member; and numerous French, German, Italian and other public figures.
86 J. Gedmin and C. Kennedy, 'Selling America short', *The National Interest*, Winter 2003.
87 Cheney is wife of the US Vice-President Richard Cheney; Bennett is President Ronald Reagan's 'drug tsar' and current head of Americans for Victory Over Terrorism (AVOT); Wilson is a conservative former Harvard academic; Mead is Senior Fellow at the CFR.
88 Thomas B. Fordham Foundation, *Terrorists, Despots and Democracy*, Washington, DC: Thomas B. Fordham Foundation, August 2003.
89 C. Kennedy, 'Defending American tolerance', in ibid, p. 28.
90 G. Scott-Smith, *The Politics of Apolitical Culture*, London: Routledge, 2002.
91 Gedmin and Kennedy, 'Selling America short'.
92 R. Kagan, 'Power and weakness', *Policy Review*, June 2002. In GMF's *Annual Report*, 2003, Kennedy notes the importance of greater recognition of the need for European military development, within NATO, and America's increasing appreciation of 'soft power' such as foreign aid and better knowledge of 'skills … to operate effectively in the Islamic world'.
93 Gedmin and Kennedy, 'Selling America short'. Colin Powell was Secretary of State in the first George W. Bush administration, 2001–2004. Immediately following 9/11, Powell commissioned Madison Avenue advertiser, Charlotte Beers, to rebrand US foreign policy; she resigned in 2002.
94 Kennedy omits mention of the failure of the US administration to grant the protections of the US constitution to detainees and violations of the Geneva Convention.
95 Gedmin and Kennedy, 'Selling America short'.
96 Scott-Smith, *The Politics of Apolitical Culture*.
97 G. Scott-Smith, 'The Congress for Cultural Freedom in retrospect', *Storiografia*, 2002, vol. 6, p. 183. CCF was formed in Berlin in 1950; key founders included Michael Josselson, James Burnham, Sidney Hook, Arthur Koestler and Melvin Lasky.
98 Saunders, *Who Paid the Piper*, p. 142.
99 G. Scott-Smith, 'The CCCF, the end of ideology and the 1955 Milan Conference', *Journal of Contemporary History*, 2002, vol. 37, no. 3, p. 442.
100 H. Wilford, *The CIA, the British Left and the Cold War*, London: Frank Cass, 2003.
101 Ibid., p. 449.
102 V. Berghahn, *America and the Intellectual Cold Wars in Europe*, Princeton, NJ: Princeton University Press, 2001.
103 Militant Tendency, *CIA Infiltration of the Labour Movement*, London: Militant Tendency, 1982, p. 30.

104 F. X. Sutton, 'Inter-Office Memorandum', to Messrs. McGeorge Bundy and David Bell, *Congress for Cultural Freedom*, 21 September 1967, Report no. 002784, Ford Foundation archives, New York.

105 F. X. Sutton, 'Confidential: Information Paper, Congress for Cultural Freedom', September 1967, report no. 002784, FF archives.

106 Unless otherwise stated, the material for this section of the article is drawn from Parmar, *Global Networks*, pp. 13–30.

107 'Grant request: international training and research. To: Mr. Henry T. Heald via Mr. Joseph McDaniel. From: Clarence H. Faust, April 14 1964', in Reel 0836, Grant PA64–277, Ford Foundation Archives (FFA), New York.

108 D. Ransom, 'Ford country: building an elite for Indonesia', in S. Weissman (ed.), *The Trojan Horse*, San Francisco, CA: Ramparts Press, 1974, pp. 93–116.

109 Ibid., p. 100.

110 H. Crouch, *The Army and Politics in Indonesia*, Ithaca, NY: Cornell University Press, 1978.

111 J. Pilger, 'Spoils of a massacre', *The Guardian Weekend*, 14 July 2001, p. 18.

112 RF *Annual Report*, 2002; emphasis added.

113 See www.rockfound.org, *Global Inclusion Program*, 2004. The goal of the Global Inclusion Program is '[t]o help broaden the benefits and reduce the negative impacts of globalization on vulnerable communities, families and individuals around the world'.

114 RF website, *Assets and Capacities Program*, 2003.

115 RF website, *Southeast Asia Regional Program*, 2004.

116 RF website, *Bellagio Program*, 2003. No details of level of financing are available.

117 *Statement by Gordon Conway President The Rockefeller Foundation*, 25 October 2001, RF website.

118 *CC Grants for Globalization Initiatives*, International Peace and Security Program, CC website.

119 Ibid.

120 *CC International Peace and Security Program: Global Engagement*, CC website.

121 CC *Grants, International Peace and Security Program*, 2004, CC website.

122 CC *Grants, Carnegie Scholars Program*, 2003, CC website.

123 CC *Grants, Special Opportunities Fund*, CC website.

124 CC *Grants, Carnegie Scholars Program*, 2003, CC website.

125 CC *Grants, Strengthening US Democracy and Special Opportunities Fund Programs, 2002–2003*, CC website.

126 CC *Grants, 21st Century Fund*, 2002, CC website.

127 'We have a framework to deal with poverty reduction and global environmental challenges. What we do not have is a world executive committee that has global legitimacy, representing the interests of the vast majority, dealing with longer term strategic issues. Such a world body would have three main tasks: to think seriously about these international issues, to monitor what happens, and to crack the whip when progress is not forthcoming and selfish national or parochial interests threaten to delay progress for the common good'. Wolfensohn, *Development and Poverty Reduction*, p. 32.

128 Q. Hoare and G. Nowell-Smith, *Selections from the Prison Notebooks of Antonio Gramsci*, London: Lawrence and Wishart, 1971, p. 146.

Thus it should not be surprising that the views of someone like Stanley Hauerwas overlap with some of the more pronounced versions of anti-liberal thought heard in the United States. Hauerwas teaches at Duke University, and there are strong similarities between his work and that of his former colleague at Duke, Stanley Fish. Fish, as it turns out, has also addressed questions involving what religious believers ought to believe, and he finds that religion is inevitably hostile to what he calls liberalism.[6] Liberalism is the great enemy, in many ways, to Stanley Fish's worldview. If believers were true to their ideas, he concludes, they would conclude that liberal ideas of tolerance and respect for different opinions are incompatible with the truths that believers uphold. If you are religious, you should struggle against tolerance. If you accept tolerance, you are not really religious.

This is ironically a view that is shared by many of religion's critics. Those who say that religious believers are too sectarian and are more committed to one version of the truth than other people, argue in their own way that liberalism and religion are incompatible. They agree that religious believers represent a culture of resistance against modern values but the critics hold that this is a bad rather than a good thing. In his enormously influential *A Theory of Justice*, probably the most important book in political philosophy in the twentieth century, John Rawls is sceptical about the capacity of religious believers to be citizens committed to liberal ideas of rationality and to have the resources necessary to engage with (rather than against) the discourse that makes liberal modernity possible.[7] Political philosophers influenced by John Rawls have endorsed his views. For example Amy Gutman (now president of the University of Pennsylvania and an enormously distinguished political philosopher) writes about the pre-conditions for democratic discourse and claims that religious believers lack the liberalism, the tolerance, the scepticism, that make democratic discourse possible.[8] So, both for defenders and critics of the faithful, one hears the argument that religion is a force of resistance against the trends of liberalism, individualism and democracy that characterize secular culture.

Rethinking the dichotomy

In my recent book entitled *The Transformation of American Religion*, I rely upon a very large, and enormously exciting literature that has been accumulating over the last three decades.[9] Most of this literature has been written by sociologists and anthropologists who are qualitative rather than quantitative in their methodology and who rely upon particularly ethnographic methods of actual observance and participation in the activities that they seek to understand. In this case these are religious activities. The name that has been given to this trend in the sociology of religion is the study of 'lived religion'. Prominent scholars writing in the tradition include historians such as Robert Orsi and Marie Griffith and sociologists such as Nancy Ammerman at Boston University and Robert Wuthnow at Princeton University.[10]

This literature provides us with a significant and extensive portrait of what religion is actually like for religious believers and what it means to be religious in the United States today. This literature does not tell us what religion ought to be. When we read Stanley Fish or Stanley Hauerwas on one side of the debate, or John Rawls or Amy Gutman on the other, we hear about what religious believers *ought* to be. Either they ought to be a source of morality and tradition that can stand against the tide of modernity, or they ought to be dogmatic and sectarian and incapable of being democratic citizens. But through the literature that sociologists have been accumulating we have access to an entirely different picture, a picture of what religious believers are actually like. On the basis of my exploration of that literature, I argue that while the United States is distinct from other comparable societies in the degree to which religion plays a role in public life and religious language is invoked in public life, the kind of religion that most Americans practise is not something that stands against the individualism, innovative, entrepreneurial character of American life. On the contrary, it is very much a part of that mainstream American culture. Indeed, American religion has been much more shaped by American culture, I believe, than American culture has been shaped by American religion.

In *The Transformation of American Religion*, I examine a number of different forms of religious practice, such as the nature of belief and fellowship, which appear to run counter to modern American culture. Religious believers talk a great deal about fellowship, about joining together with others. On the other hand the United States is often described as a kind of anti-institutional culture, a culture in which people resist joining together. If we 'bowl alone', can we really pray together? If we are a culture that puts the individual before the group how can we seek fellowship through our religious practice? How does the 'group-ness' of religion interact with the individualism of American culture? Perhaps the most controversial aspect of American religious practice involves 'witnessing one's faith'. I think we all tend to believe that religious believers, but in particular evangelical Protestants, are under an obligation to proclaim their faith, to speak out about it, to try to convert people, to proselytize, to engage in fairly aggressive and sometimes fairly invasive form of proselytizing. On the other hand, Americans put a value in everyday life to be neighbourly, to be 'nice', not to ask too many questions of other people. Elsewhere, I have discussed the extent to which the United States tends to be a non-judgmental society in which people are often reluctant to make strong judgements about other people.[11] However, you cannot reconcile non-judgementalism with proselytizing. To proselytize is to believe that you have the truth and that everyone else who does not share your truth is somehow leading an inferior life. How does the inclination or in some cases the obligation to proselytize come into conflict with the non-judgementalism of American society?

Similarly, there is a fundamental tension between the way in which Americans think about sin and the role that sin plays within American religion. So much of American religion has been influenced by the therapeutic culture and by the idea of recovery from sin. Yet the notion of recovery and the notion of sin exist in considerable tension with one another. Historically, overcoming sin, resisting temptation, has meant a long and difficult struggle. It has meant an overturning of one's role in society and a necessity to demonstrate to God how seriously one takes the question of salvation. On the other hand, American culture stands against such a notion of struggle. It is a culture of immediate gratification. The Calvinist notion of predestination, which did so much to influence the early Puritans who came to the United States, stands at odds with the culture of individualism and individual improvement. Calvinist theology stresses the pure arbitrariness of God's grace, so that you simply cannot predict what God is going to do next. Therefore to give yourself over to faith means giving yourself over to the *arbitrariness* of the process through which salvation is achieved. This theology contradicts the American emphasis upon individual initiative and the idea that you are responsible for your own faith.

We can multiply these examples of the tension between religion and culture many times. However, at the heart of these examples is a more fundamental tension between tradition and modernity that manifests itself in debates about the relationship between religion and culture in the United States. At the heart of many of our contemporary debates about religion is the idea that we in the United States have lost touch with our traditions, and indeed with the importance of tradition itself. If anything crystallizes the idea that religious believers can stand in tension with modernity, and in tension with all of those other features of modern life that I have referred to, it would be the idea that religion gives people a sense of tradition. Religious believers all identify themselves as traditional in their outlook. We all remember from the two most recent presidential elections the red map and the blue map – which depicted voters for the different candidates. Voters for the Democrat candidates Al Gore (2000) and John Kerry (2004) seemed to be concentrated on the coasts and voters for Mr Bush in both elections seemed to be concentrated in the south and the mid-west. It was said by almost everyone that what was at stake in these elections were traditional values. Particularly in 2000, it was often argued that the Republican victory was made possible by the fact that Americans had become fed up with the sexual scandals surrounding Bill Clinton, and that they wanted a return to a more traditional way of life. More specifically, they wanted to honour traditional institutions such as marriage. They wanted to go back to traditional ideas about discipline in the raising of children. The appeal of conservative Protestantism, particularly the appeal of evangelicals, is that they hold that traditional view of life. For evangelicals, men run the family as the bible commands; the woman should be to the man as the believer is to Jesus. The more traditional gender roles are embedded in evangelical Protestantism. More traditional conceptions of raising children are embedded in the evangelical outlook. A vote for a more religious candidate is a vote for a traditional conception of morality. A vote for a more liberal candidate is a vote against tradition. All this is so obvious and so prominent and so much a part of political thinking and yet in some ways I think it is almost completely wrong.

The notion that religion and tradition go hand in hand is an obvious one. In fact the use of the terms is almost interchangeable. Here is a quote from my book. In this case the particular religious believer is Jewish. 'The feeling one gets when one actually goes up to read from the torah is so intense', this person says, 'it has to do with time; it has to do with the connections from generation to generation. This is the book. This is the document that has been like a gold chain throughout the ages of Judaism. It's such an honour to stand before it and to read a part of it'. In this case the person who uttered these words was a woman who was undergoing a ritual called a *bat mitzvah*. The ritual grows out of the tradition of a *bar mitzvah*, of calling a young thirteen-year old boy to the torah and is in fact an old tradition. Although it does not go back to Moses, it does go back to about the thirteenth century, which is pretty good as traditions go. The tradition of a *bat mitzvah*, which is calling a female to the torah, goes back to 1922. The first *bat mitzvah* was performed in 1922 in a denomination called Reconstructionist Judaism, and as traditions go, 1922 is still a long time ago.

However, the 'tradition' of an adult *bar mitzvah*, when you decide as an adult that you missed it when you were thirteen and that you want it now, goes back to an episode of the television programme called the *Dick Van Dyke Show*. In the 1960s one of the characters in the show said 'Hey Rabbi, I never had the *bar mitzvah* when I was 13, I missed it, can we do it now?' Within weeks, hundreds of Jews from around the United States were calling their Rabbis. So that tradition is about forty years old. So here we have a woman undergoing an adult *bat mitzvah* invoking this gold chain throughout the generations, and proclaiming how it is such an honour for her to be part of the tradition. I submit that this example is characteristic of American attitudes towards tradition in general.

Traditions are wonderful and Americans reinvent them every five years or so. You may think that I am invoking a Jewish example because Jews are much more liberal than other religious believers and therefore it is not surprising that a more liberal person would be so cavalier towards an old tradition. In fact, Jews in the United States take tradition much *more* seriously than followers of any other of America's religions. If you were to identify any one religion that treats tradition in a classically American manner it would have to be evangelical Protestantism or 'born again' Christianity. To be a 'born again' Christian you value authenticity rather than tradition. What is important if you are evangelical is that you have an authentic faith in Jesus. In fact, 'born again' Christianity is about as untraditional a term as one can imagine. To be traditional is not to be born again. It is to participate in practices that your parents were born into and those that their parents were born into. To be evangelical, in contrast, you have to reject your tradition. George W. Bush rejected the religion of his father and his grandfather who were from the Episcopalian religion of New England. The boy from Texas reinvented his life and he reinvented his religion. One of the reasons why Mr Bush can resonate with people out in the heartland of America is *not* because he stands for traditional values but because he embodies the mobility of American culture. He embodies the idea that you have to go through a rejection of tradition in order to achieve something new.[12]

American evangelicalism goes back to the 1830s; it was one of the United States' earliest faiths. But through every one of its many forms, through Pentecostalism right up to the present time, evangelicals have been 'mavericks at heart' – that is a phrase from the historian Grant Wacker who wrote a book about Pentecostals from the 1920s onwards in Los Angeles.[13] There is, if such a thing is possible, a maverick, dissenting 'tradition' to American religion – a tradition of rejecting tradition.

Thus it happens to be the case that the states that have the largest number of evangelicals also have the highest divorce rates. Oklahoma has the largest number of evangelicals per capita in the United States and it also has the highest divorce rate in the United States. Furthermore, there is a close relationship between broken families and evangelicals. Many people believe that evangelicals tend to marry much younger than other people, and generally speaking marriages that are formed when people are very young are more likely to end in divorce. That may be the reason for the close relationship, but the idea that evangelicals embody a 'traditional' form of marriage runs against the sociological realities of the relationship between evangelicals and broken homes. Evangelicalism leads to wayward children, serious problems with alcohol, and other forms of addiction. This is a sociological reality in the contemporary United States.

It should also be noted that the most traditional religions in America are the most liberal. It is the liberal elite religions that are trying to hold on to the fact that you can actually know the difference between a Methodist and a Presbyterian, and that it is important to know what Luther stood for and that Calvin stood for something else. These are facts about religious tradition that most evangelicals don't know. We are all told that evangelicals read the bible, but what they actually read are sections of the bible. They read things taken off the Internet that translate the bible into terms of personal recovery. In fact, a biblical model with traditional readings is much more prevalent among liberal believers than among conservative religious believers.

Conclusion

In short, I believe that despite the conventional wisdom that pits religion against culture, at least in the United States this tension is often overstated. Of these two great fundamental forces (culture and religion) culture is the one that influences religion in America rather than the other way around. If this is the case, it suggests that much of the criticism of religion in the United States misses its target. If people want to be anti-American that is certainly their right; the United States is, for better or worse, an enormously powerful country and it is bound to develop more than its fair share of critics. Those who point to religion as the basis for their anti-Americanism, however, cannot correctly charge that because of the role of religion in American society, the United States is about to return to the days of the Scopes trial or fall under the sway of a particular theocracy. In contrast to Britain or Australia, the United States has a disproportionately large number of people who put God at the centre of their lives. But they have not rejected the modern world in doing so. By all means criticize Americans for their religious enthusiasm. But it gets the story wrong to criticize them for adhering to the faiths of old.

Notes

1 R. Kagan, *Of Paradise and Power: America and Europe in the New World Order*, New York: Knopf, 2003.
2 On faith-based initiatives in the United States, see A. Black, D. Koopman and D. Ryden, *Of Little Faith: The Politics of George W. Bush's Faith-Based Initiatives*, Washington, DC: Georgetown University Press, 2004; J. Formicola, M. Segers and P. Weber, *The Faith-Based Initiatives and the Bush Administration; The Good, the Bad, and the Ugly*, Lanham, MD: Rowman & Littlefield, 2003.
3 S. Hauerwas and W. Willimon, *Resident Aliens: Life in the Christian Colony*, Nashville, TN: Abingdon Press, 1989.
4 S. Carter, *Lives Without Balance*, New York: Random House, 1989.
5 D. Tracey, *Spiritual Revolution: The Emergence of Contemporary Spirituality*, New York: HarperCollins, 2003.
6 See, for example, S. Fish, *Surprised by Sin: The Reader in Paradise Lost*, 2nd edn, Boston, MA: Harvard University Press, 1998.
7 J. Rawls, *A Theory of Justice*, 2nd edn, Boston, MA: The Belknap Press, 1999.
8 A. Gutman, *Identity in Democracy*, Princeton, NJ: Princeton University Press, 2003.
9 A. Wolfe, *The Transformation of American Religion: How We Actually Live Our Faith*, New York: Free Press, 2003.
10 See, for example, R. Orsi, *Between Heaven and Earth: The Religious Worlds People Make and the Scholars Who Study Them*, Princeton, NJ: Princeton University Press, 2004; R. Marie Griffith, *Born Again Bodies: Flesh and Spirit in American Christianity*, Berkeley, CA: University of California Press, 2004; N. Ammerman, *Bible Believers: Fundamentalists in the Modern World*, Newark, NJ: Rutgers University Press, 1987; R. Wuthnow, *The Restructuring of American Religion*, Princeton, NJ: Princeton University Press, 1990.
11 A. Wolfe, *One Nation After All*, New York: Penguin, 1999.
12 On Bush's religious beliefs, see P. Kengor, *God and George W. Bush*, New York: HarperCollins, 2004.
13 G. Wacker, *Heaven Below: Early Pentecostals and American Culture*, Boston, MA: Harvard University Press, 2003.

12 Anti-Americans abroad

Tony Judt

If you want to understand how America appears to the world today, consider the sport-utility vehicle. Oversized and overweight, the SUV disdains negotiated agreements to restrict atmospheric pollution. It consumes inordinate quantities of scarce resources to furnish its privileged inhabitants with supererogatory services. It exposes outsiders to deadly risk in order to provide for the illusory security of its occupants. In a crowded world, the SUV appears as a dangerous anachronism. Like US foreign policy, the sport-utility vehicle comes packaged in sonorous mission statements; but underneath it is just an oversized pickup truck with too much power.

The simile may be modern, but the idea behind it is not. 'America' has been an object of foreign suspicion for even longer than it has been a beacon and haven for the world's poor and downtrodden. Eighteenth century commentators – on the basis of very little direct observation – believed America's flora and fauna to be stunted, and of limited interest or use. The country could never be civilized, they insisted, and much the same was true of its unsophisticated new citizens. As the French diplomat (and bishop) Talleyrand observed, anticipating two centuries of European commentary: 'Trente-deux réligions et un seul plat' ('thirty-two religions and just one dish' – which Americans typically and understandably tended to eat in a hurry). From the perspective of a cosmopolitan European conservative like Joseph de Maistre, writing in the early years of the nineteenth century, the United States was a regrettable aberration – and too crude to endure for long.

Charles Dickens, like Alexis de Tocqueville, was struck by the conformism of American public life. Stendhal commented upon the country's 'egoism'; Baudelaire sniffily compared it to Belgium (!) in its bourgeois mediocrity; everyone remarked upon the jejune patriotic pomp of the United States. But in the course of the next century, European commentary shifted perceptibly from the dismissive to the resentful. By the 1930s, the United States' economic power was giving a threatening twist to its crude immaturity. For a new generation of anti-democratic critics, the destabilizing symptoms of modern life – mass production, mass society, and mass politics – could all be traced to America.

Like anti-Semitism, to which it was often linked, anti-Americanism was a convenient shorthand for expressing cultural insecurity. In the words of the

Frenchman Robert Aron, writing in 1935, Henry Ford, F. W. Taylor (the prophet of work rhythms and manufacturing efficiency), and Adolf Hitler were, like it or not, the 'guides of our age'. America was 'industrialism'. It threatened the survival of individuality, quality, and national specificity. 'America is multiplying its territory, where the values of the West risk finding their grave', wrote Emmanuel Berl in 1929. Europeans owed it to their heritage to resist their own Americanization at every turn, urged George Duhamel in 1930. 'We Westerners must each firmly denounce whatever is American in his house, his clothes, his soul.'[1]

World War Two did not alleviate this irritation. Radical anti-Americanism in the early cold war years echoed the sentiments of conservative anti-Americanism twenty years earlier. When Simone de Beauvoir charged that America was 'becoming Fascist', Jean-Paul Sartre claimed that McCarthyite America 'had gone mad'. The novelist Roger Vailland asserted that the fridge was an American plot to destroy French domestic culture, and when *Le Monde* declared that 'Coca-Cola is the Danzig of European Culture' they were denouncing the same American 'enemy' that had so alarmed their political opponents a genera-tion before.[2] American behaviour at home and abroad fed this prejudice but did not create it. In their anger at the United States, European intellectuals had for many decades been expressing their anxieties about changes closer to home.

The examples I have quoted are from France, but English ambivalence toward America is also an old story; the German generation of the 1960s blamed America above all for the crass consumerism and political amnesia of their parents' post-war Federal Republic; and even in Donald Rumsfeld's 'new' Europe the United States, representing 'Western' technology and progress, has on occasion been blamed for the ethical vacuum and cultural impoverishment that global capitalism brings in its train.[3] Nevertheless, anti-Americanism in Europe at least has always had a distinctively French tinge. It is in Paris that European ambivalence about America takes polemical form.

The most elegant, learned, and witty history of French anti-Americanism has just been published by Philippe Roger. Entitled *L'Ennemi Américain: Généalogie de l'Antiaméricanisme Français* (2004), it richly deserves to be published in English translation, unabridged.[4] The book's argument is far too subtle and intricate to summarize briefly, but the word 'genealogy' in the title should be taken seriously. This is not strictly a history, since Roger treats his material as a 'semiotic bloc'; and he does not pay much attention to the record of French 'pro-Americanism' that would need to be discussed to present a balanced account.

Instead, in nearly six hundred pages of close textual exegesis, Roger demon-strates not only that the core of French anti-Americanism is very old indeed, but also that it was always fanciful and only loosely attached to American reality. Anti-Americanism is a *récit*, a tale (or fable), with certain recurring themes, fears, and hopes. Starting out as an aesthetic distaste for the New World, French anti-Americanism has since moved through the cultural to the political but the sedimentary evidence of earlier versions is never quite lost to sight.

Roger's book is strongest on the eighteenth and nineteenth centuries. His coverage of the twentieth century stops with the generation of Sartre – the moment, as he reminds us, when it became conventional for French anti-American texts to begin by denying that they were anti-American. That seems reasonable. There are a number of satisfactory accounts of the anti-Americanism of our own times and Roger is interested in tracing origins, not outcomes.[5] And by ending short of the present he can permit himself a sardonic, upbeat conclusion: What if anti-Americanism today were no more than a mental slavery that the French impose on themselves, a masochist lethargy, a humdrum resentment, a passionless Pavlovian reaction? That would offer grounds for hope. There are few vices, even intellectual ones, which can long withstand the boredom they elicit.

Unfortunately, there is a fresh twist in the story. Anti-Americanism today is fuelled by a new consideration, and it is no longer confined to intellectuals. Most Europeans and other foreigners today are untroubled by American products, many of which are in any case manufactured and marketed overseas. They are familiar with the American 'way of life', which they often envy and dislike in equal parts. Most of them do not despise America, and they certainly do not hate Americans. What upsets them is US foreign policy; and they do not trust America's current president. This is new. Even during the cold war, many of America's political foes actually quite liked and trusted its leaders. Today, even America's friends don't like President Bush: in part for the policy he pursues, in part for the manner in which he pursues it.

This is the background to a recent burst of anti-American publications from Paris. The most bizarre of these is a book by one Thierry Meyssan, purporting to show that the 11 September attack on the Pentagon never happened.[6] No airliner ever crashed into the building, he writes: the whole thing is a hoax perpetrated by the American defence establishment to advance its own interests. Meyssan's approach echoes that of Holocaust deniers. He begins by assuming the non-existence of a well-accredited event, and then reminds us that no amount of evidence (*especially* from firsthand witnesses) can prove the contrary. The method is well summarized in his dismissal of the substantial body of eyewitness testimony running counter to his claim: 'Far from warranting their evidence, the quality of these witnesses just shows how far the US Army will go to distort the truth.'[7]

The most depressing thing about Meyssan's book is that it is a bestseller. There is an audience in France for the farther reaches of paranoid suspicion of America, and 11 September seems to have aroused it. More typical, though, is the shopping list of complaints in books with titles like *Why do People Hate America?*, *Le Livre noir des États-Unis*, and *Dangereuse Amérique*.[8] The first two are by British and Canadian authors respectively, though they have sold best in their French editions; the third is co-authored by a prominent French Green politician and former presidential candidate.

Characteristically presented with real or feigned regret ('We are not anti-American, but ...'), these works are an inventory of commonly cited American shortcomings. The United States is a selfish, individualistic society devoted to commerce, profit, and the despoliation of the planet. It is as uncaring of its own poor and sick as it is indifferent to the rest of humankind. The United States rides roughshod over international laws and treaties and threatens the moral, environmental, and physical future of humanity. It is inconsistent and hypocritical in its foreign dealings and it wields unparalleled military clout. It is, in short, a bull in the global china shop, wreaking havoc.[9]

Much of this is recycled from earlier criticisms of America. Peter Scowen's complaints (his chapter headings include 'Les atrocités de Hiroshima et de Nagasaki' and 'Une culture vide'), like those of Sardar and Davies ('American Hamburgers and Other Viruses') or Mamère and Farbiaz ('L'américanisation du monde', 'Une croisade qui sent le pétrole' [A crusade smelling of oil]), blend traditional themes with new accusations. They are a mixture of conservative cultural distaste (America is ugly, rootless, and crass), anti-globalization rhetoric (America is polluting the world), and neo-Marxist reductionism (America is run by and for the oil companies). Domestic American critics add race into the mix. Not content with trampling over everyone else, the United States rides roughshod across its own history.[10]

Some of the criticisms of American policy and practice are well founded. Others are drivel. In their catalogue of claims against America, Sardar and Davies blame the United States for the cold war, imposed on a reluctant Western Europe: 'Both France and Italy had major Communist Parties – and still do [sic] – but with their own very specific histories that owed little to Russia.'[11] 'International communism', in other words, was an American invention. This revisionist myth died many years ago. Its posthumous revival suggests that an older, political anti-Americanism is gaining new traction from the Bush administration's foreign ambitions.[12] Once a rogue state, always a rogue state.

According to Emmanuel Todd, however, there is no need to worry. In his recent book, *After the Empire: The Breakdown of the American Order* (also a bestseller), he argues that the sun is setting on imperial America.[13] We are entering a post-American age. America will continue to jeopardize international stability. But Europeans (and Asians) can take some comfort from the knowledge that the future is theirs. American military power is real, but redundant; meanwhile its tottering economy is vulnerably dependent upon the rest of the world, and its social model holds no appeal. Between 1950 and 1990 the United States was a benevolent and necessary presence in the world, but not anymore. The challenge today is to manage America's growing irrelevance.

Todd is not at all a conventional 'anti-American' and some of what he has to say is of interest, although English readers seeking to understand the case for American decline would do better to read Charles Kupchan.[14] Todd is right to say that asymmetric globalization (in which the United States consumes what others produce, and economic inequalities grow apace) is bringing about a world unsympathetic to American ambition. Post-communist Russia, post-Saddam Iraq, and other modernizing societies may adopt capitalism ('the only reasonable economic organization') and even become democratic, but they will not mimic

American 'hyper-individualism' and they will share European preferences on many things. The United States, in Todd's view, will cling desperately to the vestiges of its ambition and power; to maintain its waning influence it will seek to sustain international tension, a 'condition of limited but endemic war'. This process has already begun, and 11 September 2001 was its trigger.

The problem with Emmanuel Todd, and it will be immediately familiar to anyone who has read any of his previous books, is less his conclusions than his reasoning. There is something of the Ancient Mariner about this writer. He has a maniacal tale to tell and he recounts it in book after book, gripping the reader relentlessly as though to say 'Don't you get it? It's all about fertility!' Todd is an anthropological demographer by training. In 1976 he published *La Chute finale: Essai sur la décomposition de la sphère soviétique*, in which he prophesied the end of the USSR based on the decline of the Soviet birth rate in the 1970s.[15] Emmanuel Todd was not the only person back in the 1970s predicting an unhealthy future for communism. Nevertheless, the link he claims to have uncovered between fertility and regime collapse has gone to his head. In his new book, world history is reduced to a series of unidirectional, monocausal correlations linking birth rates, literacy rates, timeless family structures, and global politics. The Yugoslav wars were the result of 'fertility gaps' between Slavs and Muslims. The American Civil War can be traced to the low birth rates of the Anglo-Saxon settler class. And if 'individualistic' America faces grim prospects today, this is because the 'family structures' of the rest of the world favour very different political systems.

In Emmanuel Todd's parallel universe, politics (like economic behaviour) is inscribed in a society's 'genetic code'. The egalitarian family systems of Central Asia reveal an 'anthropology of community' that made communism more acceptable there (elsewhere he has attributed regional variations in French, Italian, and Finnish voting patterns to similar differences in family life).[16] Today, the 'universalist Russian temperament' based on the extended Russian family offers a non-individualistic socio-economic model that may be the democracy of the future. Hence the unchained fury of the 'differentialist' tendencies – American, Israeli, and others.

Todd goes further. He absurdly exaggerates America's current woes, real as they are. Extrapolating from the Enron example, he concludes that all American economic data are as unreliable as those of the Soviets: the truly parlous state of the US economy has been kept hidden. And he offers his own variant on the 'clash of civilizations'. The coming conflict between Islam and the United States brings into opposition the 'effectively feminist', women-based civilization of America and the masculinized ethic of Central Asian and Arab warrior societies. Here, too, America will be isolated, for Europeans will feel just as threatened by the United States as their Arab neighbours do. Once again, it all comes down to family life, with a distinctive modern twist: 'The status of the American woman, threatening and castrating [*castratrice et menaçante*], [is] as disturbing for European men as the all-powerful Arab male is for European women.' The Atlantic gap begins in the bedroom. You couldn't invent it.

To leave Emmanuel Todd for Jean-François Revel is to abandon the mad scientist for the self-confident patrician. Revel is an Immortal of the Académie Française. He is the author of many books (thirty-one to date), as the reader of his latest essay is firmly reminded.[17] Revel's style suggests a man unfamiliar with self-doubt and unused to contradiction. He tends to sweeping, unsupported generalizations. By his account, most of Europe's political and cultural elite 'never understood anything about communism' and his version of French anti-Americanism at times approaches caricature. This is a pity, because some of what he writes makes good sense.

Thus Revel is right to draw attention to the contradiction at the heart of much French criticism of America. If the United States is such a social disaster, a cultural pygmy, a political innocent, and an economic meltdown waiting to happen, why worry? Why devote so much resentful attention to it? Alternatively, if it is as powerful and successful as many fear, might it not be doing something right? Revel is correct for the most part to charge certain French intellectuals with bad faith when they assert that they had nothing against America's anti-communist policies in earlier decades and object only to the excesses of the present. The record suggests otherwise.

As a Frenchman, Revel is well placed to remind his fellow citizens that France, too, has social problems. The much-vaunted French education system neither assimilates cultural and religious minorities nor does it support and nourish cultural difference. France, too, has slums, violence, and delinquency. And Jean-Marie Le Pen's success in the most recent presidential elections is a standing rebuke to all of France's political class for its failure to address the problems of immigration and race.[18] Revel makes legitimate fun of France's cultural adminis-trators, who can vandalize their own national heritage at least as recklessly as the barbaric Americans. No American booster could ever match Culture Minister Jack Lang's 1984 Projet Culturel Extérieur de la France, and what does it say about the sophistication of the French press and television that they devoted so much credulous space to the elucubrations of M. Meyssan?

One could go on. Mocking the French for their pretensions (and their memory holes) is almost as easy as picking apart the hypocrisies of US foreign policy. And Revel is right to describe modern anti-globalization activists with their anti-market rhetoric as a 'divine surprise' for the European left, a heaven-sent cause at a post-ideological moment when Europe's radicals were adrift. But Revel's astute observations of what is wrong in France risk being discredited by his inability to find *anything* wrong with America. His entire book is a paean of blinkered praise for a country that, regrettably, does not exist. Like the anti-Americans he disdains, he has conjured up his American subject out of thin air.

In Revel's America the melting pot works '*fort bien*' and there is no mention of ghettos. According to him, Europeans misread and exaggerate US crime statis-tics, whereas in reality crime in America is not a problem. Health coverage in America works well: most Americans are insured at work, the rest benefit from publicly funded Medicare and Medicaid. Anyway, the system's shortcomings are no worse than those of France's own provisions for health care. The American poor have the same *per capita* income as the *average* citizen of Portugal, so they cannot be called poor (Revel has apparently never heard of cost-of-living indices). There is no underclass. Meanwhile the United States has had social democracy longer than Europe, and American television and news coverage is much better than you think.

As for American foreign policy: in Revel-land the United States has stayed fully engaged in the Israel–Palestine conflict, is resolutely non-partisan, and its policy has been a success. The American missile defence programme worries M. Revel a lot less than it does some American generals. Unlike 50 per cent of the US electorate, Académicien Revel saw nothing amiss in the conduct of the 2000 presidential election. As for evidence of growing American anti-French sentiment, stuff and nonsense: '*pour ma part, je ne l'ai jamais constaté*' ('as for me, I've never seen it'). In short, whatever French critics and others say about the United States, Jean-François Revel maintains the opposite. Voltaire could not have done a better job satirizing traditional French prejudices: Pangloss in Wonderland.

Somewhere between Emmanuel Todd and Jean-François Revel there is an interesting European perspective on George Bush's America. The two sides of the Atlantic really are different today. First, America is a credulous and religious society: since the mid 1950s Europeans have abandoned their churches in droves; but in the United States there has been virtually no decline in church-going and synagogue attendance. In 1998 a Harris poll found that 66 per cent even of non-Christian Americans believed in miracles and 47 per cent of them accredited the Virgin Birth; the figures for all Americans are 86 per cent and 83 per cent respectively. Some 45 per cent of Americans believe there is a Devil. In a recent *Newsweek* poll 79 per cent of American respondents accepted that biblical miracles really happened. According to a 1999 *Newsweek* poll, 40 per cent of all Americans (71 per cent of Evangelical Protestants) believe that the world will end in a battle at Armageddon between Jesus and the Antichrist. An American president who conducts Bible study in the White House and begins cabinet sessions with a prayer may seem a curious anachronism to his European allies, but he is in tune with his constituents.[19]

Second, the inequalities and insecurities of American life are still unthinkable across the Atlantic. Europeans remain wary of excessive disparities of income, and their institutions and political choices reflect this sentiment. Moreover it is prudence, rather than the residue of socialism, that explains European hesitation over unregulated markets and the dismantling of the public sector and local resistance to the American model. This makes sense. For most people in Europe, as elsewhere in the world, unrestricted competition is at least as much a threat as an opportunity.

Europeans want a more interventionist state at home than Americans do, and they expect to pay for it. Even in post-Thatcher Britain, 62 per cent of adults polled in December 2002 would favour higher taxes in return for improved public services. The figure for the United States was under one per cent. This is less surprising when one considers that in America (where the disparities between rich and poor are greater than anywhere else in the developed world) fully 19 per cent of the adult population claim to be in the richest one per cent of the nation, and a further 20 per cent believe they will enter that one per cent in their lifetime![20]

What Europeans find perturbing about America, then, is precisely what most Americans believe to be their nation's strongest suit: its unique mix of moralistic religiosity, minimal provision for public welfare, and maximal market freedom – the 'American way of life' – coupled with a missionary foreign policy ostensibly directed at exporting that same cluster of values and practices. Here the United States is ill served by globalization, which highlights for the world's poorer countries the costs of exposure to economic competition and reminds West Europeans, after the long sleep of the cold war, of the true fault lines bisecting the hitherto undifferentiated 'West'.

These transatlantic distinctions will matter more, not less, in years to come: longstanding social and cultural contrasts are being highlighted and reinforced by irresolvable policy disagreements. Already the schism over the US war on Iraq has revealed something new. In the early years of the cold war anti-American demonstrations in Europe took their cue from Soviet-financed 'peace movements', but the political and economic elites were firmly in the American camp. Today, no one is manipulating mass anti-war protests and West European leaders have broken with America on a major international issue. The United States has been forced to bribe and threaten in unprecedented public ways, with embarrassingly limited success (even in Turkey, thanks to the unpredictable workings of democracy).

The Iraq crisis has exposed three kinds of weakness in the modern international system. We have been reminded once again of how fragile the United Nations is, how seemingly inadequate to the hopes vested in it. Yet the recent American attitude towards the UN – give us what we want or we shall take it anyway – has paradoxically strengthened practically everyone else's appreciation of the institution's importance. The UN may lack an army, but it has acquired, over the past fifty years, a distinctive legitimacy; and legitimacy is a kind of power. In any case, the UN is all we have. Those who abuse it for their own ends do so at serious risk to their credibility as international citizens.

The second ostensible victim of the crisis has been the European Union. On the face of things Europe is now bitterly divided, thanks in equal measure to American mischief and European leaders' own incompetence. But crises can be salutary. Once Iraq achieves some kind of stability the British are going to be asking hard questions about the American commitment they made in the wake of a previous Middle Eastern miscalculation, at Suez in 1956. The East Europeans will pray for short memories in Brussels, Berlin, and Paris when it comes to preparing the Union's budget. Turkish politicians are already questioning their country's once sacrosanct relationship with America. And Jacques Chirac may have his country's last, best chance to shape a Europe independent of America and its equal in international affairs. The 'hour of Europe' may not have struck, but Washington's utter indifference to European opinion has rung a fire bell in the night.

The third kind of weakness concerns the United States itself: not in spite of its overwhelming military might, but because of it. Unbelievably, President Bush and his advisers have managed to make America seem the greatest threat to international stability, a mere three years after 11 September, and in so doing the United States may have gambled away the confidence of the world. By staking a monopoly claim on Western values and their defence, the United States has prompted other Westerners to reflect on what divides them from America. By enthusiastically asserting its right to reconfigure the Muslim world, Washington has reminded Europeans in particular of the growing Muslim presence in their own cultures and its political implications. One French resident in twelve is now a Muslim. In Russia the figure is nearly one in six. In short, the United States has given a lot of people occasion to rethink their relationship with it.

You do not have to be a French intellectual to believe that an 'overmuscled' America, in a hostile international environment, is weaker, not stronger, than it was before. It is also more likely to be belligerent. What it will not be, however, is irrelevant. International politics is sometimes about good and evil, but it is always about power. The United States has considerable power and the nations of the world need the United States on their side. A United States that oscillated unpredictably between unilateral pre-emptive wars and narcissistic indifference would be a global disaster, which is why so many countries at the UN tried desperately to accommodate Washington's wishes, whatever their leaders' private misgivings.

Meanwhile, moderates in Washington insist that all these concerns will be laid to rest once stability returns to Iraq. But a military campaign is not retroactively justified by its (unlikely) success alone, and anyway much collateral harm is already done. The precedent of pre-emptive and preventive war against a hypothetical threat; the incautious, intermittent acknowledgment that this war has objectives far beyond disarming Baghdad; the alienation of foreign sentiment: these constitute war damage however successfully America handles the peace. Has the world's 'indispensable nation' (Madeleine Albright) miscalculated and overreached? Almost certainly. When the earthquake abates, the tectonic plates of international politics will have shifted forever.

Notes

1 E. Berl, *Mort de la Pensée Bourgeoise*, Paris: Bernard Grasset, 1929, reprinted 1970, pp. 76–7; A. Siegfried, *Les États-Unis d'aujourd'hui*, Paris: Colin, 1930, quoted in M. Winock, *Nationalisme, Antisémitisme et Fascisme en France*, Paris: Seuil, 1982, p. 56. See also G. Duhamel, *Scènes de la Vie future*, Paris: Mercure de France, 1930; R. Aron and A. Dandieu, *Le Cancer Américain*, Paris: Rieder, 1931; and my own *Past Imperfect: French Intellectuals, 1944–1956*, Berkeley, CA: University of California Press, 1992, Chapter 10: 'America has gone mad: anti-Americanism in historical perspective', pp. 187–204.
2 For Simone de Beauvoir, see her *L'Amérique au jour le jour*, Paris: Morihien, 1948, pp. 99–100. Sartre was commenting on the trial and execution of the Rosenbergs. Vailland's thoughts on refrigeration, from his article 'Le Ménage n'est pas un art de salon' (*La Tribune des Nations*, 14 March 1952), are discussed by P. Roger in *L'Ennemi*

Américain, pp. 483–4. And see the editorial 'Mourir pour le Coca-Cola', *Le Monde*, 29 March, 1950.

3 For German representations of the price of Americanization see Rainer Werner Fassbinder's *Marriage of Maria Braun* (1979); or Edgar Reitz's *Heimat: Eine deutsche Chronik* (1984), where the American impact on 'deep Germany' is depicted as far more corrosive of values than the passage through Nazism. And it was Václav Havel, no less, who reminded his fellow dissidents back in 1984 that rationalism, scientism, our fascination with technology and change, were all the 'ambiguous exports' of the West, the perverse fruits of the dream of modernity. See V. Havel, 'Svedomí a politika', *Svedectví*, 1984, vol. 18, no. 72, pp. 621–5 (quote from page 627).

4 P. Roger, *L'Ennemi Américain: Généalogie de l'Antiaméricanisme Français*, Paris: Seuil, 2004.

5 See P. Mathy, *Extrême Occident: French Intellectuals and America*, Chicago, IL: University of Chicago Press, 1993, and *L'Amérique dans les têtes: Un Siècle de fascinations et d'aversions*, edited by D. Lacorne, J. Rupnik, and M-F. Toinet, Paris: Hachette, 1986.

6 T. Meyssan, *9/11: The Big Lie*, London: Carnot 2002.

7 Ibid., p. 23.

8 Z. Sardar and M. W. Davies, *Why do People Hate America?*, Cambridge: Icon, 2002; P. Scowen, *Le Livre noir des États-Unis*, Paris: Mango 2003; N. Mamère and P. Farbiaz, *Dangereuse Amérique: Chronique d'une guerre annoncée*, Paris: Ramsay, 2003.

9 See also C. V. Prestowitz, *Rogue Nation: American Unilateralism and the Failure of Good Intentions*, New York: Basic Books, 2003.

10 According to Mark Hertsgaard, in *The Eagle's Shadow: Why America Fascinates and Infuriates the World*, New York: Farrar, Straus and Giroux, 2002, Americans have long been in denial about their constitution's origins in the practices of the Iroquois League, to which we apparently owe an unacknowledged debt for the concepts of states' rights and the separation of powers. So much for Locke, Montesquieu, English Common Law, and the Continental Enlightenment.

11 Sardar and Davies, *Why do People Hate America?*, p. 184.

12 We are back in May 1944, when Hubert Beuve-Méry, future founder and editor of *Le Monde*, could write that 'the Americans constitute a real threat to France… . [They] can prevent us accomplishing the necessary revolution, and their materialism lacks even the tragic grandeur of the materialism of the totalitarians'. Quoted by Jean-François Revel in *Anti-Americanism*, New York: Encounter Books, 2003, p. 98.

13 E. Todd, *After the Empire: The Breakdown of the American Order*, New York: Columbia University Press, 2003.

14 Charles Kupchan, *The End of the American Era*, New York: Knopf, 2002.

15 E. Todd, *La Chute Finale: Essai sur la Décomposition de la Sphère Soviétique*, Paris: R. Laffont, Nouv. éd. augm edition, 1990.

16 E. Todd, *La Troisième Planète: Structures Familiales et Systèmes Idéologiques*, Paris: Seuil, 1983. 'Communism's success is principally explained by the existence … of egalitarian and authoritarian family structures predisposing people to see Communist ideology as natural and good'. See *After the Empire*, p. 178.

17 J-F. Revel, *Anti-Americanism*, New York: Encounter Books, 2003.

18 On this see also P. Manière, *La Vengeance du Peuple: Les Élites, Le Pen et les Français*, Paris: Plon, 2002.

19 See <www.pollingreport.com/religion.htm and www.pollingreport.com/religion2.htm> (accessed 4 June 2005).

20 'A tale of two legacies', *The Economist*, 21 December 2002; *Financial Times*, 25–26 January 2003.

Index

ks – at www.eBookstore.tandf.co.uk

▶rary at your fingertips!

ks are electronic versions of printed books. You can
them on your PC/laptop or browse them online.

have advantages for anyone needing rapid access
▾vide variety of published, copyright information.

ks can help your research by enabling you to
▾mark chapters, annotate text and use instant searches
▾d specific words or phrases. Several eBook files would
even a small laptop or PDA.

: Save money by eSubscribing: cheap, online access
y eBook for as long as you need it.

▪ual subscription packages

ow offer special low-cost bulk subscriptions to
▾ges of eBooks in certain subject areas. These are
▪ble to libraries or to individuals.

▾ore information please contact
▾aster.ebooks@tandf.co.uk

▪ continually developing the eBook concept, so
up to date by visiting the website.

▾w.eBookstore.tandf.co.uk